T0301768

DIGITAL TRANSFORMATION DEMYSTIFIED

Digital Transformation: Accelerating Organizational Intelligence

Print ISSN: 2811-0552
Online ISSN: 2811-0560

Series Editor: Jay Liebowitz *(Seton Hall University, USA)*

According to a report released by Veritis in 2021 "the global digital transformation market size is anticipated to reach USD 1009.8 billion by 2025 from USD 469.8 billion in 2020. The demand for digital transformation services is expected to rise at a Compound Annual Growth Rate (CAGR) of around 16.5% over the forecast period from 2021 to 2025. The growing adoption of digital technologies, including Artificial Intelligence (AI), cloud computing, big data, the Internet of Things (IoT), and Machine Learning (ML), is driving the growth of the digital transformation market." To be competitive in today's fast-changing marketplace, organizations need to apply the "alphabet" of digital transformation.

The focus of the book series is unique and will cover the various perspectives on organizational digital transformation, namely business & management, technology, legal and ethics, and social aspects.

Published:

Vol. 2   *Digital Transformation Demystified*
         by Frank Granito

Vol. 1   *Digital Transformation for the University of the Future*
         edited by Jay Liebowitz

Forthcoming:

Vol. 3   *Doing Well and Doing Good: Human-Centered Digital Transformation Leadership*
         by Cheryl Flink, Liora Gross and William Pasmore

More information on this series can be found at https://www.worldscientific.com/series/dtaoi

Digital Transformation
Accelerating Organizational Intelligence
– Volume 2

DIGITAL TRANSFORMATION DEMYSTIFIED

Dr. Frank Granito

Institute for Digital Transformation, USA

Published by

World Scientific Publishing Co. Pte. Ltd.

5 Toh Tuck Link, Singapore 596224

USA office: 27 Warren Street, Suite 401-402, Hackensack, NJ 07601

UK office: 57 Shelton Street, Covent Garden, London WC2H 9HE

Library of Congress Cataloging-in-Publication Data
Names: Granito, Frank, author.
Title: Digital transformation demystified / Dr. Frank Granito,
    Institute for Digital Transformation, USA.
Description: Hackensack, NJ : World Scientific, [2023] |
    Series: Digital transformation: accelerating organizational intelligence ; vol. 2 |
    Includes bibliographical references and index.
Identifiers: LCCN 2022024393 | ISBN 9789811260452 (hardcover) |
    ISBN 9789811260469 (ebook) | ISBN 9789811260476 (ebook other)
Subjects: LCSH: Information technology--Management. | Organizational change.
Classification: LCC HD30.2 .G724 2023 | DDC 658.4/038--dc23/eng/20220603
LC record available at https://lccn.loc.gov/2022024393

British Library Cataloguing-in-Publication Data
A catalogue record for this book is available from the British Library.

For any available supplementary material, please visit
https://www.worldscientific.com/worldscibooks/10.1142/12969#t=suppl

Desk Editors: Jayanthi Muthuswamy/Thaheera Althaf

Typeset by Stallion Press
Email: enquiries@stallionpress.com

Printed in Singapore

Foreword: The Mystification of Digital Transformation

I stood on stage staring out at the large crowd of expectant faces and took a deep breath. Was anything I was about to say going to resonate at all?

I was speaking to New Zealand's business elite — CEOs, academics, and leaders of tech start-ups — at an event on so-called *digital disruption* co-hosted by the Auckland University of Technology and the U.S. Embassy.

And for the first time in my burgeoning speaking career, I was addressing an audience of non-IT people.

My first book, *The Quantum Age of IT: Why Everything You Know About IT Is About to Change,* had come out a couple of years earlier and had unwittingly launched me on a speaking career talking about IT transformation. But the organizers of this event thought that my book and the future it foretold extended beyond the realm of IT and affected, well, everyone.

That talk was the first time I used the term *digital transformation,* and while it's now bordering on overuse, it was a very new term at the time. And I had no idea if what I was going to say would make any sense at all — or whether it would have the impact I was about to predict.

Thankfully, I didn't have long to wait to find out.

© 2023 World Scientific Publishing Company
https://doi.org/10.1142/9789811260469_fmatter

A Digitally Transformed Future

By the end of my talk, and for about an hour afterward, I was the number two trending topic in the entire country of New Zealand. Digital transformation was a hot topic that people wanted to understand.

But as gratifying as my 15 minutes of fame may have been, it was what happened that weekend that solidified for me that true and lasting impact of what our digitally transformed future would hold.

A friend living outside Auckland picked me up to spend the weekend with her and her husband before my next speaking gig. Offhandedly, she mentioned that her husband's best friend would be joining us for dinner. Excited to share my newfound (albeit temporary) fame, I asked, "What does he do for a living?"

Her answer that he was a dairy farmer brought my ego back to earth. After all, who could be less impressed about someone trending because of his talk about digital transformation than a dairy farmer, right?

As we waited for my friend to finish preparing dinner, the inevitable question popped. "So what do you do for a living, Charlie," he asked. Figuring I'd better keep it simple, I responded, "I'm in IT."

"IT, huh? Mmmhmmm," he muttered as he scratched his chin.

And then he said the words that would change my life. "Yeah, IT. You know I couldn't do anything without technology. I run my entire dairy farm of 500 cows with only three people because of it."

I had to pick my jaw up off of the floor. He went on to explain that everything was automated, that he tracked consumption and waste via sensors, managed ill cows with an automated tracking system, and even had an automated milking system that allowed his distributor to pump out the milk and automatically calculate how much they owed him. "I spend most of my time traveling around the world on my motor bike," he told me.

Technology truly was transforming everything about how the world worked — and it was about far more than IT. I came home from that trip personally transformed as I realized that digital transformation was not only real but that it would fundamentally alter almost everything we knew about how the world worked.

A Mystified World

We changed the name of our organization, which up until that time we had called The IT Transformation Institute, to *The Institute for Digital*

Transformation, and set out to help the world understand the true ramifications of what digital transformation meant.

The changes we've seen in the 7 years since I gave that talk have justified much of my excitement and enthusiasm. We have seen the tremendous impact of digital transformation play out on the world stage in ways that are difficult to capture or enumerate.

But despite this impact, many business leaders — most, even — remain confused about the true nature of digital transformation. Moreover and more concerning, they seem unclear about their essential role in leading their organizations through this tumultuous period of change in which their very survival is at risk.

There are numerous reasons for this almost schizophrenic disconnect. On the one hand, consumer technologies have transformed customer expectations, forcing businesses to adapt and respond. But on the other hand, the complexities of the resulting technology stack combined with the historical organizational silos and industrial age cultural mindsets have created a consistent headwind that has pushed many business leaders to accept incremental change as transformational.

Along the way, vendors from across the full spectrum of the technology stack realized that branding something as an enabler of "digital transformation" opened wallets and broke down sales barriers.

The inevitable result was that the term digital transformation came to the precipice of irrelevance as confusion and ubiquity combined to render the term nearly meaningless.

But this mystification represents a grave danger.

The Demystification Imperative

The forces that caused me to first utter the term from that stage in Auckland have not only not abated, they have amplified.

Lying just beneath the ubiquity of this buzzword, the forces continue to demand that organizations transform themselves from the inside out. And despite what vendors and the industry might lead you to believe, the transformation required extends far beyond the technology stack to include the organization's culture, its operating processes, and virtually every facet of how it operates.

The buzz and hype created over the last few years threatens the ability of leaders to finish what was started years ago.

Digital transformation remains a strategic imperative for all companies — and one that is now even more critical than ever before. This fact means that leaders must break through the hype and demystify this term once and for all. They must get past the breathless hyperbole and understand what it really means to lead their organization through a continuous digital transformation process.

The demystification of digital transformation and understanding what it really means are critical for all leaders. And that's what this book is about.

Charles Araujo
Founder, Institute for Digital Transformation

About the Author

Dr. Frank Granito is Chief Scientist at the Institute for Digital Transformation. He has over 40 years of experience in the Information Technology field. In his role as Chief Scientist, Dr. Granito has designed the evaluation tools and analytics for the Digital Readiness Framework to assist organizations as they transition and adapt to the Digital Age. Dr. Granito holds a Doctor of Management from the University of Maryland University College, and his work in Organizational Culture resulted in a Culture Model and Assessment Instrument tailored to IT Service Management implementations. He has successfully implemented IT Service Management transformation solutions for Government and Commercial clients.

Contributing Authors

Roy Atkinson, Institute Fellow, is one of the most recognized thought leaders in IT, service management, and customer experience. He is a prolific writer, speaker, webinar presenter, and podcaster as well as an industry analyst. His expertise has been featured by The Economist, BizTech Magazine, Social Media Today, Computerworld, Oracle Customer Experience, SAP Business Innovation, and others. He was described on CIO Insight as a "model for the future digital leader" and by Nextiva as one of the "Top 50 Customer Service Experts of the Decade 2010–2020." He was HDI's 2019 Lifetime Achievement Award honoree. He holds a master's certificate in advanced management strategy from Tulane University's Freeman School of Business. Before stepping into his current role as CEO of Clifton Butterfield, LLC, a business advisory firm, he served as Group Principal Analyst for Informa Tech. He is a Professional Member of the National Speakers Association.

Jessica Carroll, Institute Fellow, is recognized as an executive who develops and articulates vision and solutions from both technical and business perspectives. She has an established history of building a culture of collaboration, trust, and respect among IT and the business. A speaker on the topics of digital transformation, cloud computing, client engagement, and team culture, she has been published in CIOInsight and BizTech magazines, and was named a 2010 Computer World Premier 100 IT Leader. She is committed to sharing, listening, challenging, and shaping the discussion around transformational business success.

Hans Gillior, M.Sc. M.B.A, Institute Fellow, is an experienced Digital Expert, Senior Advisor, and Senior Manager in the ICT/Digital industry with profound competence of value creation, agility, and innovation. He is a specialist in IT/Digital transformation and especially in the corporate effects (unpredictability) of digitalization and globalization. Hans drives research and thought leadership in the fields of Digital Transformation, Agile Governance, Innovation, and Leadership. Much of his thought leadership, expertise, and experience are packaged in the GooDIGITAL frameworks used by high-ranking consultancy firms as "best practice" for digital and agile transformation. He is a recognized writer for IDG Expert Network.

Cherri Holland, Institute Fellow, is a performance and change specialist who studied organizational psychology and how to optimize human performance through the great game of business. Influenced by leaders running successful staff-driven businesses, she sees a "partnership" approach to success as more important than ever in today's digital organization. As financial metrics are increasingly tied to customer and staff engagement, and news travels fast, organizations need quick ways to hit the reset button. Cherri has moved hundreds of clients past entrenched ways of working into self-leadership, high performance, and flow, and her clients have consistently said their high expectations of change outcomes have been exceeded. Described as commercially savvy, engaging, and inspirational, Cherri has authored four books (including *Influencing, 101*) and leads two subjects in the IT Professionals NZ *Effective CIO Series*.

Whynde Kuehn, Institute Fellow, is the Founder and Managing Director of S2E Transformation, helping organizations bridge the gap between strategy and execution, and achieve their greatest visions for business transformation in a practical and business-focused way. Whynde has extensive experience in enterprise transformation and planning, including leading large-scale transformations and her own business transformation and architecture consulting practice. Whynde is a passionate advocate for using business architecture to enable effective strategy execution and digital transformation. She is a long-time business architecture practitioner, educator, recognized industry thought leader, and community builder, with extensive experience applying the discipline at leading Fortune 500 enterprises and a range of entrepreneurial, governmental, and nonprofit organizations, and social initiatives. Whynde is the author of the book *Strategy to Reality.*

Reynaldo Lugtu Jr., Institute Fellow, is a digital and culture transformation thought and action leader, a sought-after public speaker, and an accomplished educator, author, business columnist, and innovation coach. He is the Founder and CEO of Hungry Workhorse, a digital and culture transformation consulting firm. He is also the Chairman of ICT Committee of the Financial Executives Institute of the Philippines (FINEX) and Vice Chairman of ICT Committee of the Management Association of the Philippines (MAP). He is a Professorial Lecturer in the MBA program of De La Salle University (DLSU), Philippines, and Program Director for the Digital Transformation of DLSU School of Lifelong Learning. He finished courses in business from INSEAD-Wharton University of Pennsylvania, China Europe International Business School, and Helsinki School of Economics. He is finishing his doctorate in business in DLSU.

Raymond Sheen, PMP® LSS BB, Institute Fellow, is president and founder of Product & Process Innovation, Inc. He is a veteran business leader with over 30 years of executive, engineering management, and project management experience deploying new technology and improving business performance. He has consulted and trained companies in various industries and business functions including marketing, engineering, manufacturing, service, IT, and finance. Ray is author of the book, *Guide to Building Your Business Case*, published by Harvard Business Review Press. Ray received his B.S. in Mechanical Engineering from the United States Air Force Academy and his M.S. in Astronautical Engineering from the Massachusetts Institute of Technology and has a graduate certificate in Digital Leadership and Strategy from Boston University.

John Thorp, Institute Fellow, is an internationally recognized thought leader in the field of value and benefits management with close to 60 years of experience in the information management field. A frequent speaker, and author of *The Information Paradox*, John's passion revolves around helping individuals, organizations, and society realize value from information technology-enabled change. In today's age of digital exploration, realizing this value requires going beyond frameworks and methodologies. It will require a fundamental mindset shift around the nature of value, including economic, societal, and environmental value, as well as around organizational governance, leadership, and management. In addition to being a fellow of the Institute for Digital Transformation, John is a Fujitsu Consulting Fellow and a Fellow of the Innovation Value Institute.

Jeffery S. Ton, Institute Fellow, is a sought-after speaker, author, and thought leader, having led powerful teams and built successful Information Technology departments for over 30 years. As a speaker, author, advisor, and coach, Jeff's mission is to change the face of IT. He states that "Businesses today are demanding more from their technology and their technology leaders." He serves on numerous boards and advisory councils including Forbes Technology Council, Hoosier Environmental Council board of directors, Connected World Magazine Board of Advisors, and the Mud Creek Conservancy board of directors. He is also a Fellow for the Institute of Digital Transformation. Jeff is the author of *Amplify Your Value — Leading IT with Strategic Vision* (2018) and *Amplify Your Job Search — Strategies for Finding Your Dream Job* (2020), and is a frequent keynote speaker on topics related to the evolving IT landscape and the changing role of the CIO.

About the Institute for Digital Transformation

 The Institute for Digital Transformation provides digital leaders with the resources needed to transform their organizations into Digital Enterprises.

Guided by the real-world experience of our Institute Fellows and our proprietary industry research, we produce a wide range of insightful leading-edge methodology, tools, content, and news summaries needed for a transformational journey.

Why? Because digital transformation is now a strategic imperative!

But it is not just something you do; it's an attitude and an approach. The buzz and hype created over the last few years has resulted in confusion and ubiquity that have rendered the term nearly meaningless. Transformation extends far beyond the technology stack and must include the organization's culture, its operating processes, and virtually every facet of how it functions — areas that the industry has largely ignored, with predictable results.

The Institute is your first stop for the insights, tools, and guidance needed to lead your organization past the hype into a Digital Enterprise.

Visit us to discover more. https://www.institutefordigitaltransformation.org/.

Contents

Introduction and Primer

Dr. Frank Granito

A recent Google search of "Digital Transformation Definition" yielded almost three billion results. Among them were definitions from such well-known sources as Gartner, McKinsey, Deloitte, and even Harvard. The same search under Webster brought back **zero** results. What does that tell us? It implies that until there is an agreed upon singular definition (or as close as possible) of this term, sources such as Gartner, McKinsey, Deloitte, and yes, even Harvard will all be correct. Therein lies the mystery. Which one is best? Which one's suitable for my situation? Is there a common thread to all of them?

That is the purpose of this book, *Digital Transformation Demystified*. At the Institute for Digital Transformation, we attempt to solve this mystery. We recognize there is no single definition, but a set of common threads and approaches. First, whatever definition(s) you find most useful, it should be focused on the culture of your organization, the customer experience, and the use of ever-changing digital technologies to facilitate and enable both. Second, focusing on implementing technology without understanding the consequences and impacts to your culture and your customers is shortsighted — it is merely an *Information Technology Transformation*, not a Digital Transformation. This is fine if that is your goal. However, do not delude yourself that implementing a customer service chatbot is Digital Transformation.

Let's try to solve the first part of the mystery. What is *Digital Transformation*? For some, "digital" is all about the web. For others, it

https://doi.org/10.1142/9789811260469_fmatter

is simply a more modern, updated term for all things technology. Some use the term to simply reflect the idea of a digitally powered customer experience. At the Institute, we believe that a Digital Enterprise is all those things, but it is much, much more. At the Institute, we are focused on studying the impact on organizations and their leaders as we transition from the Industrial Era into what we call the Digital Era. In its simplest form, therefore, we believe a Digital Enterprise is simply an organization that has completed this transition. But the result of that transformation is an organization that looks very different from today's typical organizations.

We believe that a Digital Enterprise is one in which Digital Technology is at the center of how the organization:

- Operates
- Produces products and services (even if they are non-digital)
- Generates revenue
- Seizes competitive advantage
- Produces value.

Your next question might be, *So what*? The "so what" is that being a Digital Enterprise results in an organization that can leverage technology in support of its overall mission in a way that makes it:

- More competitive
- More economically efficient
- More capable of dynamically adapting to new competitors and to shifts in the market.

Next, the *Now what*? The shift to becoming a Digital Enterprise is a shift away from utilizing technology at the edges of an organization and instead leveraging technology as the chief driver of every business function and business process. As a result, the core functions and structures of the organization will also shift and realign, becoming flatter and more dynamic to best leverage these new technology-driven business processes. In effect, while Digital Enterprises will not be "tech companies" in the way we think of them today, on the inside, they will think, function, and act much more like a technology start-up than they will a traditional, industrial-era organization. They will be structured and organized with a technology-first mindset and designed for speed and agility.

Now on to the mystery. Based on the paradigm above of the Digital Enterprise, your ongoing journey to Digital Transformation could take many paths — depending on your definition. But that's the paradox. A Digital Enterprise should be agile, and the purpose of this book is to provide you some context to help you solve your own mystery. The *Now what?* can take several approaches and paths — not all mutually exclusive. All those paths come with a common theme: **culture**.

Reynaldo Lugtu will tell you about the "Culture of Transformation." Whynde Kuehn offers a different perspective on **culture** in "Business Architecture as an Enabler of Transformation." The "Digital Transformation Manifesto" is rife with references to **culture** as Raymond Sheen points out. In his chapter, "Value — The Guiding Star," John Thorp laments that he did not treat **culture** as important as he should have. In "The Neuroscience of Transformation," Cherri Holland tells us that to lead continuous transformation, organizations need to create a transformation-ready **culture**. We have broached the subject of agility, and Hans Gillior, in his chapter "Agile Transformation," gives us some advice on how to create this adult, self-reliant, and team-connected work **culture**. Jeffrey Ton in his chapter "Leadership in an Era of Uncertainty" gives us a unique centuries-old lesson in diversity of **culture** required to solve the problems of today. The Digital Enterprise needs to be customer focused. Jessica Carroll in her chapter "The Client–Partner Engagement" and Roy Atkinson in his chapter, "Customer Experience and Digital Transformation" tell us the importance of a customer-first **culture** and a *culture* that is supportive and foundational to business outcomes. Finally, I discuss "Readiness" as foundational to Digital Transformation, and the digital enterprise requires a "Disruptive **Culture**" that is willing to challenge the status quo, embrace innovation, experimentation, and "fast failure," and which is perpetually focused on what's coming next.

The *Now what?* for you as a reader is to absorb all the approaches and perspectives in this book to make your own path. Create the approach that suits you. Create a **culture** that supports that approach. Be prepared to be agile and change when and where necessary. You have the power to solve this mystery. Let us help **you** *Demystify* Digital Transformation.

Chapter 1

The Culture of Transformation

Reynaldo Lugtu Jr

Introduction

Organizational Culture as a Barrier to Digital Transformation

Business executives especially in large enterprises learned about digital transformation as early as 2009, primarily driven by technology vendors promoting their ware. Much of the understanding was centered on new emerging technologies, such as cloud computing, Internet of Things, big data analytics, and artificial intelligence (Lugtu, 2020).

In fact, when the buzz peaked in the years between 2014 and 2016, majority of the trade and academic literature authors spoke about these technologies as the main driver of digital transformation (Lugtu, 2020).

This is supported by an in-depth study by Nadkarni and Prügl (2020) which systematically reviewed 58 peer-reviewed studies published between 2001 and 2019, dealing with different aspects of digital transformation. The study revealed that 33% of the papers are technology-centric, 34% are actor-centric (i.e., transformative leadership, work environment, managerial and organizational capabilities, company culture), and 33% of papers cover both technology and actor. On the actor-centric side, the review of the authors "reveals a very dominant focus on leadership and capabilities in a digital context, while in contrast company culture and work environment thus far received less recognition."

https://doi.org/10.1142/9789811260469_0001

Hartl and Hess (2017) also observed that "**culture** has surprisingly only played a **minor role** in digital transformation research," notwithstanding prior literature acknowledging the role of culture in facilitating and managing organizational transformation and the necessity of cultural transformation in IT-enabled business transformation initiatives. Kiefer (2021) also noted that "while current research on digital transformation mostly focuses on technological and management aspects, less attention has been paid to **organizational culture** and its influence on digital innovations."

But review of related research indicated that "*legacy cultures of organizations would likely present the biggest barriers to transformation and that mindset shifts would be key to successful implementation*" (Lange et al., 2018). A survey by the Singapore Management University among C-level executives revealed that "*87% of respondents agreed that culture created bigger barriers to digital transformation than technology.*"

Consulting firms and management practitioners were also quick to recognize the critical role culture plays in the success of digital transformation. Goran et al. (2017) from McKinsey & Company revealed that "*culture is the most significant self-reported barrier to digital effectiveness,*" citing the results of a 2016 McKinsey Digital survey of 2,135 business executive respondents. The study further "*highlighted three digital-culture deficiencies: functional and departmental silos, a fear of taking risks, and difficulty forming and acting on a single view of the customer.*"

Moreover, Buvat (2017) from Capgemini Consulting revealed that outdated company cultures are the number one barrier to digital transformation. Drawing from the Capgemini Digital Transformation Institute Survey of 340 organizations globally, the authors discovered that 62% of respondents consider culture as the top one hurdle to digital transformation.

Lastly, Hippold (2019) from Gartner highlighted that "many CIOs [chief information officers] see culture as a barrier to scaling digital transformation," with 64% of CIOs perceiving culture as a "barrier to achieve their digital ambitions."

What Is Culture?

Organizational culture is a collection of core values and beliefs of the members of the organization, and the policies and practices that go along with them, such as the treatment of customers and employees, and the rules on employee behavior (Lugtu, 2017). Culture can be evident in visible artifacts like logos, dress codes, and workplace designs. It also aggregates invisibly in taken-for-granted values, unspoken attitudes, and unwritten norms that have benefited the organization in the past (Soule, 2021).

Culture can be described and defined using the Competing Values Framework (CVF). Based on organizational effectiveness research, by Cameron and Quinn (2011), the CVF is organized along two major dimensions: organizational focus (internal vs. external) and versatility (stability vs. flexibility) (Figure 1). Together, these two dimensions create four quadrants of effectiveness indicators that define the dominant culture of an organization — clan, adhocracy, hierarchy, and market.

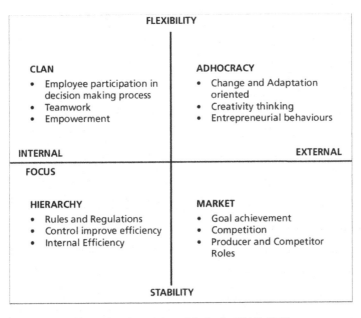

Figure 1:   Cameron and Quinn's (2011) CVF.

There is an extensive body of research on the role of culture in information systems (IS) development. One study by Leidner and Kayworth (2006) found that organizational culture influences IS development and moderates IS adoption and use. The authors discovered that people and development oriented organizational cultures as the independent variable that is supportive of IS adoption and implementation success.

Culture as Enabler of Digital Transformation

While organizational culture is seen by practitioners and business leaders as the biggest barrier to digital transformation, they also see it as an enabler. According to a Gartner research, 25% of CIOs perceive culture as an enabler (Hippold, 2019). Culture can advance digital transformation if companies can lay the groundwork by building a culture that is more adaptable to change (Andrus and Phillips, 2019). Banović-Ćurguz and Ilišević (2018) averred that culture, specifically a customer-centric one, is an enabler of digital transformation, based on their study of telecommunications industry players.

Organizational culture can be a powerful driver which influences digital transformation success (Kane *et al.*, 2017; Leidner and Kayworth 2006; Vial, 2019). Culture is a critical aspect that determines transformation, and not technology (Lange *et al.*, 2018).

In a Boston Consulting Group (BCG) study of 40 digital transformations, companies that focused on culture were five times more likely to achieve breakthrough performance than companies that neglected culture (Reichert, 2020). In this study, BCG compared digital champions and digital laggards among some 1,900 companies in the US and Europe, the author revealed that "the impact of culture was even greater than that of two other levers: investing in digital initiatives and recruiting digital talent."

What Culture Is an Enabler of Digital Transformation?

Recent literature avers that organization culture, indeed, is an enabler of digital transformation success. But what kind of culture is needed for an organization to be successful in digital transformation?

Hartl and Hess (2017) used the Delphi method to uncover "which organizational values are crucial for a successful digital transformation of businesses." Using the CVF, three cultural orientations emerged from a list of twelve (12) organizational values ranked based on the selection of the panelists in the Delphi study. The first group of values addresses an externally oriented culture comprising customer-centricity (rank 1), innovation (rank 3), and entrepreneurship (rank 7). The second group of values addresses a cultural orientation toward flexibility and adaptability comprising openness toward change (rank 1) and agility (rank 4). The third orientation is internally directed and focuses on the organization's members and their interactions; it comprises the willingness to learn (rank 5), trust (rank 6), and communication (rank 9). "These three cultural orientations match the distinct dimensions of the CVF of organizational culture" (Hartl and Hess, 2017). The ranking and definition of values are presented in Table 1.

Table 1:   Organizational value and ranking based on the Delphi study of Hartl and Hess (2017).

Organizational Value and Definition	Rank (Based on Delphi Panel Ranking)
Openness toward change: the organization's openness toward new ideas and its readiness to accept, implement, and promote change	1
Customer-centricity: the organization's orientation of all activities to meet customer needs: products and processes are designed with focus on customer needs and continuously adapted to changes thereof	2
Innovation: the organization's pursuit of improvement and growth through the development of innovations	3
Agility: the organization's willingness to work, act, and re-structure, and be flexible and adaptable in order to react to change	4
Willingness to learn: the organization's pursuit of continuous advancement through the acquisition of new skills and knowledge	5
Trust: refers to the mutual trust between the organization, its leadership, and members, as well as the organization's trust in its external partners	6
Entrepreneurship: the organization's intention to promote the empowerment of its members to act proactively and independently, and take responsibility	7
Tolerance toward failure: the organization's tolerant attitude toward reasonable mistakes and support of learning from failure	8
Communication: the organization's intention to build internal and external networks for knowledge and information sharing	9

(*Continued*)

Table 1: *(Continued).*

Organizational Value and Definition	Rank (Based on Delphi Panel Ranking)
Risk affinity: the organization's willingness to take risks and make decisions under uncertainty	10
Participation: the organization's support of open, non-hierarchical discussion and democratization of decision processes	11
Cooperation: the organization's positive stance toward teamwork, cross-functional collaboration, and readiness for cooperation with external partners (e.g., customers)	12

The organizational values were then rated by the panel in the Delphi study based on the CVF, i.e., external–internal orientation and flexibility–stability; then positioned along the dimensions in the CVF according to the average values (Hartl and Hess, 2017). The resulting CVF is depicted in Figure 2.

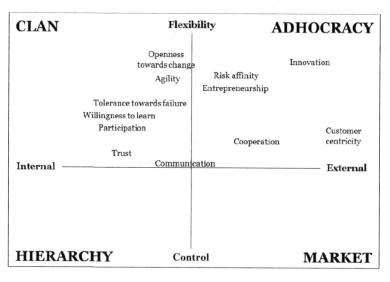

Figure 2: Delphi study results of Hartl and Hess (2017) in the CVF.

The results of the study indicate that a culture of flexibility is needed to support digital transformation (Hartl and Hess, 2017). Flexibility, alongside agility, is an essential organizational value that helps organizations constantly adapt to an increasingly unstable environment (Hartl and Hess, 2017).

A culture of flexibility requires both adhocracy and clan cultures. Clan culture promotes cohesiveness and teamwork, while adhocracy promotes innovation, creativity, and risk-taking; both culture types contribute to spontaneity and flexibility in an organization (Lugtu, 2017). This is consistent with a survey of 107 business executives which showed their highest scores in clan and adhocracy for desired cultures that will support digital transformation (Lugtu, 2017).

From the results of the study, adhocracy culture is one of the dominant culture profiles that support digital transformation. It refers to a dynamic culture that is characterized by change and adaptation orientation, creative thinking, risk-taking, and entrepreneurial behaviors (Cameron and Quinn, 2011). Successful digital transformation initiatives require a customer-centric mindset among organization members in order to innovate products and processes to address changing customer needs (Hartl and Hess, 2017). This is congruent with the study of Banović-Ćurguz and Ilišević (2018) which revealed that a customer-centric culture is an enabler of digital transformation in the telecommunications industry. Customer-centricity is a strategic approach to doing business that focuses on providing a positive customer experience both at the point of sale and after the sale, by maximizing the value that the customer derives from the product or service and converting them into loyal advocates, thereby driving sustainable profit for the company (Lugtu, 2020).

The upper left quadrant of the CVF represents the clan culture, which is characterized by an internal focus and concern for people, participation of employees in decision-making, teamwork, and empowerment (Cameron and Quinn, 2011). Successful digital transformation initiatives would require a clan culture that promotes willingness to learn among organization members and emphasizes mutual trust. In an increasingly digitalized environment of remote work and flexible work arrangements, the organization's trust in its members' commitment to the organization's cause is requisite for the success of digital transformation (Hartl and Hess, 2017).

The need for an adhocracy and clan organization culture is supported by earlier research by McConnell (2015) which surveyed 280 organizations in 26 countries. It revealed that for digital transformation to succeed, an organization should have a culture that is characterized by a strong shared sense of purpose, freedom to experiment, distributed decision-making, and openness to the influence of the external environment (McConnell, 2015). Other studies indicate innovation culture characteristics of corporate entrepreneurship, digital awareness and necessity of innovations, digital skill learning, ecosystem orientation, employee participation and agility, risk-taking, internal knowledge-sharing and collaboration, and customer orientation (Kiefer, 2021).

Innovative Culture as Enabler of Digital Transformation

The global health crisis led to the acceleration of innovation across the globe, driven by an urgent necessity to adapt to the current environment. The need to build an innovative culture in organizations has never been as pressing as it is now because an organization's culture can make or break digital transformation efforts. Chief executive officers (CEOs) have realized the need to transform company cultures into innovation-driven ones (Lugtu, 2021).

Innovation refers to the usage of novel ideas, products, services, and processes that are new to the implementing organization and create an advantage for the organization (Rujirawanich *et al.*, 2011). Innovation also refers to the organization's pursuit of improvement and growth through the development of innovations (Hartl and Hess, 2017).

Innovation culture is mentioned as a key driver to manage digital transformation (Fitzgerald *et al.*, 2013). Innovation culture is also found to have a remarkably positive effect on transformational performance (Zhang and Huang, 2010). Innovation has been a key pillar of culture that enabled digital transformation (Kiefer, 2021; Hartl and Hess, 2017).

But two key questions arise in relation to innovation culture — what is an innovative corporate culture, and if you don't have an innovative culture, is there any way an organization can build one (Rao and Weintraub, 2013)? The Six Building Blocks of Innovative Culture model was developed by Rao and Weintraub (2013) which identified key elements of an innovative culture, as well as a practical 360-degree assessment tool that managers can use to assess how conducive their organization's culture is to innovation — and to see specific areas where their culture might be more encouraging to it.

According to this model, innovative culture rests on a foundation of six building blocks: resources, processes, values, behavior, climate, and success. These building blocks are dynamically linked. For example, the values of the enterprise have an impact on people's behaviors, on the climate of the workplace, and on how success is defined and measured (Rao and Weintraub, 2013).

Rao and Weintraub (2013) define the six building blocks of an innovative culture (Figure 3).

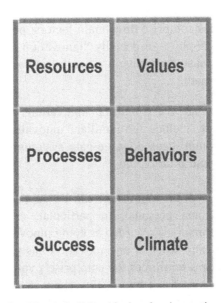

Figure 3: The six building blocks of an innovative culture.

Values: Values drive priorities and decisions, which are reflected in how a company spends its time and money. Truly innovative enterprises spend generously on being entrepreneurial, promoting creativity, and encouraging continuous learning. The values of a company are less what the leaders say or what they write in the annual reports than what they do and invest in. Values manifest themselves in how people behave and spend, more than in how they speak.

Behaviors: Behaviors describe how people act in the cause of innovation. For leaders, those acts include a willingness to kill off existing products with new and better ones to energize employees with a vivid description of the future and to cut through red tape. For employees, actions in support of innovation include doggedness in overcoming technical roadblocks, "scrounging" resources when budgets are thin, and listening to customers.

Climate: Climate is the tenor of workplace life. An innovative climate cultivates engagement and enthusiasm, challenges people to take risks within a safe environment, fosters learning, and encourages independent thinking.

Resources: Resources comprise three main factors: people, systems, and projects. Of these, people — especially "innovation champions" — are the most critical because they have a powerful impact on the organization's values and climate.

Processes: Processes are the route that innovations follow as they are developed. These may include the familiar "innovation funnel" used to capture and sift through ideas or stage-gate systems for reviewing and prioritizing projects and prototyping.

Success: The success of an innovation can be captured at three levels: external, enterprise, and personal. In particular, external recognition shows how well a company is regarded as being innovative by its customers and competitors, and whether an innovation has paid off financially. More generally, success reinforces the enterprise's values, behaviors, and processes, which in turn drive many subsequent actions and decisions: who will be rewarded, which people will be hired, and which projects will get the green light.

In my consulting work in the Philippines, an organization's innovative culture is diagnosed by running a 54-question survey across the organization that rates the employees' perceptions on a scale of 1 to 5 in the six building blocks of innovation. The resulting average rating is what is called the organization's innovation quotient, with 5 being the highest (Lugtu, 2021).

The organization is then evaluated along the digital maturity scale (Lugtu, 2020), which consists of the following five dimensions:

- **Leadership and strategy**, which spans from lowest maturity, i.e., having no strategy and no clear ownership of the digital initiatives to highest maturity, i.e., having clear strategy and ownership;
- **Execution and delivery**, which ranges from less than 40% of processes digitized to more than 75% of processes digitized;
- **Customer experience**, which extends from ad-hoc updates, no strategic plan, and slow to deliver to ground-breaking initiatives continually delivered;
- **Organization and culture**, which range from continual resistance from parts of the organization and business as usual thinking prevails to having no barriers and we are having a successful digital transformation program fully supported by the organization; and
- **Digital platform**, which ranges from the lowest where there is no integrated platform and many separate applications in place to the highest where there is fully operational and integrated platform through which the organization delivers all of its digital solutions.

With all these five dimensions, the digital maturity of an organization is then rated: the lowest as "emerging," moderate as "progressing," and most digitally mature as "optimizing" (Lugtu, 2020).

Table 2: Innovation quotient and digital maturity, organizations in the Philippines.

Organization Type	Digital Maturity	Innovation Quotient
Diversified Technology Firm	Optimizing	4.10
Energy & Utilities Firm	Progressing	3.65
Manufacturing Firm	Progressing	3.57
Shipping & Logistics Firm	Progressing	3.54
Financial Services Firm No. 2	Progressing	3.45
Financial Services Firm No. 1	Progressing	3.44
Regional Shared Services Company	Emerging	3.14

Table 2 shows the different organizations surveyed and studies by the author from 2019 to 2021, with their corresponding digital maturity and innovation quotient. It can be observed that as innovation quotient progresses, digital maturity likewise progresses. While there are limitations in this study, qualitative interviews with senior executives from these firms under study confirm that an innovative culture is a critical component for the success of digital transformation.

Barrier to Culture Transformation

Cultural transformation is difficult because it requires changing many things: the behaviors and mindsets of your employees, the organizational practices that influence them, and the company values that guide them (World Economic Forum, 2021).

Business transformations can only be successfully implemented if change is accepted (Hartl and Hess, 2017). An organization that values openness toward change fosters the willingness to accept, implement, promote, and ultimately establish a change-oriented mindset, which is required to master digital transformation and considered a key skill for digital talents and leaders (Kane *et al.*, 2017).

Professor Deborah Ancona of the MIT Sloan School of Management avers that "employees will resist because they still see the old behaviors as critical to their success and central to who they are while seeing the new norms as risky" (Buvat, 2017).

Some of the reported obstacles to digital transformation success (McConnell, 2015) are as follows:

- **Decision-making**: decision-making by consensus, internal politics, and competing priorities;
- **Value perception**: lack of ROI or proven value and lack of senior management sponsorship;
- **Willingness to address deep change**: hesitation to rethink how we work and too much focus on technology;
- **Operational awareness**: lack of understanding of operational issues at the decision-making level and difficulties when going from theory to practice;
- **Fear and control**: fear by management of losing control, fear by central functions of losing control, and fears that employees will waste time on social platforms.

Therefore, changing culture requires a methodical approach (Lugtu, 2021) to build the right mindsets, norms, and behaviors.

How to Transform Culture

Business owners and leaders need to embrace the kind of culture that promotes innovation and risk-taking to support the digital transformation of their businesses (Lugtu, 2017). The question is how?

The best-known model for change management is the three-stage process of change by Kurt Lewin, known as unfreeze–change–refreeze (Klee, 2021). Another popular model is Kotter's 8-Step Change Model (Kotter, 2009); see Figure 4. But these change models follow the sequential and planned approaches which are relatively slow (Burnes, 2005). Culture change is a complex and dynamic process consisting of accommodations and adaptations to produce fundamental change (Hartl, 2019).

Figure 4:   Kotter's 8-Step Change Model.

This dynamic approach to managing change is rooted in the need to meet uncertainty regarding digital change requirements and to stay agile within a volatile business environment. While digital culture change was initiated by top management, change itself was decisively shaped by the firm's employees through participation and active involvement in the process: by defining goals, co-developing and conducting change methods, and often driving cultural change through "coalitions of the willing" or as change ambassadors (Hartl, 2019).

Therefore, culture transformation is a journey where digital transformation and the cultural changes that make it successful are multi-stage processes that require in-depth planning and oversight.

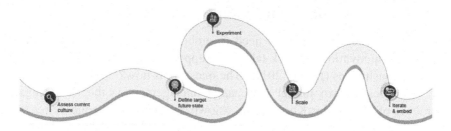

Figure 5:   Stages of a cultural transformation journey.

In this model, there are five (5) stages which need to be considered by C-level leaders positioned to implement these changes at scale (Figure 5).

Stage 1. Assess current culture: This is when the creation of and empowerment of the transformation office begins. A transformation office is typically a temporary governance and delivery vehicle whose sole purpose is to govern and drive the successful implementation of critical projects and programs that enable the organization to be transformed. This stage also covers the culture baselining through data collection from focus groups discussion, surveys, and reviews of policies and procedures. In the consulting work of the author, the Six Building Blocks of Innovation (Rao and Weintraub, 2013) is used to baseline the culture of innovation in an organization.

Stage 2. Define target future state: This involves defining the future state, i.e., digital mindset, customer-centric culture, and analyzing gaps. This is also where the digital competency model is crafted, i.e., a set of knowledge, skills, attitudes, and abilities needed in the successful execution of digital transformation.

Stage 3. Experiment: This stage of experimentation involves piloting new programs such as enablement of employees, introducing new ways of working, conducting skills workshops, and running experiments to determine what works in an organization.

Stage 4. Scale: This is when digital learning journeys and upskilling programs are instituted to the rest of the organization. New policies are introduced, and new organization structures are implemented. This is when communication campaigns are run to institutionalize a digital mindset. Progress is tracked through leadership dashboards.

The stages of culture transformation are further operationalized in the consulting work of the author. Figure 6 shows the stage process of culture transformation with a customer-centric culture as the end-state objective of C-level executives.

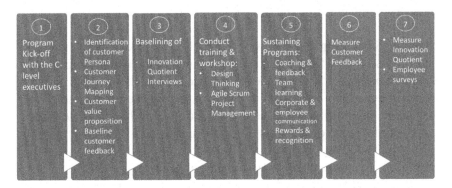

Figure 6:   Stages of customer-centricity culture transformation program.

Stage 1. Program kick-off: This is when the culture transformation program is launched as a pilot in select business units in an organization. The CEO's involvement and messaging are crucial here for the employees to see the urgency of the transformation program, as well as covey ownership.

Stage 2. Baselining of customer-centricity culture: This is where customer feedback is baselined through a customer satisfaction survey. Identification of customer personas, mapping the customer journeys, and crafting of the value proposition are necessary baselining activities to understand the vies of the customers toward the organization. These are conducted through workshops with the target participants on the customer-centricity culture change.

Stage 3. Baselining of innovation quotient: The Six Building Blocks of Innovation (Rao and Weintraub, 2013) interment is administered to the target participants. This gives a baseline of the organizational values, behaviors, and climate, as well as the employees' perceptions on processes, resources, and success building blocks that support innovation.

Stage 4. Conduct trainings and workshops: These are run to impart behavioral skills related to customer-centricity. Workshops such as design thinking and agile scrum project management are some of the trainings conducted among the target participants, intended to address some of the gaps that come out from the Six Building Blocks of Innovation Survey.

Stage 5. Sustaining programs: After running the skills-building workshops, this is when sustaining programs are conducted over a period of several months to a few years, with the objective of allowing the employees to practice the learned skills and sustain the new behaviors. Four sustaining program activities are included — coaching and feedback, team learning, employee communication, and rewards and recognition. In this stage, new key performance indicators are assigned to the target employees to ensure the display of the right behaviors.

The objectives of coaching and feedback sustaining activity are to reinforce learning by application of the lessons and then get feedback on how they are doing. The tactics involved are assigning coaches from within who will regularly run coaching sessions to ensure that the right skills and behaviors are applied and displayed.

Team learning sessions are group learning activities where small groups of the target participants convene regularly to share their experiences in applying their new skills. Team learning is an ongoing process of reflection and action, characterized by learning-oriented behaviors such as asking questions, seeking feedback, experimenting, reflecting on results, and discussing errors or unexpected outcomes (Edmondson, 1999). Team learning is found to moderate the individual learning on organizational performance (Dayaram and Fung, 2014).

Employee communication sustaining program involves using multiple media to reinforce the content and messages related to the new skills and behaviors developed. The messages will serve as an inspiration or call to action for the target participants to display and practice the new skills related to customer-centricity.

Lastly is the rewards and recognition sustaining program. This is to recognize and reward employees who learn the new behaviors and begin getting results. Rewards can vary — from vouchers to public recognition from the CEO. This approach is effective in reinforcing the new behaviors.

Stages 6 and 7: Measure customer feedback and employee innovation quotient: After running the sustaining programs for a period, feedback from customer through a survey is conducted. The best judges of the effectiveness of the customer-centricity culture transformation program are naturally the customers. But employee innovation quotient is also gathered through a survey and interviews to understand if indeed the new behaviors, values, and norms are institutionalized across the organization's employees.

The author has applied this framework and approach to companies in the Philippines. One case study is a financial services firm, where the CEO's mandate was to transform the organization's culture to a customer-centric one. The program was run over two years — first as pilot in the first year and then expanded to the rest of the organization in the second year. After one year of the program, the company reported the highest customer satisfaction scores, while increasing its revenue significantly despite the pandemic.

Conclusion

Organizational culture can be a barrier to or an enabler of digital transformation. The elements of culture, i.e., employee behavior and mindsets and organizational practices can slow down decision-making and stunt innovation in organizations. Cultural norms, values, behaviors, and practices that involve customer-centricity, flexibility, agility, and innovation are requisites in helping organizations to constantly adapt to an increasingly unstable environment.

In particular, an innovative culture that rests on a foundation of six building blocks — **resources, processes, values, behavior, climate, and success** — is a key driver to the success of digital transformation initiatives.

But transforming organizational culture is not an easy undertaking as it involves employee resistance. It requires a methodical approach to build the right mindsets, norms, and behaviors among organization members. The 7-stage culture transformation framework of the author has been field-tested, yielding positive outcomes for organizations in the Philippines.

Bibliography

Banović-Ćurguz, N. & Ilišević, D. (2018, July 02) "Customer-centric culture as enabler of digital transformation," 2018 41st International Convention on Information and Communication Technology, Electronics and Micro-electronics (MIPRO), 2018, pp. 0400–0404, doi: 10.23919/MIPRO.2018. 8400076.

Boston Consulting Group. (n.d.). *How to Drive a Digital Transformation: Culture Is Key.* https://www.bcg.com/capabilities/digital-technology-data/digital-transformation/how-to-drive-digital-culture.

Burnes, B. (2005). Complexity theories and organizational change. *International Journal of Management Reviews*, 7(2), 73–90.

Buvat, J., Solis, B., Crummenerl, C., Aboud, C., Kar, K., El Aoufi, H., & Sengupta, A. (2017). *The Digital Culture Challenge: Closing the Employee-leadership Gap.* Capgemini. Retrieved August 20, 2021, from https://www.capgemini.com/wp-content/uploads/2017/12/dti_digitalculture_report.pdf.

Cameron, L. & Quinn, R. (2011). *Diagnosing and Changing Organizational Culture: Based on the Competing Values Framework.* Jossey-Bass.

Dayaram, K. & Fung, L. (2014). Organizational learning in the Philippines: How do team and individual learning contribute? *Asia Pacific Journal of Human Resources*, 52(4), 420–442.

Edmondson, A. (1999). Psychological safety and learning behavior in work teams. *Administrative Science Quarterly*, 44, 350–383.

Fitzgerald, M., Kruschwitz, N., Bonnet, D., & Welch, M. (2014). Embracing digital technology. A new strategic imperative. *MIT Sloan Management Review*, 55(2), 1.

Goran, J., LeBerge, L., & Srinivasan, R. (2017). Culture for a digital age. *McKinsey Quarterly*, 3(1), 56–67.

Hartl, E. (2019). A Characterization of Culture Change in the Context of Digital Transformation. In *AMCIS*.

Hartl, E. & Hess, T. (2017). The role of cultural values for digital transformation: Insights from a Delphi study.

Hippold, S. (2019, April 26). *CIOs: Break Through Culture Barriers to Enable Digital Transformation.* Gartner. https://www.gartner.com/smarterwithgartner/cios-break-through-culture-barriers-to-enable-digital-transformation.

Kane, G. C., Palmer, D., & Phillips, A. N. (2017). Achieving digital maturity. *MIT Sloan Management Review*, 59(1), 1–29.

Kane, G. C., Phillips, A. N., Copulsky, J. R., & Andrus, G. R. (2019). The Technology Fallacy: How People Are the Real Key to Digital Transformation (Management on the Cutting Edge). *Copyright material MIT Sloan Management Review*, Boston, USA.

Kiefer, D., Dinther, C. V., & Spitzmüller, J. (2021, March). Digital innovation culture: A systematic literature review. In International Conference on Wirtschaftsinformatik (pp. 305–320). Springer, Cham.

Klee, C. (2021). Digital transformation in property development and the role of change management: Structured literature review and future trends. *In ICMBF 3rd International Conference on Advanced Research in Management, Business & Finance.*

Kotter, J. P. (2009). Leading change: Why transformation efforts fail. *IEEE Engineering Management Review*, 37(3), 42–48.

Leidner, D. E. & Kayworth, T. (2006). A review of culture in information systems research: Toward a theory of information technology culture conflict. *MIS Quarterly*, 30(2), 357–399.

Lugtu, R. (2017, November 3). The culture of digital transformation. *Manila Times*. https://www.manilatimes.net/2017/11/03/business/columnists-business/culture-digital-transformation/360412.

Lugtu, R. (2020, January 10). The evolution of digital transformation. *Business World* Online. https://www.bworldonline.com/the-evolution-of-digital-transformation/.

Lugtu, R. (2020, February 14). Digital maturity. *BusinessWorld Online*. https://www.bworldonline.com/digital-maturity/.

Lugtu, R. (2020, February 27). Building a customer-centric organization. *Manila Times*. https://www.manilatimes.net/2020/02/27/business/columnists-business/building-a-customer-centric-organization/696935.

Lugtu, R. (2021, June 11). Building blocks of innovation. *Manila Times*. https://www.manilatimes.net/2021/06/11/business/top-business/building-blocks-of-innovation/1802779.

McConnell, J. (2015, August 1). Digital transformation and work cultures. NetJMC. https://www.netjmc.com/digital-transformation-and-work-cultures/.

Nadkarni, S. & Prügl, R. (2021). Digital transformation: A review, synthesis and opportunities for future research. *Management Review Quarterly*, 71(2), 233–341.

Rao, J. & Weintraub, J. (2013). How innovative is your company's culture? *MIT Sloan Management Review*. Retrieved September 12, 2021, from https://sloanreview.mit.edu/article/how-innovative-is-your-companys-culture/.

Rujirawanich, P., Addison, R., & Smallman, C. (2011). The effects of cultural factors on innovation in a Thai SME. *Management Research Review*, 34(12), 1264–1279.

Soule, D. (2021). Why culture is a critical component in your digital transformation journey. Copyright Clearance Center, Inc. https://www.copyright.com/wp-content/uploads/2019/09/CCC_Becoming-Digital-Culture-WP-2_FNL_WEB.pdf.

Vial, G. (2021). Understanding digital transformation: A review and a research agenda. *Managing Digital Transformation*, 13, 66.

Westerman, G., Bonnet, D., & McAfee, A. (2014). *Leading Digital: Turning Technology into Business Transformation*. Boston: Harvard Business Review Press.

World Economic Forum. (2021, June 29). Digital culture: The driving force of digital transformation. https://www.weforum.org/reports/digital-culture-the-driving-force-of-digital-transformation.

Zhang, W. & Huang, X. (2010, August). A research on the relationship between innovation culture, transformational capabilities and transformational performance. In *2010 International Conference on Management and Service Science* (pp. 1–4). IEEE.

Chapter 2

Business Architecture as an Enabler of Transformation

Whynde Kuehn

Introduction

Finally, your holiday is here, and you are about to embark upon the road trip of which you have been dreaming. With your vehicle all packed, you slide into the driver's seat. You open the map application on your smartphone and enter the destination. You are presented with three routes and choose the most scenic one, which also avoids the construction roadblocks that are in place this time of year. You tap *Go*, and the adventure begins.

We have become so accustomed to this scenario as part of our daily lives that we may not give it a second thought. However, it is worth marveling for a moment at the elegance that makes this possible. First, we take it for granted that a map exists in the first place, which is documented and agreed to. Maps provide us with a common mental model about how we see the world along with a common vocabulary for describing places. Second, we have incredible technology that guides us. GPS (Global Positioning System) tracks where our vehicle is at all times, and an application presents us with moment-by-moment directions and options to inform our decisions.

How would we ever plan a road trip across the United States from New York to California if we had no map (or concrete boundaries for New

York and California), did not know where we were starting from, and had only a conceptual idea of where we were going? We either would not try or if we did attempt the trip, it might take a long time and convoluted path to get there. We laugh at the idea, but conceptually this is not so far off from how many organizations approach digital transformation.

Organizations do not come with a map or a guidance system. We need to intentionally put them in place and for the same reasons: to give us a shared understanding of where the organization is today and where it is going in the future, to define how we will get there, and to inform our decisions along the way.

Business architecture serves as that map and guide for an organization, and it is the gateway to successful digital transformation.

Business Architecture is a Blueprint to Create Understanding and Activate Change

What is business architecture? Business architecture is simply a set of views or *blueprints* of an organization that creates common understanding and aligns strategy and execution. It represents everything an organization does through a pure business lens, comprehensively, and at a high level of detail.

A business architecture describes how an organization is structured to deliver value to its customers (or equivalent such as patients for healthcare or constituents for government or non-profit organizations) as well as support its operations. There are no other views or techniques like it. In our world of complexity and detail, what makes business architecture so unique is that we can see an entire organization and the business ecosystem in which it operates from a bird's eye view and through a refreshing new lens: *the whole*.

A business architecture comprises multiple different business perspectives: value streams, capabilities, information, organization, strategies, metrics, products, stakeholders, policies, and initiatives. At the heart of an organization's business architecture are value streams and capabilities. Value streams represent how value is delivered from end-to-end to a customer, partner, or employee. Capabilities define the *whats* of the business — the unique abilities that the organization performs across all business units and product lines. Capabilities are a crucial construct to organize and optimize the resources needed to deliver stakeholder value and evolve the organization through change initiatives. They are the one domain that connects to all the others. Capabilities are like reusable building blocks that may be used many times within or across value streams.

Information forms the vocabulary of an organization through defined information concepts such as Customer, Product, Partner, and Asset. **Organization** represents business units, which may be internal business units or external partners. **Strategies** capture various aspects of business direction, and **metrics** measure the performance of the organization. **Products** represent the goods and services that an organization offers to its customers. **Stakeholders** represent the external or internal players that participate in value streams to receive and/or contribute value. **Policies** guide the organization and may be externally driven such as a regulation or internally driven such as an internal human resources policy. Finally, **initiatives** represent any current or planned scope of work to implement change.

Each of these perspectives is valuable on its own but becomes even more valuable when connected. For example, from a capability perspective, we can understand which capabilities enable a value stream, which capabilities deliver a product or service to a customer, which capabilities need to be matured to realize a strategy and which initiatives are delivering on those changes, which policies guide capabilities, and how the aggregate set of changes being made to the capabilities across initiatives will impact the stakeholders collectively.

These business architecture perspectives (with a focus on value streams and capabilities) can also be connected to other domains outside the scope of business architecture. A few common connection points for business architecture include **journeys** (part of the customer experience design discipline), **business processes** (part of the business process management discipline), **applications** and **software services** (part of the IT architecture discipline), and **requirements** (part of the business analysis discipline).

There are a few key characteristics that distinguish business architecture from other documentation and approaches:

A business architecture represents the business — Business architecture is *not an IT view* or discipline. It is wholly business focused, describing the scope of what the business does, in the language of the business. A business architecture can, however, be connected to an organization's IT architecture, which illuminates how the business is supported by applications and services, data and data deployments, and infrastructure.

A business architecture represents the entire scope of an organization and the ecosystem in which it operates — Business architecture is the big view. A business architecture does not exist in fragments across an organization. A business architecture is one, top-down, cohesive view of everything an organization does.

A business architecture is described at a high level of detail — To make that scope of documentation attainable and usable, a business architecture is described from a higher elevation. In contrast to the detailed processes, rules, data, and systems we are immersed in daily, business architecture allows us to see the forest for the trees. This is by design for the value business architecture is intended to deliver.

A business architecture is reusable — Unlike the many documents, presentations, and deliverables which we create and archive, an organization's business architecture persists in a knowledge base that is accessible to anyone. This translates into great time savings for onboarding and making changes to an organization because an understanding of the current state is always readily available.

Every organization has a business architecture. This is true for organizations of all sizes and across all sectors. An organization's business architecture may not be written down and some aspects may have been created unintentionally, but it does exist. The key is documenting it in a principled manner and maintaining it in a shared repository so that it can be used to support a multitude of business and technology decision-making scenarios.

Business Architecture Underpins Successful Digital Enterprises and Transformations

Whether an organization is already a digital enterprise or on the transformation journey to become one, three abilities are necessary, which often require building new muscle. Each of these abilities is underpinned by business architecture and includes:

- Effective organization and ecosystem design and redesign.
- Continuous end-to-end execution of strategies and transformations.
- New mindsets and ways of working that are value-focused, agile, and innovative.

Effective organization and ecosystem design and redesign is necessary to reimagine and articulate the future state of an organization leveraging digital technologies strategically, such as to transform business models, as well as operationally such as to gain new efficiencies with automation. Business architecture provides the fundamental structure for digital transformation and evolution, allowing people to readily view what the organization does today and then methodically redesign how it will change.

To successfully achieve transformation, organizations need a way to define and implement people, process, and technology changes across business units, products, and locations for potentially the largest scope they have encountered to date. Of course, constant change is now the new normal, so organizations need to become good at **continuous end-to-end execution of strategies and transformations**. The organizations that can execute upon their digital strategies in a coordinated way, and with agility, will win. The ability to move strategy into action, and continually innovate and adapt to change, has now become competitive advantage in itself.

Business architecture plays an important — and often missing — role to inform and translate strategies into a harmonized set of actions for execution. It provides a mental image and framework to help people within the organization as well as any external partners grasp the breadth and complexity of change. The business architecture knowledge base serves as an enterprise-wide impact analysis tool that can be used to identify how a strategy or transformation will impact the business and technology environments as well as the customer, partner, and employee experiences. These impacts can be cataloged and assessed, and then collectively architected across products and business units — using capabilities (in a value context) as the focal point for organizing the changes.

The planned business and technology changes can even be visualized in a target state architecture, which provides a shared picture of the organization of the future at a more actionable level of detail than strategy documentation — to help everyone see and work towards the same vision. The resulting target architecture(s) can then be scoped into a set of transformation initiatives in the most effective way across business units — without fragmentation, redundancy, conflicts, or dependency issues. This macro-level translation of direction applies equally whether waterfall or agile approaches are leveraged for delivery.

In addition, the business architecture knowledge base also manages the traceability from strategy and objectives through the business architecture to initiatives, which also provides assurance that initiatives actually deliver on the expected business results. This top-down, cross-business unit approach to strategy execution is not only essential to carrying out the digital transformation, but it also builds an organization's ability to continually adapt to change and replan when necessary.

Figure 1 provides a simplified perspective on the major activities involved to define and deliver digital transformation along with the role of business architecture and business architects throughout. (Note: Many additional teams collaborate iteratively across this end-to-end perspective but are not shown here.)

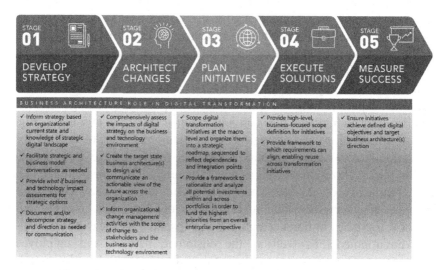

Figure 1:   The role of business architecture in digital transformation.

"...a great strategy is valuable only if a company is capable of executing that strategy. And whether or not a company can execute its strategy depends largely on whether it is designed to do so. In other words, it depends on business architecture — the way a company's people, processes, systems, and data interact to deliver goods and services to customers."

Jeanne Ross, Architect Your Company for Agility

Leveraging business architecture to execute strategies and transformations bridges an important gap between ideas and actions, but also provides additional benefits such as:

- **Exceptional, integrated, and consistent experiences for customers, partners, and employees**: Because the experience design can be operationalized across silos, and because the business and technology environments can be streamlined to support a better experience.
- **Decreased complexity of the business environment and decreased complexity and technical debt of the IT environment**: Because business and technology solutions can be built once and reused; business architecture can also be used to identify areas for further simplification.
- **Decreased time and cost to develop and maintain solutions**: Because business and technology solutions can be built once and reused as well as integrated up front.
- **Decreased business risk and potential for non-compliance**: Because business architecture creates transparency and the business and technology environment is simpler.
- **Decreased brand and reputational risks**: Because customer and partner solutions are designed more effectively, and risks related to compliance, security, or other matters are lowered.
- **Better quality in products and services as well as operations**: Because of better design, integration, execution, and transparency.
- **Better ability for stakeholders to consume the changes implemented**: Because the collective impact on stakeholders is known up front and can be adjusted.
- **Increased organizational agility and faster time to market for implementing strategies and changes**: Because of a common business vocabulary and mental model, a streamlined environment, and an effective end-to-end strategy execution approach that can continually react to change.

Digital transformation is a fundamental business change which also requires a rewiring of the way an organization operates. To sustain transformation, organizations need to adopt **new mindsets and ways of working that are value-based, agile, and innovative**. For example, some key shifts required, particularly for non-digital native organizations, include:

- Leading with value for customers and stakeholders (focus from the *outside-in*), not the organization's *inside-out* view.
- Developing transformational strategies and a culture of continual strategy and innovation, not tactical improvements.

- Taking responsibility for the business, not allowing digital transformation to be technology-led or vendor-led.
- Embodying an enterprise-first mindset, not a silo-first mindset.
- Building end-to-end organizational agility, not just execution agility.

These shifts require changes to the underlying structures and culture of an organization, but business architecture can be leveraged as a catalyst and enabler to help shift peoples' mindsets and behaviors. For example, an organization's business architecture is naturally politically agnostic and can help inform tough decisions and priorities in a way that transcends organizational silos and illuminates what is best for the customer and the enterprise.

We will now explore a few ways in which business architecture can be and has been leveraged by organizations to enable digital transformation.

Business architecture gives structure to and helps scale strategy formulation and innovation

True digital transformation is just that: *transformational*, going beyond digital operations and leveraging technology as part of the strategy, and embedding digital thinking into the core of what the organization does. This may be reflected in how an organization reimagines its business model and value propositions, or in the digital products and services that it offers.

Business architecture provides a high-level structure for strategy formulation and innovation activities that articulate what is in place today and help unlock new creative ideas. For example, an organization's documented business model canvas is an ideal structure upon which methodical analyses can be performed to evaluate and redesign it, and then communicate those changes with others. On the other hand, an organization's capabilities can be looked at like *Lego blocks* that can be reused and reconfigured in new ways to deliver new value propositions to existing or new customers. Of course, business architecture may also be used to assess the viability and impact footprint of strategic options and innovation ideas, as mentioned earlier with the *what if* concept.

In addition, business architecture can also be used to scale innovation ideas across an organization. For example, where an innovation idea may have been identified for just one use case, a business architecture pinpoints additional ways of leveraging it for other business units, capabilities, value streams, products, or locations.

Business architecture facilitates the shift to customer centricity

Digital customer engagement is another important aspect of leveraging technology for strategic business value. This includes selling, servicing, and engaging with customers through digital channels, including self-service.

First and foremost, a business architecture is entirely oriented around an organization's end customers and the products, services, and value offered to them. In other words, in a business architecture, products and services represent the things an organization offers in the market, and customers are defined as the individuals or organizations that have an agreement with the organization for those products and services, or otherwise benefit from them. This orientation gives everyone in an organization a shared guiding light of what is important, and continually emphasizes the *outside-in* perspective. Furthermore, when business architecture combines with customer experience design (and the broader umbrella of Human-Centered Design) it creates a powerhouse for marrying the outside-in with the inside-out to help organizations maximize their customer value delivery and results.

For example, business architecture helps create consistent, streamlined customer experiences. Capabilities that leverage reusable solutions help create consistent experiences for customers, even when delivered across many business units and external partners. Value streams orchestrate the capabilities, information, stakeholders, products, and technology across the customer journey, making sure that all the pieces are available at the right place and right time to deliver the best possible experience. This concept can even be expanded to include situations such as a government that wants to define and deliver reusable government services across agencies, leading to a more integrated citizen experience as well as operational efficiencies.

Business architecture also safeguards the customer experience. This is especially critical during times of transformation when many different teams and initiatives are making changes that could potentially have negative impacts on the experience. For example, if a significant change is planned to a process or solution, it can be traced to the impacted capabilities, then to the impacted value stream stages, and ultimately to the specific customer journey stages that could be affected. Or, a business architecture-based checkpoint could be inserted in the initiative decision-making process to assess the potential customer experience impact of any proposed initiatives before they are prioritized and approved.

In addition, business architecture can also help pinpoint the root causes of customer-related issues. A customer experience issue that is occurring at a certain stage(s) within a customer journey can be traced through to the value stream stages that are enabling that portion of the journey, and then further traced to the potentially problematic capabilities within those value stream stages. From there the people, process, technology, or other focal points can be explored to uncover the root cause. For example, the customer issue may be occurring because a team is understaffed, or an internal policy is misaligned with customer needs.

Business architecture helps scope and prioritize transformation

Scoping a digital transformation can feel a bit intimidating, like *eating an elephant*, because the changes are typically far reaching and intertwined across an organization's business units, products, and locations. Business architecture value streams and capabilities serve as focal points to scope the macro set of work in a logical and interlocking way — and bring the conversations up to a higher level.

Different leaders and teams may be responsible for delivering shared capabilities or orchestrating cohesive value streams. For example, one set of teams may be responsible for delivering ready-to-use capabilities (with people, process, and technology enablement) organized around customer information and preferences, customer communications, or money movement. Another set of teams may be responsible to ensure that different value streams such as Acquire Product or Settle Financial Account are streamlined, unified, and integrated across business units and products, and ready to leverage the capabilities. These value streams and capabilities can then be assembled to deliver cohesive, consistent journeys for customers, partners, and employees. Figure 2 shows a simplified example of this concept for a retail customer journey.

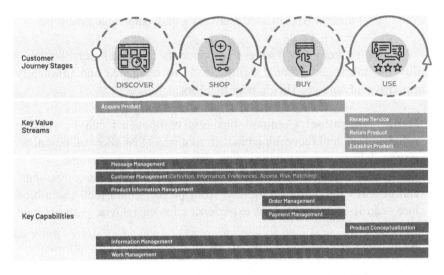

Figure 2: Alignment of journeys, value streams, and capabilities.

Furthermore, a business architecture-scoped transformation creates the foundation for long-term business ownership. A business executive or steering committee can be established to set the direction for a set of capabilities or value stream(s) and govern the evolution to them. Target architectures and strategic roadmaps provide ideal structures for business leaders to make decisions and govern because they are high-level and entirely business oriented.

Business architecture creates a composable organization

The concept of a *composable organization* — and the mindset that goes along with it — has become increasingly important for continuously delivering innovation and responding to the accelerating pace of change.

> *"As business needs change, organizations must be able to deliver innovation quickly and adapt applications dynamically — reassembling capabilities from inside and outside the enterprise. To do this, organizations must understand and implement the 'composable enterprise.'"*

Leveraging common business components facilitates organizational agility — and organizational agility leads to resilience and ultimately competitive advantage. This is beneficial for:

- **Rapid innovation**: Common business components can be reused, reconfigured, and recombined in different ways that allow an organization to deliver new value, products, and services to customers.
- **Integrated experiences and solutions**: Common business components can be built internally or sourced from partners, and then assembled into seamless and consistent experiences for customers, partners, and employees.
- **Rapid business changes and strategy execution**: Common business components allow changes to be made faster because those changes only need to be made one time. (Compare this to many instances of processes and automation that may exist in siloed or legacy environments.)

So, what are these common business components? Capabilities. Of course, an entire business architecture is essentially a componentized view of an organization, comprising reusable, interconnecting pieces, but capabilities are the Rosetta stone that knits them all together.

Capabilities set the stage for composable technology such as reusable software services that can be exchanged within an organization as well as outside of it with partners. In addition, capabilities facilitate a composable thinking mindset in business leaders and beyond, to inspire new ideas for innovation and agility.

Business architecture facilitates cross-team communication, coordination, and collaboration

A digital enterprise has high functioning teams that can work autonomously, and integrate, communicate, coordinate, and collaborate effectively with each other. A business architecture framework helps empower teams to work more autonomously since they can readily identify key intersection and collaboration points. A shared language is of course a necessity for effective team communication, but capabilities also serve as a Rosetta stone to facilitate team collaboration. For example, teams can identify when they are building or enhancing the same capabilities to identify opportunities for reuse, consistency, or coordination. Capabilities also illuminate dependencies, such as when a capability (or service) such as customer preference management must be established before other capabilities such as communication delivery can leverage it. Value streams provide additional context for capabilities to identify all usage scenarios so that solutions can be built holistically, such as for a payment capability which is used by customers, partners, and employees.

An organization's business architecture can also be heat-mapped to reflect current strategic priorities. This enables teams, such as agile or continuous improvement teams, to decide where to focus, making sure their actions are aligned with only the highest strategic priorities. If policies are tied to capabilities, teams can also become readily aware of regulations, internal policies, ethics, or other guidelines that should be adhered to.

The big picture view of business architecture is also a highly effective way for team members to understand how they fit within the organization and contribute to the overall value delivery. For example, value streams provide a higher-level, value-based context for processes. This not only helps team members understand where they fit, but also what happens upstream and downstream. This type of knowledge can ultimately lead to more effective, proactive, and empowered team members.

Business architecture ensures strategic alignment

Even if an organization's digital strategy was translated into initiatives through the business architecture as described in Figure 1, misalignments still can arise as work executes over time. In addition, a large organization will likely have a high volume of initiatives that are in-flight beyond the digital transformation. The golden thread in Figure 3 is a visual representation of how the end-to-end traceability of business architecture can be used to assess and align strategies to architecture to initiatives.

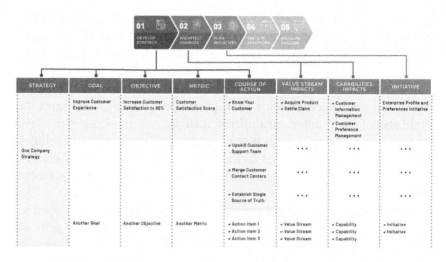

Figure 3:   Aligning strategy and initiatives through business architecture.

Leveraging business architecture to assess and ensure strategic alignment is relevant to different audiences at different points across the strategy execution perspective. For example:

- **Leaders and strategists** can assess alignment across strategies to ensure that objectives and courses of action are not conflicting.
- **Business and IT architects** can assess alignment of enhancements being made to the same value streams, capabilities, and other architecture focal points across strategies and transformations.
- **Portfolio leaders** can assess alignment from proposed initiatives back to strategies as well as alignment across proposed initiatives.
- **Initiative stakeholders, including sponsors and program or project managers**, can assess alignment of initiative results back to the original strategies and objectives. In-flight initiatives can even be assessed for alignment back to the business objectives they are supporting and the value streams and capabilities they are uplifting, and any necessary course corrections made.
- **Business analysts** can assess alignment of initiative requirements back to the value streams, capabilities, and business objectives they are enhancing.
- **Business architecture provides a business lens for technology decision-making.**

While technology is of course at the heart of digital transformations and digital enterprises, it is ultimately guided by and in service to the business — through people that it supports and the value that it enables. This means that technology decisions and investments are essentially *business* decisions and investments.

Business architecture helps to facilitate business and IT partnership and co-creation. It allows people to communicate and have productive conversations about technology-related decisions in a simple, shared business language and context, regardless of their business or technology backgrounds. This not only results in better decision-making, but also better understanding, engagement, and ownership by the business for issues such as technical debt and modernization. It also enables important conversations about building a scalable, adaptable, and future-ready technology foundation to support the business as it evolves.

Within an application portfolio management context, business architecture elevates the conversation from focusing on specific system applications to focusing on business capabilities, which may be automated by many applications. This puts the application landscape into a business context which inevitably leads to different decisions. For example, measurements of the level of automation, application redundancy, application risk, or technical debt can be aggregated and assessed at the capability level. When combined with the business priority and strategic importance of those capabilities, it leads to prioritization and decision-making that is best for the business overall. Business decisions can be made with eyes wide open, including areas where risk is acceptable, or technical debt is tolerable because it provides strategic or operational value.

In addition, business architecture is a critical driver of the direction and investment priorities of IT architecture transformation. Business architecture drives changes to the IT architecture based on business direction and planned changes of all sizes, from creating a new software service to address a capability gap to supporting a reinvented business model. Business architecture also provides the business lens for other IT architecture transformation, such as a shift towards a service-oriented architecture or microservices architecture. Business architecture also facilitates business-driven approaches and roadmaps for IT architecture transformation. For example, the level of application technical debt and business misalignment aggregated by capability can guide whether targeted investments are needed to improve the IT architecture or whether a major architectural investment is needed to address foundation.

Capabilities can also guide on when IT architecture investments should be made based on business priority and the timing of other initiatives.

Business architecture also provides critical business context to inform decision-making for cloud strategy and migration. Business architecture articulates an aggregate view of business direction related to planned strategies, transformations, improvements, and structural changes (e.g., internal department changes or external ones related to mergers, acquisitions, divestitures, and joint ventures) along with their collective impact on various aspects of the business and technology environment as well. Business architecture also provides the business context and priority for defining what an organization should put in the cloud and when.

Business architecture can also guide organizations as they make decisions, implement, adopt, and govern emerging technologies. This may include artificial intelligence, blockchain, virtual reality, and others. For example, business architecture can ensure data is rationalized around a common business perspective, particularly important for use by emerging technologies such as AI. Business architecture can help uncover workforce implications related to emerging technologies and guide workforce planning and upskilling. Coupled with human-centered design, business architecture facilitates cohesive experiences and interactions between humans and technology. It is also an ideal framework to facilitate governance and risk management, as described in the next section.

Business architecture provides a framework for transparency and governance

The power of technology and our connected world also introduces some new challenges and considerations for organizations and their stakeholders, including customers, workers, the environment, and society at large. For example, using artificial intelligence, generating large volumes of data stored in the cloud, or producing certain types of digital products can have far-reaching implications to the well-being of humans and the environment. The need for good long-term decision-making and transparency in compliance and responsibility as it pertains to ethics and sustainability has become even more urgent.

Business architecture embeds compliance, ethics, and sustainability into the structure of an organization. It is essentially the scaffolding that helps to keep these important considerations top of mind. For example, if an organization has its regulations, internal policies, ethics, and sustainability metrics tied to its capabilities in the business architecture knowledge base, then this becomes a natural trigger for conversation anytime a team or initiative plans to make any changes to a capability.

The business architecture knowledge base also provides transparency. It enables repeatable, defensible analysis and shows the end-to-end traceability between everything. For example, compliance can be demonstrated by tracing through a regulation or internal policy to its impacted capabilities, business units, and value streams — with the ability to drill down to the relevant processes and systems that implement them. Business architecture can also help people to understand and govern AI within a familiar business context. For example, as shown in Figure 4, an algorithm can be traced through to the capability it enables (Agreement Eligibility Determination), the value streams in which that capability is used (Acquire Product), the business units involved (Group Sales), the policies or rules that guide the algorithm (Non-Discrimination Policy), and the technology in which it resides (Sales System).

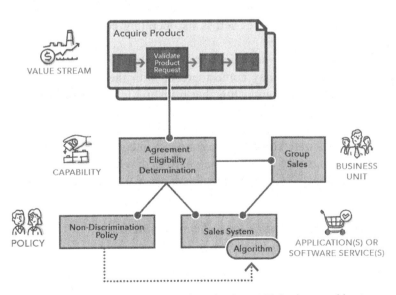

Figure 4:   Facilitating transparency in technology with business architecture.

Business architecture facilitates ecosystem design

The concept of a business ecosystem is multiple organizations working together towards a shared purpose, to create greater value for customers, society, and themselves beyond what they can do individually. The global movement towards business ecosystems — accelerated and enabled by technology — provides unparalleled opportunities to solve some of the greatest challenges of our time while also fostering business growth and prosperity. It represents an important shift in how we think about the role of a firm and how value is defined by society.

Business architecture inherently helps to drive a new ecosystem mindset because it encourages thinking big picture, working across silos, and applying a value lens to decisions and design. The structure of business architecture also lends itself well to working across organizational boundaries because it already represents the scope of an organization and its entire business ecosystem, focuses on end-to-end value delivery which can transcend organizations, and it includes external perspectives such as customer, partners, and regulators.

Business architecture can facilitate:

- **Cross-entity coordination within an organization's scope**: For example, a company may want to facilitate opportunities for sharing innovations and resources across its operating companies, brands, or other entities.
- **Collaborative cross-organizational ventures**: For example, two or more organizations may come together with the intent to deliver an extended customer journey together from end-to-end, each contributing capabilities as a customer moves seamlessly from one stage to the next.
- **Ecosystem architecting and collaboration**: For example, multiple organizations may come together around integrated solutions such as smart homes, smart cities, or the connected vehicle — or within ecosystem perspectives such as open banking or the circular economy.

The time to start leveling up to leverage business architecture for digital transformation is now

To be clear, business architecture is not a silver bullet. It takes an entire ecosystem of teams working in harmony for an organization to execute strategy from end-to-end and transform into a digital enterprise. Business architecture is also not a quick fix, because let's face it, the challenges that many large, non-digital native organizations need to overcome were not created overnight.

Business architecture does, however, help to connect teams, bridge the gap between strategy and execution, and provide a foundation for digital readiness and transformation — as well as sustainable organizational agility and success. Establishing a business architecture practice accelerates and improves the outcomes of digital transformation and enhances other teams in the process.

Digital transformation can be the ideal impetus for introducing or scaling business architecture within an organization. Organizations that already have a mature practice in place are best positioned to leverage business architecture for digital transformation. In cases such as these, a business architecture knowledgebase likely exists, the strategic value and role of business architects is recognized, and a supporting practice to ensure consistency and scale of the discipline is established. However, since the existence of a mature business architecture practice is still fairly uncommon in organizations, it is possible to establish or mature one *while* leveraging it for digital transformation. Transformation does require a solid level of business architecture maturity, but it can be built *just enough just in time*, especially with the right business sponsorship and investment behind it.

Ensure the Business Architecture Essentials Are in Place to Support Transformation

Business architecture knowledgebase

While it is ideal to have a business architecture knowledge base that includes content for all domains of business architecture, the *minimum* to consider for digital transformation includes:

- An organization-wide capability map decomposed to three levels of capabilities.
- The value streams within the scope of transformation, especially customer-facing ones.
- A value stream/capability cross-mapping to provide context for capability usage.

- Connections to additional business architecture perspectives, especially strategies and objectives, initiatives, products, business units, and information.
- Connections to related discipline perspectives, especially journeys, processes, and software applications and services.

The volume of business architecture content and cross-mapping necessary for digital transformation usually requires an automated repository tool to support information capture, analysis, visualization, and reporting.

Business architects and business architecture practice

Leveraging business architecture for a digital transformation not only requires the knowledge base, but also business architects who play an invaluable role in informing digital business models and strategy, assessing the impacts, translating the strategy into a future state for the organization, defining the initiatives required to achieve it, and ensuring continual strategic alignment. The business architect role must be defined and socialized, and filled with individuals who are trained and certified, and who have a range of experience and talents.

A supporting practice must also be put into place (e.g., through a Center of Excellence) to orchestrate and ensure consistency of activities such as business architecture training and mentoring, methodology, governance, and tooling. An intentionally built business architecture practice will continually deliver value and scale to meet the organization's demand for the discipline over time.

Focus on maturing your organization's business architecture practice over time

Whether your organization already has a business architecture practice or plans to establish one alongside your digital transformation efforts, here are some steps you can take:

Assess your overall business architecture maturity: Request a third-party business architecture maturity assessment or perform a self-assessment using a business architecture maturity model. Create a roadmap to address any areas of opportunity or gaps.

Assess your business architecture essentials for transformation: Refer to the section above and identify any gaps in your business architecture knowledge base, team, or practice to make sure you have the essential elements in place to support transformation.

Partner with transformation leaders and teams: Educate and build relationships with business and technology leaders as well as any related teams you will work with such as customer experience or organizational change management. Help them understand what business architecture is, where it fits in, and how it brings unique value to the outcomes they are trying to achieve.

Position and engage business architecture and business architects: Engage business architects in the digital transformation as soon as possible, involving them upfront within the strategy execution perspective, starting with direction-setting. In addition, make sure business architects are positioned at the right level of authority, and that the role of business architecture is formally reflected in any transformation or planning frameworks.

Learn from the best practices of successful business architecture teams

First and foremost, successful business architecture teams leverage business architecture as an *enterprise discipline*, not as a toolbox of available techniques. One shared business architecture helps bring together an entire organization. On the other hand, offering business architecture as a set of tools and templates for each business unit to use as they wish will only reinforce the silos that exist.

The foundation for business architecture as an enterprise discipline is ensured by two immutable principles. The first is there is one shared business architecture for an organization (unless it is a conglomerate or other structure which warrants multiple). The second is business architecture practitioners share one methodology. The first principle ensures the same architecture is used and the second ensures that the architects use it consistently and have a shared education and frame of reference.

Beyond these important principles, there are proven critical success factors for business architecture. These include:

- **Executive sponsorship**: Obtain visible, committed executive-level sponsorship as high in the organization as possible, as soon as possible.
- **Business and value orientation**: Focus on the business in the business architecture and remember that the architecture is just a means to an end. Define a clear value proposition for business architecture in an organization, deliver it through repeatable services, and build the knowledge base and practice just enough just in time.
- **Partnerships**: Build strong partnerships with other roles and teams. Successful business architecture teams see themselves as an internal service provider to their organization. They focus relentlessly on helping people and building bridges.
- **Ubiquitous business architecture**: Make business architecture for everybody. Having this aim from the start instills the right mindset and accelerates the adoption and usage of business architecture.

Chapter Take-Aways

Business architecture is often a missing piece that can help organizations articulate their current state and desired state, and then illuminate the most effective pathway to transformation. It also helps guide immeasurable critical decisions along the way. Business architecture gives organizations their own map and guidance system to navigate transformation. Leveraging this discipline and the expertise of business architects not only leads to more successful transformations, but also helps build the organizational capacity necessary to adapt to continuous change in the future as well. Business architecture is a powerful tool for continual strategy execution, organization and ecosystem design, and decision-making.

Here are three key take-aways:

1. **The What**: Business architecture is a blueprint to create understanding and activate change. It comprises multiple different business perspectives, with value streams and capabilities as the centerpiece.

Every organization has a business architecture, but the key is documenting it in a principled manner and maintaining it in a shared repository so that it can be used to support a variety of business usage scenarios.

2. **The Why**: Business architecture underpins successful digital enterprises and transformations by ensuring exceptional, integrated, and consistent experiences for customers, partners, and employees as well as business benefits such as decreased complexity, cost, and risk. It is also an essential aspect of the transformation process to help scope and prioritize the changes, ensure stakeholders can consume those changes, and facilitate collaboration and mindset shifts.

3. **The How**: Successful business architecture teams focus on continually delivering business value. Once the business architecture baseline is in place with value streams and capabilities, build out the rest of the knowledge base along with other aspects of the business architecture practice and role *just enough just in time, directly in support of business value.*

As we carry forward on our digital journeys, we are making some of the most pivotal decisions that we will perhaps ever make, that will shape our organizations — and impact our societies — for years to come. Considering all that is at stake, can we afford to do digital transformation *without* business architecture?

Bibliography

BIZBOK® Guide from the Business Architecture Guild. https://www.business architectureguild.org/page/publications.

Gaughan, D., Natis, Y., Alvarez, G., & O'Neill, M. (2020). *Future of Applications: Delivering the Composable Enterprise.* Gartner. https://www.gartner.com/ en/doc/465932-future-of-applications-delivering-the-composable-enterprise.

Granito, F. (2017, February 27). *What is a Digital Enterprise?* The Institute for Digital Transformation. www.institutefordigitaltransformation.org/what-is-a-digital-enterprise/.

Kuehn, W. (2019, February 7). *The Gateway to Successful Digital Transformation.* The Institute for Digital Transformation. https://www.institutefordigitaltrans formation.org/the-gateway-to-successful-digital-transformation/.

Kuehn, W. (2019, October 10). *A Keystone for Digital Readiness*. The Institute for Digital Transformation. https://www.institutefordigitaltransformation. org/a-keystone-for-digital-readiness/.

Kuehn, W. (2022). *Strategy to Reality: Making the Impossible Possible for Business Architects, Change Makers and Strategy Execution Leaders*. New York: Morgan James Publishing.

Ross, J. (2018). Architect your company for agility. *Staying Agile*, 26.

Chapter 3

The Digital Transformation Manifesto

Raymond Sheen

Introduction

The term manifesto often brings to mind wild-eyed fanatics or authoritative dictators making bold claims about their intentions. We are neither wild-eyed fanatics nor authoritative dictators, but we are making bold statements to clarify the fundamental principles of successful digital transformation. People often focus on the term "digital" in digital transformation, but that is just the adjective. Digital is the enabler, but it is not the most important aspect. The true impact is the transformation. Transformation of an organization, an industry, and even our society is the ultimate outcome from digital transformation.

Digital transformation is a journey. While there are many paths to success, there are also many paths to failure. In our experience, success is not dependent upon the particular digital technology, rather it is based on organizational culture and characteristics. For many organizations, there is a dual application to the term digital transformation. One aspect is the transformation of their industry and their business model as new opportunities and threats emerge based on the digital technologies. The other aspect is the transformation of the organization and society. Long-established "industrial age" organizations must transform how they manage, interact, and even their culture. Both transformations can be formidable.

For this reason, the Institute for Digital Transformation has developed a Digital Transformation Manifesto. The Manifesto articulates the core tenets of successful digital transformation. This Manifesto doesn't discuss

45

https://doi.org/10.1142/9789811260469_0003

specific technologies, it addresses changes in organizational culture and operating practices that are imperatives for organizations embracing digital transformation. To assist in the adoption of this Manifesto, we have also created a digital transformation metrics framework.

Digital Transformation Manifesto

Digital transformation is the continuous journey of organizational evolution and technological advancement in order to drive outcomes that align with an organization's business purpose.

To successfully remain on the path of digital transformation, an organization should strive to have these core tents as part of their organizational fiber.

- *We proactively embrace change*
- *We have the agility to pivot quickly*
- *We create purpose-based value*
- *The stakeholder experience is at our core*
- *Our decisions are driven by data*
- *We are reimagining business practices*
- *Our culture is one that empowers individual leadership*
- *Ethics are integral to our organization*

http://www.DTManifesto.com

The Need for the Digital Transformation Manifesto

The purpose of the Digital Transformation Manifesto is to create a commonly accepted understanding of principles and drivers for successful Digital Transformation. We have found that there are many digital technologies available and most of these are constantly improving. Successful digital transformation is much more than a project to incorporate the latest version of a technology. It occurs when the organization's culture and mindset have embraced the capabilities and potential for a radical shift of operations and strategy that are enabled because of the digital technologies.

The challenge for most organizations is the culture change, not the technology change. That is one of the reasons why many of the digital leaders are "*digital natives*," meaning the organization was founded in the digital age and relies on digital systems and technologies. These organizations, although not as well funded or long-established as other mainline organizations, were able to start with a digital culture. They did not need to undergo the difficult challenge of culture change.

In the late 20th century, Dr. Edward Deming revolutionized many industries through his continuous improvement and quality principles. But the application of these concepts has been to become better and better at achieving a specific level of performance and then maintaining the organization at that performance level. In this context, change and variation are bad things. *In the new digital world, the performance goal is constantly changing.* And the changes may not be incremental. In addition to the changing goals, the nature of interactions between individuals and business entities has been transformed by digital technologies and is continuing to transform. This impacts the speed of business, the breadth of the market, and the nature of competition. In this environment, we found that the core principles that made many organizations successful in the past had to change. This led to the development of the Digital Transformation Manifesto.

In this chapter, we will explain each of the eight tenets in more detail and provide an example of the tenet. Following this, we will discuss a metrics framework that can be used to assess your progress with respect to embracing these tenets and embedding them into the fabric of your organization. As we discuss these eight tenets, you may find yourself thinking, *"We already do that."* Your organization probably does follow some of these to a limited extent. However, these are no longer "nice to have," they are **imperatives**. We have found that these tenets must characterize the day-to-day operations and decision-making of all areas and levels of the organization. The eight tenets of the Manifesto apply to all aspects of the organizational culture as it exists from the C-suite out to every individual and operating location. Further, there is a synergy between these tenets. The full transformational impact occurs when all eight are characteristics of the organization, not just one or two.

We Proactively Embrace Change

There is a familiar paradox, *"the only thing that is constant is change."* The paradox is a reality with digital transformation. Digital transformation is fundamentally changing the products, processes, systems, industries interactions, and the environment of an organization and society. This is done through the application of digital technologies, often in new and unique ways, which brings us back to our paradox, the only thing that is constant is change.

Traditionally, one of the goals and metrics for an organization was to find the sweet spot of performance and maintain that level. Whether it was product performance, customer service delivery, manufacturing process quality, or system uptime, an optimum level was determined. The management control systems and metrics then focused on maintaining that level. That approach has become obsolete with digital transformation.

Managing for the sweet spot of performance is looking backward not forward. It assumes that what was required in the past will continue to be the expectation for the future. However, when you embrace digital transformation, you are embracing proactive change. As agents of digital transformation, we seek out changes enabled by digital technology and leverage their continuous improvement for ourselves, our organizations, and society. These can be changes in products, services, business processes, and the way we interact both internally and externally. Also, there are both changes we initiate and changes that are occurring in the environment and culture around us.

Let's consider an illustration. The first commercially successful smartphone, the iPhone, was released in January 2007. The technology was transformative but so has been its impact on business models and interpersonal communication. Today, when we look globally, there are over 3 billion users of smartphones — both iPhones and Androids. The average American checks their smartphone every 10 minutes. But here is one of the transformative changes. Even though it is a smartphone, people are seldom using it for phone calls. Only 18% of the usage of the smartphone is for telephone calls. The primary use of a smartphone is apps. There are now literally millions of apps available on both iPhones and Android phones. Apps have changed how we interact with people and organizations, how we buy products and services, and they have even changed our forms of entertainment. Yet the entire app industry is only a few years old. We doubt that Steve Jobs and Apple envisioned what it has become when they launched the iPhone.

And who knows what is next? Is it wearables clothing with sensors and controls? Is it autonomous devices — planes, trains, and automobiles? Is it integrating augmented reality with real-world interactions? Or is it some new technology still being created? **The point is continuous change is now inevitable. The requirements of the past are obsolete**. The agents of digital transformation are embracing, leveraging, and amplifying that change — not trying to maintain the status quo. It really is true, the only thing that is constant is change.

The first tenet of Digital Transformation is to proactively embrace change because this tenet is foundational. An organization that embraces the other seven tenets but is resistant to change, or even just slow to change, will be left behind. They may know what they should do, but they are too slow to be effective.

We Have the Agility to Pivot Quickly

Speed is exhilarating! We love fast cars, fast boats, fast planes, fast bikes, and even fast horses. But speed can also be frightening when we lose control. Thanks to digital transformation, our industry and society are changing, and it is changing fast. If we can keep ourselves in control, that speed is exhilarating, if not it is frightening and likely will lead to a crash.

The capability of digital technologies is constantly increasing at a rapid pace. Computer processing speed doubles every two years. Data being created doubles every 12 months although memory storage is only increasing at 19% per year. The internet is continuing to expand after growing more than 1,300% during the past 10 years. Add to that the rapid increase in availability and capability of digital technologies like artificial intelligence (AI), Internet of Things (IoT), virtual reality, and connected platforms. The impact is that the rate of technical change is fast and accelerating. **But it is more than just technical change that is occurring**.

Businesses and industries are affected by change leading to significant business moves that have happened in the past few years. Banking, publishing, and entertainment are primarily online operations now. The retail industry's focus has changed to virtual marketing and delivery systems instead of storefronts and square footage. The transportation and hospitality sectors are being transformed to self-service instead of relying on travel agents. Automobiles and home appliances respond to voice commands and tell us when they need maintenance. Manufacturing lines have been automated. Even educational institutions are now virtual. Almost every sector of the industry is undergoing profound change. Some elements are quickly becoming obsolete as whole new products, services, and interactions are created.

With rapid change happening everywhere, you and your organization must decide whether to be proactive in your approach or to become victims of digital transformation changes. To be proactive, you must develop the personal and organizational skills to pivot quickly. That requires a regular sensing of both your industry and technology to identify opportunities and threats. Then the organization must rapidly respond to what is happening with Agile projects and proactive decision-making. Whether the changes are positive or negative, a rapid pivot is often needed in order for an organization to direct its destiny and not become a victim.

As an example, let's consider the ride-sharing business, Uber. Uber as a company was enabled by digital transformation. The creation of the smartphone as a platform for the Uber app and the processing power of cloud computing were the critical digital technologies for Uber to be successful. Uber and similar companies were changing the industry for urban transportation. But then the COVID-19 pandemic occurred, and Uber was in trouble. With everyone on lockdown, no one needed a ride. *So, it was time to quickly pivot.* Everyone was staying at home, but they still needed to eat. Uber pivoted from ridesharing to Uber Eats, providing restaurant and grocery delivery.

The ability to pivot quickly is one of the critical elements of successful digitally transformed organizations. We already discussed the need to embrace change. This tenet is necessary to implement the required changes.

We Create Purpose-Based Value

Most organizations have a mission statement. The mission is normally focused on the purpose of the organization. It answers the question, "Why does this organization exist?" or "Why do we provide these products and services?" The purpose is the motivation for the employees and stakeholders of the organization.

You may be thinking to yourself, "What does this have to do with digital transformation?" The answer is that *your organization's purpose also provides the motivation for your digital transformation.* New digitally enhanced systems and operations enable an organization to greatly magnify its ability to achieve its purpose or mission. At the same time, digital improvements can allow an organization to remove waste and inefficiency that hinders its mission.

Digital transformation has two core components, the application of digital technologies and the transformation of products, processes, operations, and culture to a new or unique level of performance and achievement. Each component is powerful in its own right. Upgrading existing products and processes with digital technologies will lead to faster, stronger, or more accurate performance. In this case, the organization is still doing the same thing but doing it much better. Transforming an organization with new products, processes, personnel, and culture has often led to enhanced performance. A transformation can reposition your organization in the competitive landscape, but it does not necessarily revolutionize or create an entire industry.

Digital transformation combines both components. The synergy creates a dramatic effect. It helps your organization be faster, stronger, and more accurate while it is creating entirely new industries and entirely new ways of operating. That is why the purpose becomes so important. The purpose provides direction, alignment, and motivation for the changes. Through the transformation, the purpose is achieved and often expanded and enhanced.

An organization with a great mission or purpose can use digital transformation as an enabler for achieving the mission. But *an organization can also transform its mission to take advantage of the new horizons that are opened to it through digital transformation*. Instead of being confined to a small geographical area, it can reach the world. Instead of being limited in its offering to its customer base, it can create a platform with many interconnected products and services. As an organization, it can scale and grow exponentially. Added to this is the attribute of the mission that goes beyond a profit motive. Through digital transformation, an organization can add environmental or social causes within its purpose without destroying profitability.

As stated in IBM's 2020 Annual Report, *"IBM's essential and transformative role in the world is a reminder that few companies have the trust, talent, and ingenuity to help clients solve their greatest challenges."* The emphasis is on solving customer's problems. Historically, the IBM approach was focused on technology development, and technology is still what they are selling. However, the aspect of creating value for customers is a transformation of the culture to an external focus and realignment of processes and systems.

Today's cultures place a priority on societal and environmental issues and initiatives. Many people today are searching for more than a paycheck. They want meaning in their professional life and the organization's mission, or purpose is a consideration when seeking employment. The employees, members, and stakeholders need to believe the mission is both meaningful and achievable. The application of digital transformation can clear the way to achieve what was previously viewed as a "mission impossible."

We have discussed embracing change and pivoting quickly. **The principle of creating purpose-based value will direct and focus your digital transformation**. It guides an organization on what changes to embrace and what pivots are needed.

The Customer and Stakeholder Experience Is at Our Core

Almost every organization's mission is to create value for its customers, members, owners, or stakeholders. Value is created when one individual or organization believes the benefits they are receiving are greater than the cost they are paying. In addition, value often depends upon the customer experience. A frustrating or irritating interaction undermines the inherent value of the product or service, and a positive, friendly experience can enhance the value. With the advent of digital technologies, almost all interactions now have a digital component. This could be through personal account communication, product/service delivery, or transaction processing.

There can be a great deal of subjectivity in value creation based on the stakeholder's expectations for the digital interaction. Therefore, *focusing on the customer experience is a core principle of digital transformation.* Each individual, organization, and transaction is unique. They are unique to the parties involved but also unique to the circumstances surrounding the parties involved. To deliver maximum value to a customer or stakeholder, one must understand the customer's or stakeholder's circumstances and customize the interaction for those circumstances. Most products and services are just commodities until the personalization aspect of the transaction is added.

Digital transformation enables organizations to gather real-time data from their customers, members, and stakeholders. In addition, digital transformation enables the organization to constantly assess the business situation. This allows the organization to customize the experience which creates value for the customer or stakeholder. The transaction experience is enhanced by the digital elements used in that experience.

A major challenge and force for change in many organizations is the rapid advancement of digital technologies. As industries have globalized, there are almost no closed markets. Essentially, there are multiple competitors for everything in every market. However, competition in an industry is no longer based solely on other organizations offering similar products or services. The customer's and stakeholder's expectations are influenced by all their transactions. For instance, when shopping online, the customer's expectations for the online experience are based on their best-ever online shopping experience. The experience expectation is not dependent upon the commodity being purchased, rather it is dependent upon the technologies used.

A great example is Amazon Prime. Amazon has worked hard to streamline and simplify the customer online shopping experience. In addition, it has specialized accounts for its Amazon Prime customers. This emphasis on customer shopping experience has allowed Amazon to leapfrog other retailers and go from selling books to selling virtually anything a consumer might buy. The customer experience is their core competitive advantage, not the actual products or even the pricing.

In this environment, convenience, personalization, and trust are the dominant attributes of interaction value. A focus on customer or stakeholder experience is needed to build and strengthen each of those attributes. The digital tools, systems, and platforms available are essential elements when designing and delivering customer transaction value within the customer experience.

We have embraced change and quickly pivoted to create purpose-based value. However, **the customer and stakeholder experience must be positive for the organization to gain any traction with its transformation**. And keep in mind as the digital technologies change, the customer expectations will change. This will require yet another pivot in order to provide stakeholder value.

Our Decisions Are Driven by Data

A well-known American politician, Daniel Patrick Moynihan, is noted for saying, *"Everyone is entitled to his own opinion, but not his own facts"* (Wikipedia). Facts have always been a critical element in decision-making within businesses and organizations. But facts are often elusive. In many cases, when the facts became available, they were already obsolete or irrelevant due to other more recent events.

One of the challenges is that facts are based on data and in the past, reliable data was hard to acquire. Data collection methods had to be created and validated before reliable data could be obtained. The data collection process was often expensive and time-consuming. If the data was collected or recorded using manual methods, the data acquisition was constrained by the availability of qualified data collectors. And once the data was collected, it needed to be analyzed to identify the facts and insights in the data while separating out the noise and clutter that often was found in the dataset. All of this took time and expertise.

As a result, most organizations relied more on the judgment, wisdom, and "gut feel" of those who were experienced. These individuals could quickly grasp a situation and make a decision. Many times, their decisions were correct, especially if the situation they face was closely similar to a previous experience. But in times of uncertainty or change, the "gut feel" can be wrong.

In the era of digital transformation, there are continuous changes occurring in business and society. **"Gut feel" cannot be trusted**. Fortunately, a benefit of adopting digital systems and processes is that they normally are able to collect real-time data. Plus, the advances in business analytics and AI that have accompanied the digital transformation make it easy to analyze the data in real-time and identify critical facts.

Data is empowering for an organization. Digitally transformed organizations capture customer data and process data to understand what is happening in their environment. Digital tools such as IoT, Natural Language Processing, AI, and Big Data have enabled any organization to collect and analyze virtually any type of data in real-time. This data is being made available to employees and associates at the front line of customer interface and process operation. This empowers them to make the best business decision without needing to refer everything to managers and supervisors.

The culture change associated with this tenet is the shift in decision-making to rely on data and not "gut feel." At all levels and positions in the organization, data becomes the driver for critical decisions. Data can be used to make real-time operational decisions, and data can be used to make strategic decisions, even if the expert's gut says differently. Netflix's initial success was built upon the easy customer experience associated with renting DVDs. However, when data showed that customers were starting to use live-streaming apps, they shifted their entire business model, discarding the very profitable DVDs, and now dominate the entertainment streaming market.

Building the structure of an organization to collect, analyze, and then rely on data for decision-making is a core principle of digital transformation.

Whether embracing change, pivoting when necessary, or understanding the customer experience, data guides an organization and allows it to continually stay aligned with the creation of purpose-based value.

We Are Reimagining Business Practices

A law of nature formulated by Arthur C. Clarke, the well-known science fiction writer, is *"Any sufficiently advanced technology is indistinguishable from magic."* In the second half of the 20th century when Clarke was writing, that seemed an appropriate line for fiction, but preposterous for real-life. However, digital transformation has changed our perspective.

I have a friend who visited a Third World country several years ago on a business trip. He and his host were sitting at an outdoor café in a large mountain village, and they did an informal poll to see who had a smartphone. Everyone who passed their café had a smartphone. And my friend, who is a techy millennial, was embarrassed to find that everyone in that village had a newer and more powerful smartphone than he had. Ten years before, that village had no internet, no smartphones, and if you had tried to describe one it would have been considered magic. Now it is commonplace.

Changes like this are not unique to mountain villages in Third World countries. Every process, product, and even interaction is being regularly reimagined and transformed. And every aspect of our lives is being affected. We recently sold a house to someone thousands of miles across the country who never visited the house in person but toured it online. A dairy farm near where my father lived uses robots, AI, and analytics to manage the milking process and the herd. There are many days when no human being even enters the barns, but cows are milked several times a day and the quality and quantity of milk are the best ever produced at that farm. An individual can even monitor and activate every appliance in their home by using an app on their phone.

All of this would have been considered science fiction or magic just a few years ago. However, through digital technologies, we have begun to transform every aspect of an organization, individual activities, and the environment. **The limitation now is based on what can be imagined**. That is why agents of digital transformation look beyond applying technology to what they currently do. They are inventing new products, services, systems, and applications.

Digitally transformed organizations understand the continuous nature of change that is enabled by technology. They are not satisfied with only optimizing an existing product or service. They are always searching for new opportunities and applications. And as they adopt digital technologies it opens doors to more reimaging. FedEx switched to digital systems for taking and tracking orders in order to save on the cost of 5-copy carbon paper. But once the digital systems were in place, they enabled new products and services that transformed the shipping experience by providing real-time information and updates to their customers through the process.

Agents of digital transformation are searching for the next magical application of technologies that can change an industry or delight a customer. With that new idea, they embrace the change and quickly pivot the organization to address it. Then they rely on the value of the stakeholder experience and data-based decision-making, guided by their purpose, to bring that imagined new reality to life.

Our Culture is One That Empowers Individual Leadership

Jeff Bezos, the CEO of Amazon, commented in a discussion on digital transformation, *"The only sustainable advantage you can have over others is agility"* (Bezos, 2021). A digitally transformed organization is one that embraces continuous change. Technology today is rapidly advancing, the competitive landscape in every industry is going through upheaval, and even the patterns of interaction throughout society are rapidly changing. Continuous change is ubiquitous in the world in which we now live. But continuous change can be a strain on individuals and organizations. Effective leadership is needed whenever there is change underway.

Digitally transformed organizations tend to have a flat organizational structure. They do not require myriad layers of management controlling information and decision-making. They are not dependent upon top-down control. As previously stated, individuals at all levels of the organization have the real-time information needed to understand a situation and the authority and responsibility to make decisions. The managers do not control, rather they *coach, train, mentor, and facilitate.* The leadership skills that encourage and empower are at a premium in this organization, not those that direct and control.

The implication for digitally transforming organizations is that they need to recruit, hire, and train leaders throughout the organization. The organization does not rely upon automatons doing only what they are told — they have robots to do that. Rather, they need their employees and associates to assess a situation and take appropriate action, be problem solvers, and be proactive implementers of change. In other words, **the digitally transformed organization relies on leaders at every level and position in the organization.**

The upheaval in work practices due to the COVID-19 pandemic illustrated the power of this tenet. Organizations around the globe sent their employees home and told them to work from there using the digital technologies available to them. The supervisor was no longer watching everyone to be sure they stayed busy. In many organizations, productivity went up as the workforce was empowered to manage themselves.

A question often asked is whether leaders are born or made. Unquestionably some people have the personality and ability to be effective leaders. But even these individuals will tell you that leadership is something that can be taught and practiced. A digitally transformed organization is in the business of developing leaders and improving leadership skills for everyone.

This is not something that depends upon technology, it is a culture within an organization. The culture starts at the top with executives and is amplified throughout the organization. This culture is reinforced by the hiring, training, promotion, and human resource management within the organization. For many organizations, this culture is the most difficult aspect of implementing digital transformation. It is not something that can be changed by installing a new system or downloading an app. Rather, it requires changes in the behaviors and interactions of individuals throughout the organization. It gets to the heart of how people think and interact on a day-to-day basis.

An absolutely critical element of this transformation is the development of trust between individuals. Senior leaders must trust that the people in their organization will make the right decision when given the right tools and information. And individuals must trust that senior leaders will support them in their work and help them to grow both personally and professionally. Different departments within an organization must trust that the actions of individuals in other departments are in the best interest of the organization and its customer. Trust is built on a track record of positive interactions. An organization that does not have a track record of empowering everyone to lead will need a steady stream of new interactions to overcome the mistrust. Creating and sustaining that stream of interactions can take years, which is why this is possibly the most difficult of the elements of digital transformation.

Creating a culture that empowers everyone to lead is necessary for the new environment being created by digital transformation. Reimaging the organization and industry leads to continuous change and frequent pivots. This requires leadership. These leaders must be aligned with the organization's purpose and rely on data to build trust. When the leader is focused on ensuring the customer and stakeholder experience is improving, the organization will progress in a positive direction creating purpose-based value.

Ethics Are Integral to Our Organization

Stan Lee, the author of the Spider-Man comic, restated the principle found in the Biblical story of the Faithful Servant and popularized for today as the Peter Parker principle, *"With great power comes great responsibility."* Organizations that have achieved sustained growth and performance in the digital era have also created confidence that their actions and motives are rooted in an ethical foundation. The power of their innovation and transformation that was enabled through digital technology is magnified and elevated when their stakeholders and customers are convinced of their ethical behavior. However, when customers begin to doubt that; they quickly change to someone else for the product or service.

A key element of organizational ethical behavior is establishing and maintaining trust between an organization and its stakeholders. Trust relies on constancy in purpose and the alignment of actions to support that purpose. A characteristic of the digital era is the widespread availability of data and information. An organization cannot sustain a public persona standing for one set of values and in private violate that same standard. The information leaks out, and when it does, it goes viral in a very short time. When an organization says it stands for one set of values and behaves differently, the stakeholders lose confidence in everything else the organization says.

But it is not only the external stakeholders who are concerned about ethics in the digital era, internal stakeholders are also a factor. Digital technologies have enabled a global job market and workforce. Many organizations now have virtual "gig workers" who are based around the world. Often these individuals are actively seeking to work for organizations whose values they share. Just as with external stakeholders, when internal employees and associates find that an organization's actual ethics differ significantly from the public persona, they quickly move onto an organization with which they are aligned. Because of the digital technologies that are available, the barrier for an individual to change employers is very low.

A key point to make at this time is that technology is ethically neutral. The digital technologies are available to both highly ethical and highly unethical organizations and individuals. However, ethics are key in the ability to transform. The transformation process often requires an extended time as old habits are retired, and new ones are formed. To change the organization's processes and systems, many interactions are needed. This is where the ethics of an organization are revealed. Constancy of purpose, a genuine care for customers and employees, and trust in the integrity of an organization are built over time. While it may take months or years to establish the reputation for integrity, that same reputation can be destroyed in a matter of days or hours. If that happens, the organizational transformation becomes derailed.

These eight tenets of digital transformation, ethical behavior, empowered leadership, reimaged practices, data-driven decisions, stakeholder experience, purpose-based value, rapid pivots, and embracing change are synergistic. While each of these is a positive organizational characteristic, they become transformational when all are woven into the fabric of the organization. **None of these require digital technologies**. However, when married with the capabilities of ever-changing digital technologies they produce a transformed organization. If you wish to succeed in your digital transformation, your organization should embrace these tenets.

Digital Transformation Metrics Framework

While establishing and strengthening the eight tenets is the foundation, there is no "12-step process" or "right way" to digitally transform. The strategy and purpose of digital transformation vary from industry to industry and organization to organization. Each organization is starting from a different place and operating in an environment with competitors and stakeholders who are at different stages of transformation. Therefore, the digital transformation journey of every organization will be different. To assist you in the development and monitoring of your organization's digital transformation, we have created a digital transformation metrics framework as a companion to the eight tenets of digital transformation. This framework can guide you on your journey. The framework is based on the concept of a balanced scorecard. This business management approach was introduced by Norton and Kaplan in 1996 in their book by that name. In this framework, an organization has an articulated strategy or high-level business goals. The organization then identifies a small set of metrics that are directly related to the goals or strategy. These metrics are in different aspects of the organization to ensure that the entire organization is aligned with the strategy. By involving all the key aspects of business performance, the scorecard stays "balanced." There are generally two or three metrics associated with four categories or operational domains:

- Financial Metrics
- Customer/Market Metrics
- Operational Metrics
- Organizational Development Metrics.

The organization's leadership team regularly reviews these metrics for progress in all four domains, which keeps the scorecard balanced. This has become one of the standard business scorecard approaches.

We have adapted this same approach to create a measurement framework for an organization's digital transformation journey. This framework does not replace the organization's existing measurement system or analytics. That system is often unique to an industry and competitive environment. That system should stay in place. However, this additional framework is used to assess the organization's progress in digital transformation. This digital transformation framework uses four domains that are linked to the eight tenets of the Digital Transformation Manifesto.

- **Change Governance Perspective**: Tracking how quickly your organization can react to change and effectively implement it.
- **Customer and Market Perspective**: Tracking how well your organization anticipates shifts in customer expectations and market changes.
- **Cultural Perspective**: Tracking how receptive your organization is to implementing change.
- **Business Operations Perspective**: Tracking operational sustainability and readiness within your organization.

Each of these domains is discussed in more detail. The tenets from the Manifesto that are linked to the domains are identified. In addition, several example metrics for that domain are shown. These metrics are for illustration, they are not an exhaustive or exclusive list. These may not be appropriate for your specific organization or industry. In addition, different organizations may place higher weighting upon some metrics based on their assessment of the progress they have made along their digital transformation journey.

Digital transformation strategy

A key principle of the balanced scorecard approach is that all the domains are focused on supporting the organizational strategy. This principle is followed in the digital transformation metrics framework. However, the strategy is the digital strategy. This strategy will include a combination of the innovative digital technologies being deployed and their strategic impact on business mission and goals. This strategy is unique for every organization. The technologies selected and the roadmap of implementation will vary based on strengths and weaknesses. The strategy will also vary based on organizational vision and mission.

Creating the strategy is the first step in creating the Digital Transformation Metrics Framework. The domain metrics will point back to the strategy. The measurement goals will be aligned with achieving strategic goals.

Change governance perspective

The change governance perspective tracks how quickly the organization reacts to change. It is a measure of agility and responsiveness. The perspective includes identification of needed changes and implementation of appropriate changes. The governance aspect of this domain is that the changes are intentional and controlled. **It is proactive change management, not reactive change accommodation**.

Two tenets from the Digital Manifesto have a significant impact on this domain:

- We have the agility to pivot quickly.
- Our decisions are driven by data.

While these are the primary tenets, there are attributes of the other six tenets that contribute to the metrics of this domain. Organizations that need to improve in this domain should focus on their implementation of Agile project management and the deployment of business analytics. As with most skills, improvement comes with practice. The organization should identify changes that can be quickly implemented and start with those. The lessons learned from those changes are used to improve the overall change management process and the threshold levels used for data-driven decisions (Table 1).

Table 1:   Governance domain example metrics.

Objective	Performance Metric	Performance Metric Definition
Respond quickly to market/ supply chain opportunities and threats	Decision Time	# of days from investment proposal (new digital transformation initiative) to final approval or rejection
Have the financial power to enable the digital transformation	Resources Allocated to Digital Transformation	% of organizational annual revenue available for digital transformation investments
Master business unpredictability and reliance on relevant data for decisions	Strategic Planning Frequency	# of days of lead-time for the strategic planning review
Protect organization from cyber-threats and information breaches during times of change (breach of proprietary or confidential information)	External Information Security Incidents	% of successful information security hacks during the last 12 months
	Internal Information Security Breaches	# of information security breaches by employees or associates during the last 12 months
Improve collaboration between different units of the organization and key service providers	Value Chain Collaboration	Customer Satisfaction score of service providers (internal units and external partners) meeting or exceeding internal stakeholder expectations

Customer and Market Perspective

The Customer and Market Perspective tracks how well an organization anticipates shifts in customer expectations and market changes. This is an external focus within the organizational culture. It includes the impact the organization has on the customer, industry, and society. **Survival of an organization is based on how it adapts and interacts with other organizations within its environment**. The measurements in this domain consider this external impact.

Three tenets from the Digital Manifesto have a significant impact on this domain:

- The customer and stakeholder experience is at our core.
- We create purpose-based value.
- Ethics are integral to our organization.

While these are the primary tenets, there are attributes of the other five tenets that contribute to the metrics of this domain. Organizations that need to improve in this domain should adopt a two-prong approach. First, ensure the organization is receiving direct unfiltered feedback from customers and stakeholders and then acting on it. Second, focus on clarifying their mission and purpose and ensuring they have communicated that to all levels of the organization and key partners. This domain can be the most difficult to effect permanent change since it often will require a track record of continuous actions to demonstrate that these tenets are truly foundational principles for the organization. **The metrics in this domain are externally focused**. It may be difficult to get an accurate assessment since the information will be based upon others and not under the direct control of the organization (Table 2).

Table 2:   Customer and market domain example metrics.

Objective	Performance Metric	Performance Metric Definition
Boost customer experience and engagement to world-class levels	Net Promoter Score (NPS)	Subtract the percentage of Detractors from the percentage of Promoters. Bain & Co, the source of the NPS system, suggests that above 50 is excellent, and above 80 is world-class

(Continued)

Table 2: (*Continued*)

Objective	Performance Metric	Performance Metric Definition
Rapidly respond to customer needs with new product or service releases	Time to Market	# of days from idea to launch of new feature or service
Improve customer experience and engagement	Time to Delivery	# of days from customer order to delivery
	Outbound Marketing Performance	# of connection, likes, and shares of web content on preferred platforms
Increase traffic and presence on preferred platforms	Revenues Based upon Platform Interactions	% of all revenues coming from each revenue-generating platform
Increase organizational innovation power	Innovation Contribution	# of innovation ideas contributed by employees and partners
Strengthen customer connections	Customer Lifetime Value Score	Average order value divided by one minus the repeat purchase rate
Establish a profile as a sustainable business and organization	Business Sustainability	# of UN Global Compact Principles certified by external experts

Cultural perspective

The cultural perspective tracks how receptive an organization is to change. It is a measure of the organization's willingness to make changes and its ability to effectively implement changes. **The cultural aspect of this domain is the extent to which the organization proactively seeks needed changes or is resistant to change.** Change can create fear in an organization. This domain includes assessments of attitude. This is in contrast with the first domain, Change Governance, which focused on the actual performance of projects and activities that support digital transformation.

Two tenets from the Digital Manifesto have a significant impact on this domain:

- We proactively embrace change.
- Our culture is one that empowers individual leadership.

While these are the primary tenets, there are attributes of the other six tenets that contribute to the metrics of this domain. Organizations that need to improve in this domain should focus on their workforce development. This includes the hiring, training, and promotion of employees and associates. In addition, the workforce is organized to enable leaders to develop at all levels. The entire organization is motivated and incentivized to implement productive change on a continual basis (Table 3).

Table 3:   Culture domain example metrics.

Objective	Performance Metric	Performance Metric Definition
Increasing employee engagement and commitment	Employee Engagement	% of employees with high engagement and empowerment on employee satisfaction surveys
	Vision and Values	% of employees committed to the organizational vision and values based on employee satisfaction survey
	Training and Development	% of employees who participate in voluntary work-related training programs
	Employee Retention Rate	% turnover of staff during the last 12 months
Increase performance of all employees and staff	Digital Transformation Employee Performance	% of employee goals relating to CX and DT met during the last 12 months
	Digital Transformation Leadership Performance	% of leaders' goals relating to CX and DT met during the last 12 months
Improve organization's ability to change	Change Readiness	Maturity of organization's change management capability as assessed by a third-party auditor
Embrace change	Change Initiative Success	% of change initiatives successfully completed on time

Business Operations Perspective

Business Operations Perspective tracks the levels of operational sustainability and readiness within an organization. *Given that digital transformation entails continuous change, it is possible that operational performance may erode if the various digital transformation projects and initiatives are poorly implemented.* In addition, the constant change can sap the energy and focus for an organization. By the same token, appropriately selected digital transformation projects that are aligned with the purpose and values of the organization and are well managed can continually improve performance and move the organization to higher levels of sustainability. There is only one primary tenet from the Digital Manifesto that has a significant impact on this domain:

- We are reimagining business practices.

While this is the primary tenet, there are attributes of the other seven tenets that contribute to the metrics of this domain. Organizations that need to improve in this domain should focus on benchmarking and encouraging innovation within the organization. In addition, a regular survey of digital technologies and their impact on other industries should become an element of strategic planning. "Reimagined products and processes" in other industries are excellent starting points for an organization's efforts in this area (Table 4).

Table 4: Business operations domain example metrics.

Objective	Performance Metric	Performance Metric Definition
Increase business productivity	Business Productivity	% year over year change in the ratio of business output and input (cost)
	Workforce Productivity	% year-over-year change in output metric per labor hour (output metric is related to the activity of the organizational department)
	Business Hours Saved	% of hours reduced within a business process by implementation of digital technology and services

Table 4: (*Continued*)

Objective	Performance Metric	Performance Metric Definition
	Level of Technical Debt	% of infrastructure budget used to maintain end-of-life and/or obsolete systems
	Level of Digital Automation	% of administrative processes supported by digital process automation (robotics or AI)
Increase business quality	Business Project Quality	# of change orders or updates to complete a business project (note this does not include backlog updates on Agile projects)
	Business Transaction Quality	% of customer complaints (external or internal) of transactions processed within a fixed time period
Increase power of ecosystem	Value of Business Ecosystem	% of ecosystem partners contributing to the mission and strategy of the organization

Digital transformation metrics example

It is important to create a strategy and then take all four perspectives into account when designing metrics to track the performance of a digital transformation initiative. **All four domains must be considered and measured to "balance" the scorecard**. A one- or two-dimensional approach increases the probability of failure of your digital transformation initiative. Based on your specific industry and business objectives, some domains may be weighted higher (or considered more important) than others. Those domains would likely contribute more metrics. In addition, your business strengths and weaknesses may indicate a need for emphasis in one area or another.

To illustrate how this metric framework can be applied, two examples are provided. The first example is a manufacturing operation. In this case, the manufacturing operation is an equipment manufacturer that builds equipment that is customized for each order. The manufacturing operation has both fabrication processes using automated computer numerical control equipment and manual assembly operations. The fabrication processes are high volume and an expectation of high quality. The assembly processes are lower volume, but still have an expectation of high quality. On-time delivery is a critical need identified from customers (Table 5).

Table 5:   Manufacturing operations example.

Strategy: Leveraging digital technologies become the lowest cost manufacturer in Europe in our industry while maintaining above-average quality and delivery.		
Perspective	**Performance Metric**	**Rationale**
Business operations	Level of Digital Automation	Automation typically lowers product cost and improves quality
Business operations	Business Transaction Quality	Ensure the required customization is understood and effectively implemented
Business operations	Level of Technical Debt	Incorporation of continually improving technology
Customer and market	Time to Delivery	Ensure that a customer KPI is met
Change governance	Resources Allocated to Digital Transformation	Ensure strategic pivots are implemented to stay competitive
Cultural	Employee Engagement	As automation expands through the organization, roles of workers will change

The emphasis for the manufacturing operations is the Business Operations Domain since operational excellence is the foundation of their business competitiveness. The business operations domain includes both internal and external measures and considers both product and process performance. The Customer and Market domain recognizes that time is an element of customer requirements. The Change Governance Domain and Cultural Domain metrics focus on internal capability to respond and lead digital transformation initiatives.

The second example is a retail operation with storefronts scattered across the country and extensive online sales. The products they sell are name-brand products and the products categories are consumer commodities. The organization has high overhead costs because of the storefronts and logistics systems, so it relies on fast product turnover in order to be profitable. From a competitiveness perspective, customer experience is the key for attracting and retaining customers (Table 6).

Table 6:   Retail example.

Strategy: Integrating storefront and online systems and processes to establish top-rated customer experience for consumer products in the USA in both categories.		
Perspective	**Performance Metric**	**Rationale**
Customer and market	NPS	Assesses the overall customer experience based upon real customer feedback
Customer and market	Time to Market	The industry has supply chain challenges and product availability directly correlates with sales
Customer and market	Revenue Based on Platform Interactions	Understanding of channel performance so as to pivot when needed
Business operations	Level of Digital Automation	Reduce overhead and operating costs while improving process quality
Change governance	Strategic Planning Frequency	Ensure relevant data is used when planning the pivots
Cultural	Employee Engagement	Due to relatively high worker turnover, monitor for quick identification of problems

In this example, the Customer and Market Domain dominates since this is most closely aligned with the Digital Transformation strategy and is the focus of business operations. These metrics are based on customer engagement and the impact of digital systems on this engagement. The Business Operations Domain focuses on internal cost structure. Notice the focus is not on the money spent on automation but rather on the actual adoption of the automation. The Change Governance Domain is focused on strategic pivots. In the digital age, retail changes rapidly as products quickly go viral and just as quickly die out. This metric will indicate one aspect of the organization's ability to pivot quickly, the recognition of the need for a pivot. Finally, the cultural metric is looking at the workforce. The organization, as described, will still have a large workforce because of the storefronts. Therefore, a metric is needed to ensure they enable digital transformation and do not block it.

The two examples demonstrate how each organization will likely balance its scorecard in different ways. This is due to different characteristics of the industry, size of the entity, scope of their work, market pressures, and other factors. The specific Digital Transformation Balanced Scorecard has different metrics in the two industries, reflecting their unique needs and strategies. However, the purpose remains the same. The scorecard is used by the organization to ensure they are making progress on their digital transformation journey.

Key Take-Aways

The Digital Transformation Manifesto articulates the core tenets of digital transformation. These eight tenets illustrate the set of drivers for successful digital transformation, regardless of the specific digital technologies being deployed and implemented. When digital transformation fails, it is typically due to culture, not technology.

We have described each of the eight tenets and provided illustrations or examples of their application. While discussing the tenets as individual principles, they work together and reinforce each other. You can't decide to pick four to implement and four to ignore and hope to be successful.

We also described a Digital Transformation Metrics Framework based upon the Balanced Scorecard methodology. Applying this framework to an organization's digital transformation initiative will use business performance metrics to judge the success of the initiative and prevent the initiative from getting out of balance.

Bibliography

Asurion. (2019). Americans Check Their Phones 96 Times a Day. *Cision PR Newswire.*

Clarke, A. C. (1973). *Profiles of the Future: An Inquiry Into the Limits of the Possible.* Harper and Row.

Deming, W. E. (1982). *Out of the Crisis, reissue.* MIT press.

Gaskell, A. (2020). Productivity in times of Covid. *Forbes Magazine.* https://www.forbes.com/sites/adigaskell/2020/12/08/productivity-in-times-of-covid.

IBM. (2020). *IBM 2020 Annual Report.* https://www.ibm.com/annualreport/assets/downloads/IBM_Annual_Report_2020.pdf.

Institute of Directors. (2017, August 14). *Digital Transformation and Becoming an Agile Business*, https://www.iod.com/resources/blog/science-innovation-and-tech/digital-transformation-and-becoming-an-agile-business/.

Internet World Stats. (n.d.). *Internet World Stats: Usage and Population Statistics.* Accessed on October 9, 2021, https://www.internetworldstats.com/stats.htm.

Iqbal, M. (n.d.). *App Download Data (2022).* BusinessofApps. Accessed on October 9, 2021, https://www.businessofapps.com/data/app-statistics/.

Kaplan, R. & Norton, D. (1990). *The Balanced Scorecard: Translating Strategy into Action.* Cambridge: Harvard Business Review Press.

Misra, A. (2020, September 13). *Netflix — Constantly Pivoting its Business Model to Success. The Strategy Story.* https://thestrategystory.com/2020/09/13/netflix-pivoting-business-model/.

O'Connell, B. (2019, March 23). *The Search for Meaning.* Society of Human Resource Management. https://www.shrm.org/hr-today/news/all-things-work/pages/the-search-for-meaning.aspx.

Richer, F. (2022, February 4). *Amazon's Incredible Long-Term Growth.* Statista. https://www.statista.com/chart/4298/amazons-long-term-growth/.

Shah, H. (2021, January 5). *App usage statistics 2021 that'll surprise you (updated).* Simform. Accessed on October 9, 2021, https://www.simform.com/blog/the-state-of-mobile-app-usage/.

Statista. (n.d.). *Number of smartphone subscriptions worldwide from 2016 to 2027.* https://www.statista.com/statistics/330695/number-of-smartphone-users-worldwide/.

Statista. (n.d.). *Volume of data/information created, captured, copied, and consumed worldwide from 2010 to 2025.* https://www.statista.com/statistics/871513/worldwide-data-created/.

Wikipedia. (n.d.). *Daniel Patrick Moynihan.* https://en.wikipedia.org/wiki/Daniel_Patrick_Moynihan.

Wikipedia. (n.d.). *With great power comes great responsibility.* https://en.wikipedia.org/wiki/With_great_power_comes_great_responsibility.

Wikipedia. (n.d.). *Timeline of Apple Inc. products.* https://en.wikipedia.org/wiki/Timeline_of_Apple_Inc._products.

Williams, G. (2020, July 23). *Uber Eats Growing Through COVID-19 via Connectivity, Delivery.* Investing News Network. https://investingnews.com/daily/tech-investing/emerging-tech-investing/mobile-web-investing/uber-eats-growing-through-covid-19/.

Chapter 4

Value — The Guiding Star

John Thorp

Introduction

> *"In the near future somebody will write a book about how executives in the 1990's spent too much money on information technology because they were afraid to manage it properly. They put their trust in technological experts to deliver business value from I.T. investments."*

Editorial, Wall Street Journal, 12/20/96

> *"It is safe to say that so far nobody has produced any evidence to support the popular myth that spending more on information technologies will boost economic performance. The presumption that more IT spending is better remains one of the most cherished beliefs of computerdom. It took experimental science to dispel the dogmas of the ancients. It may take better research and better metrics before executives will come to recognize that IT is a subtle influence where an overdose of what works can also disable."*

The Squandered Computer, Evaluating the Business Alignment of
Information Technologies, Paul A. Strassman, 1997

I have worked close to 60 years with and around technology, starting as a computer operator back in 1963. From my very first day, I have had two interests — the technology itself and, more importantly, the value that

https://doi.org/10.1142/9789811260469_0004

the users of the technology were expecting to get from its use. Over the years, living in several countries, and working in many more, my focus has been on helping clients, specifically boards and executives get clarity around the outcomes they expected from their IT investments. In most cases, I discovered that what they needed was not what they thought they wanted and, more importantly, that they needed to think way beyond the technology itself. They had to think about how it was being used, the business change that it enabled, and indeed required if the expected value was to be realized, and recognize, understand, and accept their role in leading and managing that change.

In 1997, in collaboration with several colleagues, I wrote *The Information Paradox, Realizing the Business Benefits of Information Technology*. The book was aimed at addressing the issues identified in my opening quotes. It introduced three fundamentals and three necessary conditions for realizing those benefits. The fundamentals were program management, portfolio management, and full-cycle governance. The necessary conditions were activist accountability, relevant measurement, and proactive management of change. The book was well received at the time and has influenced the thinking and work of many colleagues. Beyond that, I would like to think that it has contributed to organizations doing much better at realizing value from their increasingly large investments in technology, or as it is now more commonly referred to as Digital Technology.

"A staggering 70% of digital transformations fail."

> Companies That Failed At Digital Transformation
> and What We Can Learn From Them,
> Blake Morgan, Forbes, 2019

"84% of Digital Transformation projects fail due to the failed adoption of technology."

> Why Digital Transformations Are Failing,
> Forbes, quoted by Silverstorm, May 2021

As you can see from the more recent quotes above, billions of dollars have been wasted and continue to be wasted on failed investments.

Indeed, if you go back to the Standish Group Chaos reports which started in 1997, the failure rate of IT projects across a broad range of enterprises, both public and private, has stayed consistently between 70 and 90%. In many cases such as healthcare, those failures resulted in significant financial losses, and/or societal harm.

So, why is this? A 2016 McKinsey article states that *"Common pitfalls include a lack of employee engagement, inadequate management support, poor or nonexistent cross-functional collaboration, and a lack of accountability. Furthermore, sustaining a transformation's impact typically requires a major reset in mind-sets and behaviors — something that few leaders know how to achieve."*

Technology is becoming embedded in everything, we as individuals, businesses, and societies do, and, indeed, we are increasingly becoming embedded in everything technology does. However, the technology simply provides a capability and it's how we use the capability that results in value, and that requires addressing the pitfalls described above. If we are to deliver on the promise of the digital revolution, we must acknowledge that the way we have governed and managed IT in the past has proven woefully inadequate, and that continuing on this path will be a huge impediment to delivering on that promise.

The labeling problem

Labeling and managing investments in IT-enabled business change as IT projects and abdicating accountability to the CIO are the root cause of the failure of so many to generate the expected payoff. Business value does not come from technology alone; technology in and of itself is simply a cost. Business value comes from the business change that technology both shapes and enables. Change of which technology is only one part and increasingly only a small part. Back in 1991, Michael S. Scott Morton introduced the MIT90's framework. This framework was a key eye-opener for me and was a significant influence on my subsequent work. I included it in *The Information Paradox*, and subsequently used a somewhat modified version in practice which I called the BTOPP model (Business, Technology, Organization, Process, and People). As I look back now, I realize that, to keep it simple I left out a few key parts of the original model, notably culture and the exterbal socioeconomic and technological environment. I'm including the original Scott Morton version below as these are key factors at work today (Figure 1).

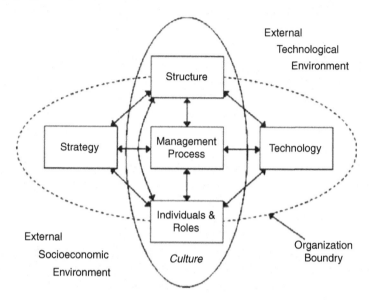

Figure 1: BTOPP model.

The model illustrates that technology only contributes to business value when complementary changes are made to the business — including increasingly complex changes to the organizational culture, the business model, the operating model, and people skills, as well as to relationships with customers and suppliers, business processes and work practices, staff skills and competencies, reward systems, organizational structures, physical facilities, etc. Ultimately, it is the intelligent and innovative use of the data captured, organized, distributed, visualized, and communicated by technology that creates and sustains value. This is not a technology issue, it is a business issue.

The failure of business leadership to understand this and the lack of focus on value have been a subject of much discussion over the last three decades.

- An all too often blind focus on the technology itself, and the cost of the technology, rather than the change (increasingly significant and complex change) that technology both shapes and enables, and requires if value is to be created and sustained.

- The unwillingness of business leaders to get engaged in, and take ownership of this change, preferring to abdicate their accountability to the IT function.
- Failure to inclusively involve the stakeholders affected by the change, without whose knowledge, understanding and "buy in" failure is pretty much a foregone conclusion.
- A lack of rigor at the front-end of an investment decision, including, what is almost universally a totally ineffective business case process.
- Not actively managing for value.
- Not managing the journey beyond the initial investment decision.

We still have what is predominately a "culture of delivery," "build it and they will come," rather than a "culture of value;" one that focuses on creating and sustaining value from an organization's investments and assets.

We have been having the wrong conversations. If organizations are to succeed in the digital economy, we need to change that conversation!

What Is Digital Transformation?

While the term digital transformation means many different things to different people, and indeed its manifestation will likely be different for every organization, it does help to ground the discussion with a definition (Figure 2).

Figure 2: Digital transformation.

Digital transformation is an ever-evolving digitally driven and enabled journey of exploration and experimentation. It represents a cultural and mindset change which involves continually challenging all aspects of the status quo. It requires reimagining and fundamentally transforming government, business, and society in a way that is inclusive of and creates value for all stakeholders.

What is value?

"Everything is worth what its purchaser will pay for it."

(*Source*: HBR, Nov–Dec 1998, James C. Anderson and James A. Narus)
Publilius Syrus, first century B.C.

"Things only have the value that we give them."

Molière 1622–1673, French actor and playwright

"Price is what you pay. Value is what you get."

Warren Buffet

Most businesses have no clear idea of the value that they expect to realize from the use of the technology. **They still see digital transformation as being largely about implementing the technology and have little understanding of the significant changes they will need to make to realize value from their use of technology**. Changes to the nature of their business, how they are organized, their processes, the skills of their people, their reward system, and, most importantly, their culture and mindset.

A more fundamental problem in many businesses is that there is limited understanding of what constitutes "value" for the business, or how value is created. Strategies to create and sustain value are often poorly defined and even more poorly communicated. In a recent Harvard Business Review article, the authors suggest that most executives cannot articulate the basic elements of strategy of their business (objective, scope, and advantage) in a simple statement of 35 words or less — and that if they can't, neither can anyone else. Research at the IT Leadership Academy suggests that the main reason for over 60% of IT projects that were deemed to be "underperforming" or "disappointing" was not the technology or project management, it was a bad business strategy.

It would appear ironic that executives who cannot adequately define what is of value to their enterprise express frustration that they cannot measure the value received from their IT investments. Many years ago, I asked the CEO of a large financial institution what value he was expecting from what was seen as his pet project, an over budget and behind schedule major ERP implementation. His response was "I don't know, but I'll know it when I see it." He was gone within a year.

The reality is that "value is in the eye of the beholder." There are many types of value, including, but not limited to functional, monetary, environmental, social, and psychological, and a broad range of beholders, in this case, stakeholders. In marketing, value is generally considered customer-perceived value, but a better and broader definition would be stakeholder-perceived value. In the digital era, there are an increasing number of stakeholders, some of this driven by the emerging, albeit slow adoption of the triple bottom line approach which encompasses social, environmental, and financial performance, often summarized as people, planet, and profit.

How do you manage for value?

I learned early that boards and executives, the "guys" who must get this, don't respond well to complex presentations on frameworks, methodologies, or processes. Their response was usually what does all this mean in simple terms that we can all understand. I addressed that response by introducing four simple questions which became the four "Ares":

- Are we doing the right things?
- Are we doing them the right way?
- Are we getting them done well?
- Are we getting the benefits?

Over the last few decades, these four questions have become the foundation of my work, and that of others. In my case, they have framed *The Information Paradox*, numerous chapters in other books, articles and blogs, several frameworks, and methodologies, and supporting processes and tools. I do however now tend to change "Are we getting the benefits?" to the broader question "Are we getting the expected value?".

"Are we doing the right things?" the strategic question, and "Are we getting the benefits?" the value question, raise key business issues relating to both strategic direction and the organization's ability to produce the targeted business benefits. "Are we doing them the right way?" the architecture question, raises a mix of business and technology integration issues that must be answered to design successful [digitally enabled] change programs. "Are we getting them done well?" the delivery question, directs attention to traditional technology project delivery issues, as well as to the ability of other business groups to deliver the necessary business change projects.

I always open my discussions with boards and executives with these questions. They are simple, and they can understand and relate to them. In one case, shortly after introducing these questions, the CFO, went down the list one by one. Yes, he said, I think we're doing the right things. Yes, also, we're doing them the right way, and, yes, we're getting them done well. Then, when he got to "Are we getting the benefits?" he paused for a while, then said, I think I'd better go back to "Are we doing the right things?" I've had a similar response many more times over the years.

This is not saying that processes are not needed. They are absolutely needed, but the four "Ares" provide a context to engage the leadership in helping them understand the relevance and importance of the processes, and their role related to them. I'll return to this later, as it is key to the realization of value. However, first I'll briefly discuss the core processes as well as the key related processes, and several tools that can be applied to make them more effective.

The Core Processes

Portfolio management

> *"There is nothing worse than doing well that which should not be done at all."*

> Peter Drucker

> *"If you don't know where you're going, any road will take you there."*

> Lewis Carroll

The term portfolio originated in the 1700s in Italy describing a case based on Latin words meaning to carry papers. Its use has since been extended to describe, categorize, and evaluate almost anything that is of interest to us. In the context of value, its use here is in describing, categorizing, and evaluating investments in digitally enabled enterprise change.

The board and executive team are accountable to a broad range of stakeholders for ensuring and assuring that their enterprise creates and sustains value. Portfolio management supports the **board and executive** in making objective selection of **investments**, including business change **programs**, in line with their **strategy** in order to maximize overall **enterprise value**. It also includes proactive monitoring and adjustment of the portfolio of investments and resulting **assets** based on their performance and changes to the business context through their **full life cycle**.

Other factors to be considered in maximizing the value of the portfolio include:

- Managing risk systematically both by diversifying the portfolio across varied investment programs and by improving the risk profile of each program.
- Managing program interdependencies with a focus on the four central issues of sequencing, overlaps, resource competition, and change bottlenecks, so as to turn potential conflicts into mutual reinforcement so that programs leverage each other whenever possible, and to cut down on pointless inter-program competition for resources.
- Continuously adjusting portfolio composition as programs are completed, new ones are selected, and priorities change to reflect shifts in the business environment.

Program management

The terms project and program management have been used interchangeably since the 1960s. It was only in the early 2000s that the distinction between projects delivering capabilities (outputs), and programs delivering business/organizational change (outcomes) that are closely aligned to and directly support an organization's strategic objectives started to emerge. However, there still appears to be a common belief within the project community that program management is part of or an extension of project management.

Program Management supports **business sponsors** in the identification and management of programs that include a structured grouping of projects encompassing all the elements of **change** (BTOPP) that are both necessary and sufficient to **realize** the expected **benefits** of the program.

Project management

Project management is a structured set of activities concerned with delivering a defined capability based on an agreed schedule and budget. It is a relatively mature discipline, having been around for quite a while.

Project management supports **project managers** in managing a structured set of activities concerned with delivering a defined **capability** that is necessary but NOT sufficient to realize the expected benefits of an investment.

As organizations move from traditional application development and maintenance, and IT infrastructure into a cloud and ecosystem world, there is an evolving discussion around how the nature of projects could

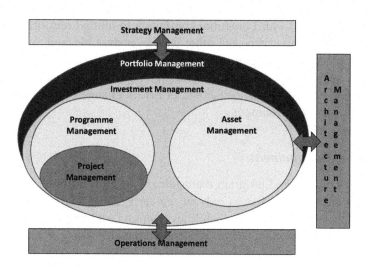

Figure 3: Portfolio management.

change. McKinsey suggests that we could be moving to a rejuvenate, innovate, and pioneer business-technology model.

The relationships between Portfolio, Program, and Project Management, which are often referred to as P3M, as well as Asset Management and Investment Management are illustrated in Figure 3.

This view illustrates that if we are to look at how we realize value from projects and programs, we need to introduce the investment and asset management views. Program management is only the first part of the investment view. Benefits and value are only realized when the capabilities delivered by the programs of change become operational assets. Portfolio management must be applied at the investment level, including both programs of change and the resulting assets.

Furthermore, there are more linkages required to ensure that we are doing the right things, doing them the right way, and getting them done well. These start with the links to strategy, architecture, and operations, as described as follows.

Strategy

The concept of strategy can be traced to its roots in military history. The term "strategy" comes from the Greek word stratego, which means "a general."

Michael Porter stated in 1980 that competitive strategy was the blueprint for how a business would compete in the marketplace, including its goals and objectives. In other words, strategy is the schematic, the framework for how an organization will operate. An organization's strategy guides every aspect of how the firm conducts business. Marketing plans, sales processes, capital investments, expansion strategies, and even the hiring of new employees are guided by the organization's strategy. This is true whether you work for a non-profit, a family-owned business, a public corporation, or a multinational operating in several countries.

The strategic planning process model presented in Figure 4 is based on the concepts of strategic thinkers including Michael Porter, Peter Drucker, Larry Bossidy, and Ram Charan.

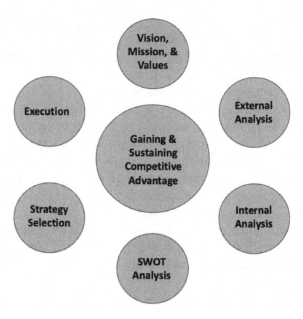

Figure 4:   Strategic planning model.

Architecture

Architecture involves maintaining an enterprise perspective on an organization's assets and their relationships, and includes structure, systems/ processes, and skills. It supports and informs strategy, identifies opportunities for integration, and helps to avoid unnecessary duplication of effort. Architecture must also consider organizational culture. An appropriate and effective architecture can increase business agility, thus creating competitive advantage, and increasing value. In the digital world, with the increasing adoption of cloud computing, and the emergence of ecosystems, it provides a platform to join different internal and external applications in a timely and agile way.

Operations

Operations are concerned with ensuring quality, repeatable and secure execution of the delivery of services daily. The nature of operations of a business varies across enterprises, including public and private sector, and small and large organizations, and must be structured according to the requirements of the specific enterprise. Operations evolve as enterprises grow, and changes to operations must be managed in such a way as to avoid disruptions. As in the case of architecture above, in the digital economy, enterprise operations will have to adapt to providing both traditional stability and the agility and responsiveness that the digital world requires.

There are still other several necessary conditions that must be met for value to be realized. These are in the areas of managing change, metrics, and governance, including accountability.

Management of change

Change doesn't just happen, it must be managed, and it must be done with all the stakeholders who will be affected by the change, not to them. In most cases, they understand more about what will be required than the leadership. If they are to embrace and support the change, they must be involved throughout the investment life cycle. When I was involved in writing proposals, I would always include a significant amount on managing change. As a rule of thumb, **I would plan for 30% of the effort being managing change**. In the digital age, this is even more so. Digital transformation impacts all the aspects of the BTOPP model introduced earlier and, again, it is the cultural and people aspects that will require the greatest attention.

Relevant metrics

"You can't manage what you can't measure."

Peter Drucker

"You can't measure what you can't describe."

Kaplan & Norton

Traditional IT metrics have tended to focus on outputs related to solution delivery in terms of delivering the desired capabilities on time and on budget, and service operation in terms of reliability and usage. Limited attention has been given to outcomes, the benefits and value realized from the use of the services. Similarly, with digital transformation, many organizations still measure the success of their investments using traditional financial and operational efficiency metrics, which are not usually effective. In both cases, the metrics used are generally output metrics, rather than outcome metrics. Managing for value requires two types of outcome metrics, **lead and lag**. Lead metrics measure intermediate outcomes which are necessary on the way to realizing the end outcome. They provide early warning when the necessary conditions to realize your end outcome are at risk. Lag outcomes measure the attainment of the expected final outcomes of the investment over time. Lead metrics are even more important in the digital era, where there is a need to rapidly adapt and up-scale or fail fast and pivot depending on progress towards desired outcomes.

Digital transformation will also look different for every enterprise, and will be continually evolving, so establishing metrics is a challenge. According to Peter Sondergaard, VP of Research at Gartner, the indicators that measure the success of the digital transformation almost always answer these questions

- How fast are changes occurring within the enterprise such that more agile and flexible models being adopted?
- To what extent have the barriers between departments been removed to promote and ensure collaboration between functional areas of the enterprise?
- How is the digital strategy integrated with the general strategy such that the particular objectives of each area or department are aligned with the overall enterprise strategy?
- To what extent is innovation in management and recruitment of talent, and continuous training integrated in talent management?
- To what extent is personal development linked to personal and group involvement such that people feel involved and see it as an opportunity for continuous growth?
- Are the enterprise's culture and values consistent with what the team is doing so as to avoid contradictions or resistance?
- To what extent are people and teams taken into account such that each person feels important in their teams and valued and involved in the joint success?

Value/benefits mapping, described in the tools section below, is an important tool to help define both lead and lag metrics.

Full-Cycle Governance

If value is to be created and sustained, value and benefits need to be actively managed through the whole investment lifecycle. Most programs are considered complete when the capabilities are delivered. There may be some form of post-implementation review shortly after that, but that's it. Benefits are only realized, and value is only created once the capabilities are delivered. Benefits and value need to be managed throughout the full life cycle of an investment, from the original idea through to the retirement of the resulting assets.

This requires an effective approach to governance throughout the full life cycle of investments and resulting assets. This must be done with a strong focus on ownership and accountability that promotes and supports a culture of value, with accountability being much more than a tick-box exercise, or a signature on a form. Effective accountability requires:

- Clear mandate and scope
- Sufficient authority and latitude to act
- Requisite competence
- Commensurate resources
- Clear lines of accountability
- Understanding of rights and obligations
- Relevant performance measures
- An aligned reward system.

And, most importantly, there must be acceptance of accountability.

The Bigger Picture

Figure 5 brings all the above together and makes it clear that when we look at how value is created, it goes way beyond project management, indeed way beyond P3M. Value and benefits management are part of portfolio, program, and project management, but they are much more than that. They are behaviors that need to be embedded in all management domains from strategy through to business operations.

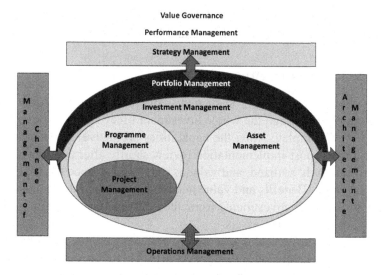

Figure 5:   Value governance.

If value and benefits are not appropriately addressed in any of the domains, strategic, structural, or execution, value leakage can occur. Figure 6 indicates where most of that leakage has occurred in the past, and still occurs today. The greatest leakage, 85%, is strategic and structural leakage, with only 15% being project leakage. It is the missing link between strategy, structure, and execution that is the problem.

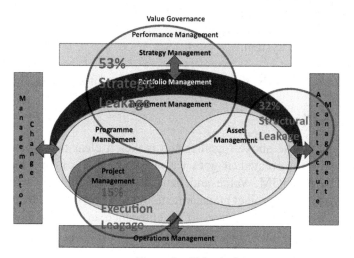

Figure 6:   Value leakage.

Portfolio management at the board and executive level provides that link; managing portfolios of investments, comprising programs of enterprise change and resulting assets, and providing input to, and receiving direction from enterprise strategy and architecture. Unfortunately, boards and executives continue to see this as a technology project issue.

Organizations such as PMI and APM continue to evolve their offerings to increase awareness and understanding of P3M, and to provide relevant training and support materials for the project community. A recent PMI report recognizes the extent of change in the evolving digital age saying that *"Relentless technological evolution, shifting customer demands, and global socioeconomic volatility are forcing a revolution in how problems are solved and how work gets done."* They then go on to say that all change happens through projects and describe this new era as "The Project Economy." Their doing so adds to the perception that P3M is all about projects, and that all elements of P3M belong in the project space. Certainly, projects have a key role to play, and the way projects are managed will have to change, but the digital economy is much more than a project economy, and the change required is much broader.

The ongoing reluctance of boards, executive management and, in many cases, business management to get appropriately engaged in what they erroneously see as technology projects has left project managers to do the best that they can on their own. However, labeling P3M and more as project work, and labeling the digital era as the project economy is misleading at best, and certainly will not help with the challenge of getting that engagement. Even within P3M, portfolio, program, and project management, while closely related, are quite different in terms of their role, what they deliver, the skills that are needed, who they involve, and who should be responsible and accountable for them.

Figure 7 illustrates that the board, CEO, and executive management are accountable for establishing the strategic context for realizing value, while line of business management, working with IT management are accountable for ensuring that change programs include the full scope of change (BTOPP) required to realize the expected benefits. This is shown as a dotted line in Figure 7 as the line between the responsibilities of business and IT management is becoming less clear in the digital world.

Four "Ares" & Accountability

		Accountability	Focus	Domains
ARE WE DOING THE RIGHT THINGS? The *strategic* question	**ARE WE GETTING THE BENEFITS?** The *value* question	Board, CEO & Executive Team	• Value Governance • Investment eval'n, selection & oversight • Value Optimisation across investments	Value Governance Portfolio Mgmt Strategy Mgmt Architecture Mgmt Mgmt of Change Performance Mgmt
		LOB Management	• Benefits Realisation for individual investments • Business change • Delivery of new/ improved business capabilities/ processes	Programme Mgmt Architecture Mgmt Asset Mgmt Mgmt of Change Operations Mgmt Performance Mgmt
ARE WE DOING THEM THE RIGHT WAY? The *architecture* question	**ARE WE GETTING THEM DONE WELL?** The *delivery* question	IT Management	• Technology change • Delivery of new/ improved technology capabilities/ services	Project Mgmt Architecture Mgmt Asset Mgmt Mgmt of Change Operations Mgmt Performance Mgmt

Figure 7: The 4 "Ares" and accountability.

Tough questioning is critical to get rid of silver bullet thinking about IT and lose the industrial-age mind-set that is proving extremely costly to organizations. Asking the four "Ares" helps to define the business and technical issues clearly, and thus to better define the distinctive roles of business executives and IT experts in the investment decision process.

For the board and executive, the two most important questions in the Four "Ares" are the strategic and value questions. They are accountable for ensuring and assuring that their organizations are doing the right things. They are also accountable for identifying key metrics for their investments, including both programs and resulting assets to determine that they are realizing the expected benefits and value, have effective oversight, and can take appropriate action when things are not going to plan. Effective portfolio management is a key tool to address this issue. However, in all too many enterprises, it is the missing link.

Without the appropriate level of engagement of boards and executives, we will continue to see the failure of organizations to realize value from their past and current technology investments, and even more so from their current and future investments in digital transformation.

At this point, you might be thinking that this is too much work to expect the board and executive to do, and to be at too detailed a level. That doesn't have to be the case. Many organizations today have a Project Management Office (PMO). The PMO can do most of the detailed legwork for the board and executive. More than that, they can facilitate the work that the board and executive must do themselves, including:

- Providing sufficient clarity and substance to the strategy process.
- Clearly defining expected outcomes, both intermediate and end outcomes.
- Establishing performance metrics, both lead and lag metrics to monitor those outcomes.
- Ensuring that business cases are aligned with the enterprise strategy, have a clear statement of the expected value (benefit net of costs), with an acceptable level of risk (both delivery risk and benefits risk), that they are provided in a succinct and consistent way, and kept up to date through the full life cycle of an investment decision.
- Taking timely action when there are risks to attainment of those outcomes, both intermediate and lag outcomes, either because of concerns with individual investments, or changes in the external context.

One of the benefits of an effective PMO is that their work in ensuring that the ducks are all lined up for the board usually results in those business cases that really have no chance of approval, are withdrawn by the sponsor before they get to the board/executive, thus removing more workload from them.

Portfolio Management: The Bridge to Value

Portfolio management involves:

- managing the evaluation, selection, monitoring and on-going adjustment of different groupings of investment programs or assets, which are
- categorized by their type/characteristics
- with clear and consistent evaluation criteria for each category, and
- assigning weightings to those criteria based on their contribution to strategic objectives
- while meeting clear risk/reward standards, thus

- enabling decisions to be made on how to best manage entities in the portfolio, in order to
- optimize the value of the portfolio for the overall enterprise.

Again, this can sound time consuming. However, not all investments require the same level of scrutiny, and not all investments need to be managed at the enterprise level. This is where categorization comes in.

Categorize programs

Different types of investments require different handling, depending upon the degree of freedom in allocating funds, and the complexity of the investment. A sound system for categorizing programs lets executive management focus on the key business decisions they need to make based on the nature, size, complexity, and strategic importance of the programs, and their expected contribution, benefits, cost, and risk over time. An example of such an approach is shown in Figure 8.

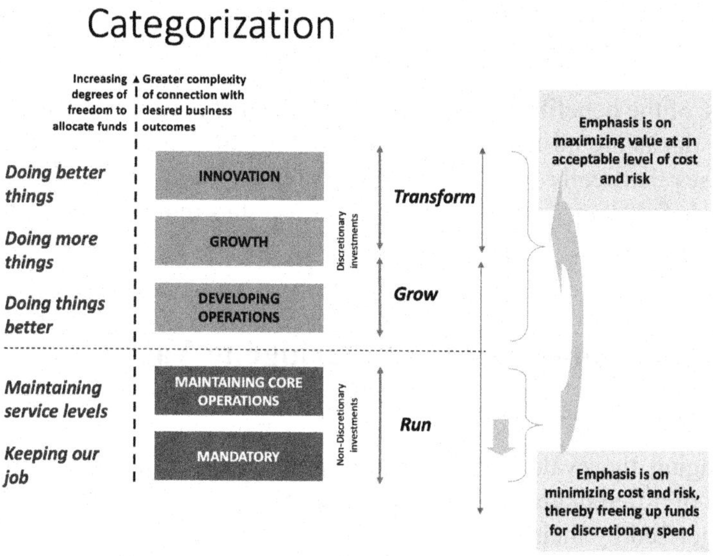

Categorization

Figure 8: Categorization.

Source: Gartner (Meta).

Effective categorization determines the level of rigor required in the business case. Some business cases can be just a few pages; few should be more than 30 pages.

The Business Case

"Business cases are generally viewed only as documents for gaining funding. Once approved they are put away...few track the business benefits the projects actually achieve."

Gartner, Building Brilliant Business Cases

"Largely works of fiction based on 'delusional optimism' and 'strategic misrepresentation'"

Stephen Jenner quoting Daniel Hahneman & Brent Flyvbjerg

I can hear the groans now, "Oh no, not the business case!" It does often appear that the quality of a business case is measured by its weight. Business cases are all too often seen as a necessary bureaucratic hurdle, and rarely revisited after the initial approval. However, the business case process is the foundation that sows the seeds for success or failure for any investment.

While much of the work identified below should be done at the program level, I have included the material here as the board and executive will evaluate the program using portfolio management and will set the criteria for what they expect to see in the business case. They may require the use of a modeling tool, an example of which, the Results Chain, is described in this section, to clarify the outcomes that they expect programs to contribute to, and the metrics that they will use to measure that contribution.

Business cases should:

- Go beyond delivery of technology projects to include realization of value from investments in digitally enabled business change.
- Focus on managing the "journey" as well as achieving outcomes (both intermediate and end outcomes).
- Ensure that relevant and appropriate metrics (both lead and lag), accountability and reporting are included.
- Be a living, operational management tool, updated through the full life cycle of an investment decision, with timely corrective actions taken as required.

The basic steps in developing a business case include:

- Defining the expected end outcome(s).
- Identifying the initiatives required to realize the outcome(s).
- Defining the metrics, both lead and lag, which will be required for effective oversight.
- Surfacing any assumptions that are being made, which should either be removed by identifying additional initiatives or tested regularly using appropriate metrics as the investment moves forward.
- Estimating the expected value over time, including benefits and costs and risks.

Value/benefits mapping

Depending on the categorization of the program, and where there is a choice of where to allocate funds, or where the realization of value is complex, programs merit appropriate assessment in the competition for scarce resources. Beyond financial impact, consideration needs to be given to broader investment criteria, including the alignment of programs with business strategies, the degree of risk around delivery of benefits and interdependencies within and between programs. A key tool for doing this is value/benefits mapping. Figure 9 illustrates one such tool, which identifies end and intermediate outcomes, initiatives, contributions of initiatives and intermediate outcomes, and assumptions. There are several similar tools available in the marketplace.

Benefits Mapping - Completing and Connecting the Dots

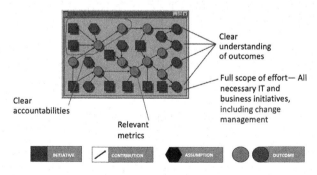

Figure 9:   Benefits mapping.

Source: The results Chain™, Fujitsu.

Value mapping can be used at several levels:

- An overall map showing the contribution of a portfolio of investments.
- A high-level map for one investment showing the intermediate and end outcomes, and key initiatives for one investment.
- A detailed map showing all the elements for one investment (or for parts of the investment).

The value of benefits/value mapping is not so much in the maps that are created, although that is certainly useful, but in the process of extensive interviews and workshops with stakeholders that are involved in developing the maps. The sponsor and key stakeholders are also involved in the development of the maps, which promotes discussion, consensus, and commitment. It develops a shared understanding of the expected outcomes, which often change because of the mapping process. It identifies the full scope of BTOPP change required to achieve those outcomes, along with the contribution of the initiatives, and the metrics required to measure that contribution. Its power is in making explicit what is implicit and surfacing assumptions. In doing so, it facilitates communication and enables better decision-making. It also helps solidify the "team" and clarifies ownership and accountability.

Again, you may be thinking that this takes too much time. While it can take time to develop the more detailed program maps, at the higher level, a lot can also be accomplished with executives in a few hours (Figure 10).

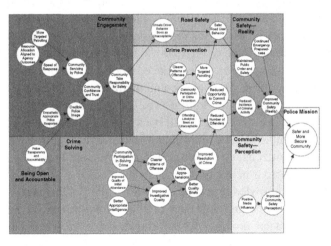

Figure 10:   Benefit/value mapping.

Source: Val IT Police Case Study — ITGI — used with permission.

Benefits/value mapping is about much more than an abstract map, once used then forgotten. It is a key part of developing the business case, and when completed, it can become a living model of the benefits/value realization process. Living in the sense that it can and should be continually revised to monitor and communicate progress, reflect any changes, and identify actions that might be required to ensure that value is created and sustained.

The ever-evolving digital economy, the pace of change in the areas of big data, analytics, artificial intelligence, machine learning, deep learning, etc., as well as increased adoption of cloud computing, and the emergence of ecosystems, and Cloud Partner Ecosystems is impacting all aspects of the above. While the processes described above are still required in the digital age, they will need, from strategy to operations, to be applied in a much more agile and dynamic way.

Moving Beyond Words to Action

With COVID-19, we have seen the ability of organizations and individuals in all sectors to pivot to new ways of delivering their products and services. As Satya Nadella, Microsoft's CEO, summed it up, "Social distancing rules have brought forward the adoption of a wide range of technologies by two years." In the case of healthcare, digitally enabled services that have been discussed for years or, in some cases, decades have been delivered in a few weeks. The Economist, under a heading "Creative Disruption" discusses the pandemic "liberating firms to experiment with new ideas," and being to do so at breakneck speed, and without huge financial outlays. But, as evidenced above, it's more than that. It is liberating organizations of all types, and in all sectors, as well as individuals of all ages across the world to do so. We need to ask ourselves, when the crisis abates, are we going to fall back to the traditional world of ineffective leadership, bloated inefficient bureaucracies, and disengaged employees and citizens, or are we going to learn from the crisis and move forward together to a better world.

The body of knowledge related to the realization of business value from today's increasingly significant and complex investments in information technology has been growing for several decades. However, it could be argued that while every addition makes a positive contribution, the fundamentals have not changed for some time. Many current writings present these fundamentals as new ideas, often using slightly different language or models to describe what are essentially the same fundamentals. At the same time, the take-up of these fundamentals continues to move at little more than a snail's pace. As Craig Symons of Forrester once commented to me, "*One of the things that never ceases to surprise me is that IT investment management as a management process has been around since 1981 yet remains very immature in many organizations.*" He went on to add that "*Another issue is [my IT clients'] inability to get the business leadership interested in IT governance and engaging more actively with IT.*" These comments certainly support my own experience and are in line with discussions that I have had with many other individuals and institutions. Whilst we should certainly continue adding to and improving the body of knowledge around this topic, we will not turn words into action until we put much more focus on understanding the constraints to adopting proven solutions that already exist and identifying and implementing approaches to overcoming those constraints.

We need leaders who lead

The real challenge as it relates to managing the organizational change has been getting awareness and understanding of the problem by those who need to commit to the solution. In the more than 30 years that I have been speaking around the world on this topic, a comment that I invariably get at the end of any presentation is "**My boss should have been here!**" Middle managers and practitioners, including consultants, are generally aware of and in many cases understand the problem. They often recognize what needs to be done but are not usually the decision-maker. And in most cases, they do not have the authority or resources to do it. Most executives, those that do have the authority and the ability to deploy resources to do something about it, are not always aware of the need, rarely understand the nature of the problem, and, as a result, have little interest, let alone commitment, to do anything about it.

The CFO of a Fortune 100 company that I worked with once confided: "*I know the way we are doing things isn't working, but I don't know a better way.*" **A better way that is not simply about thinking differently about IT, but about doing things differently**.

There is certainly not a lack of proven value management practices. **The issue is the lack of serious and sustained adoption of them**. The real challenge is one of overcoming the "knowing–doing gap," as described by Jeffrey Pfeffer and Robert Sutton in their book of the same name. We know what to do, and the knowledge is available on how to do it. Yet, so far, there has simply been little or no appetite for, or commitment to the behavioral change required to get it done.

For enterprises, public and private, large and small, to survive, let alone thrive in the digital economy, and for the potential individual, community, and societal benefits of the digital economy to be realized, the status quo is not an option! To quote General Erik Shinseki, a former Chief of Staff of the US Army, "*If you don't like change, you're going to like irrelevance even less!*" Success in the digital age will require a major cultural change.

The digital age requires a cultural change

While we are still wrestling with getting more traditional investments right, we are now facing a new, rapidly evolving world of digitally enabled business transformation, one which includes a broad and ever-evolving group of stakeholders. One in which, while the fundamentals of value and benefits management remain the same, our approach to implementing them will have to adapt significantly to be more agile in this new context. One which will require a culture that is:

- **Obsessed with value and reducing complexity**
  - ○ Challenging all aspects of the status quo
  - ○ Continually unlearning, reimagining, and reinventing
  - ○ Transcending traditional roles, silos, and hierarchies, and dismantling bureaucracy
- **Inclusive, open, transparent, and collaborative**
  - ○ Decision-making driven by data rather than hierarchy, politics, and ego
  - ○ Embracing openness and transparency with empowerment and accountability "at the edge"
  - ○ Getting things done through teamwork and responsible autonomy
  - ○ Leadership as a behavior to be recognized, nurtured, empowered, and rewarded throughout the organization

- **Open-minded and embracing diversity**
  - o In recruiting new talent, as well as integrating external talent and partners
  - o Challenging existing organizational paradigms and mindsets
  - o Recognizing that great ideas and creativity can come from anywhere in the organization or its ecosystem
- **Comfortable with risk, uncertainty, and continuous change**
  - o Willing to try new things
  - o Having the capability and agility to rapidly adapt and up-scale or fail fast and pivot depending on progress towards desired outcomes
- **Guided by ethics**
  - o Ensuring and assuring positive outcomes to stakeholders
  - o Constantly aware of, pro-actively guarding against, and preventing harmful misuse, either accidental or deliberate.

Final Thoughts: Moving beyond Leadership as a Role to Leadership as a Behavior

"The typical medium- or large-scale organization infantilizes employees, enforces dull conformity, and discourages entrepreneurship; it wedges people into narrow roles, stymies personal growth, and treats humans as mere resources — a small but growing band of post-bureaucratic pioneers are proving that it is possible to capture the benefits of bureaucracy — control, consistency and coordination — while avoiding the penalties — inflexibility, mediocrity and apathy."

Humanocracy, Gary Hamel

The challenge ahead is to break out of the straitjacket of more than a century of hierarchical, siloed industrial age mindsets which are controlling, risk-averse, and "know-it-all." To evolve them into mindsets that are enabling, learning, and willing to try new things and fail. To move to a more agile and inclusive approach to governance, leadership, and management. A value-focused, data and analytics-driven, agile, sense and respond approach that transcends functional and organizational boundaries, and engages employees, customers, and other key stakeholders. One that places accountability and decision-making at the most appropriate level, while supporting decisions with broader and more knowledgeable input. One that can survive and thrive in an ever-evolving, complex, and chaotic context. Only when this is done will we come close to realizing the full value of the digital age.

An era in which leadership is a behavior, recognized, nurtured, and rewarded throughout an organization, with leadership at the top playing a role akin to some combination of an orchestra conductor and an air traffic controller. A world in which: Bureaucracy, a term coined roughly two centuries ago is no longer fit for purpose when today's employees are skilled, not illiterate; Competitive Advantage comes from innovation, not sheer size; Communication is instantaneous, not tortuous; and the Pace of Change is hypersonic, not glacial. A world in which employees, as in the case of China's Haier, are engaged as "energetic entrepreneurs, and an open ecosystem of users, inventors, and partners replaces formal hierarchy."

The technology exists to support this today. What is needed is the leadership mindset, will, and capability to make the behavioral change required to get it done.

Bibliography

Allen, T. J. & Morton, M. S. S. (Eds.). (1994). *Information Technology and the Corporation of the 1990s: Research Studies*. Oxford University Press on Demand.

Avora, C., Catlin, T., Forrest, W., Kaplan, J., & Vinter, L. (2020, July 21). *Three Actions CEOs can Take to Get Value from Cloud Computing*. McKinsey Quarterly. https://www.mckinsey.com/business-functions/mckinsey-digital/our-insights/three-actions-ceos-can-take-to-get-value-from-cloud-computing.

Bolland, A., Singla, A., Sood, R., & van Ouwerkerk, J. (2016, October 3). *Transforming Operations Management for a Digital World*. McKinsey Digital. https://www.mckinsey.com/business-functions/mckinsey-digital/our-insights/transforming-operations-management-for-a-digital-world.

Clancy, T. (1995). The chaos report. *The Standish Group*.

Elkington, J. (1994). Towards the sustainable corporation: Win-win-win business strategies for sustainable development. *California Management Review*, 36(2), 90–100.

Forrest, W., Gu, M., Kaplan, J., Liebow, M., Sharma, R., Smaje, K., & Van Kuiken, S. (2021). Cloud's trillion-dollar prize is up for grabs. *McKinsey Digital*.

Goran, J., LaBerge, L., & Srinivasan, R. (2017). Culture for a digital age. *McKinsey Quarterly*, 3(1), 56–67.

Hamel, G. & Zanini, M. (2018). The end of bureaucracy. *Harvard Business Review*, 96(6), 50–59.

Kestenholz, P. (2020, January 30). *The Identity Crisis Of A PMO In Times Of Digital And Agile Trends*. Forbes. https://www.forbes.com/sites/forbes-techcouncil/2020/01/30/the-identity-crisis-of-a-pmo-in-times-of-digital-and-agile-trends/.

Lloyd, R. & Aho, W. The Four Functions of Management: An Essential Guide to Management Principles. https://fhsu.pressbooks.pub/management/front-matter/the-four-functions-of-management/.

Paredes, D. (2018, April 22). *A Kiwi Global CIO's Framework for Building a Change-Ready, Growth-Minded ICT Team*. CIO. https://www.cio.com/article/204225/a-kiwi-global-cio-s-framework-for-building-a-change-ready-growth-minded-ict-team.html.

Pascale, R., Millemann, M., & Gioja, L. (1997). Changing the way we change. *Harvard Business Review*, 75(6), 126.

Pfeffer, J. & Sutton, R. I. (2000). *The Knowing-Doing Gap: How Smart Companies Turn Knowledge into Action*. Harvard business press.

PMI. (2020). *Tomorrow's Teams Today*. https://www.pmi.org/learning/library/pulse-indepth-tomorrows-teams-toady-11941.

Saleem, F. & Fakieh, B. (2020). Enterprise architecture and organizational benefits: A case study. *Sustainability*, 12(19), 8237.

Steyn, P. & Zovitsky, E. (2018). The Evolution of Programme Management towards Governance of Industry 4.0 Organisations.

Thorp, J. (2017, May 1). *The Dark Side of Digital*. Institute for Digital Transformation. https://www.institutefordigitaltransformation.org/the-dark-side-of-digital/.

Ungoti. (n.d.). *How To Measure Digital Transformation Evolution*. https://ungoti.com/blog/how-to-measure-digital-transformation-kpi/.

Chapter 5

The Neuroscience of Transformation

Cherri Holland

Introduction

Transforming organizations in the digital era and Neuroscience have to do with healthy, functioning brains, and brains that are not functioning at potential in otherwise healthy people.

Digital transformation affects human brains, and in turn, transformation is affected by the "brain state" of those involved, both inside and outside an organization.

It is widely acknowledged that transformation "programs" don't have a high success rate. Gartner estimates that over 70% of transformation initiatives fail, and Forbes reports that 84% of Digital Transformation efforts fail.

This chapter gives a neuroscience rationale for this poor success record and explores how you can better facilitate transformation outcomes through an appreciation of the neuroscience of transformation — what we know about human beings and the organizations they work in.

The chapter addresses these challenging questions about poor transformation outcomes:

- As the human brain is continuously monitoring (internally and externally) to adapt to signals and ensure you stay alive, what is it about people in organizations that makes continuous adaptation so difficult?

© 2023 World Scientific Publishing Company
https://doi.org/10.1142/9789811260469_0005

- What is it about human beings as individuals, in groups, and in organizations that makes change so challenging?
- How does this adaptation challenge play out in the digital era organization?
- How can you ensure transformation delivers on expectations?

This Introduction to the chapter gives some assumptions, so you can more quickly make sense of the information, and it ends with a list of the sections in the chapter. The following contain consistent themes that explain common challenges with digital transformation, and are referred to throughout:

- Systems Theory
- Social-psychology frameworks such as Transactional Analysis
- The emotional and social brain research of Daniel Goleman
- The science of power research of Dr. Dacher Keltner
- Research into super-performance from the latter half of the last century.

Human reactions to change

While organizations in a digital era are different in many ways to those in the analog era, human beings (and certainly human brains) haven't changed much in thousands of years. Human reactions to *certain kinds of change* are a constant.

> *"More and more companies are trying to make a fundamental change in the way they operate. For years, they have struggled with growing competition by introducing improvements (or at least improvement programs) into every function and process. But the competitive pressures keep on getting worse, the pace of change keeps accelerating, and companies keep pouring executive energy into the search for ever higher levels of quality, service and overall business agility. The treadmill moves faster, companies work harder, results improve slowly or not at all."*

> Richard T. Pascale, *et al.*

While that was written over two decades ago, the results today are no better. It could even be that the digital era has magnified the issue when we may have expected it would evolve systems and processes that better *enable* continuous change, given that organizations have never been so connected.

Transformation failure

Failure matters most in these two ways:

- The benefits that the transformation strategy was developed for are not realized which could threaten actual survival in a fiercely competitive industry.
- The delays and disengagement that accompany many transformation strategies burden the organization at a time when stakeholder expectations are at an all-time high, and patience is at an all-time low. At the very time, when an organization needs to get more done in less time, productivity plummets.

Why have organizations not got better at this? **The average person has had at least one bad organizational change experience, and the healthy brain never forgets**. Yet, it can be different. A manager at a Change workshop I ran many years ago said a department head presented an organization restructure as a great opportunity for those in that department. There was no inherent reason why that department was any better off, yet everyone in that team was positive, engaged, and enthusiastic throughout. As they were the only people with a smile on their face, and a bounce in their step, it is highly likely that they were more favorably considered for opportunities and therefore more likely to find the experience validating (Self-fulfilling prophecy). Same organization, same challenge, same people, but different perspective, and a different transformation memory (and outcome) for those people.

Human brains within organizations

This is what we know:

- Change is not inherently negative (above example, and ask any lotto winner).
- Transformation is an ongoing process, but is often experienced in organizations as a series of "initiatives" each of which causes (forces?)

change in people and the entire organization as a system, rippling out to the wider ecosystem.

- Human brains are designed for continuous change that is iterative; not sudden, unexpected, and pervasive (perceived as threatening, if not traumatic, in the primal brain).

"Five times a second your brain is scanning the environment, asking: Is it safe here? Or is there threat?"

Michael Bungay Stanier

In an emotional state of both safety and positive anticipation, more of the human brain is available for nuanced, sophisticated thinking. Ambiguity and pressure are more gracefully navigated. The brain opens up to new possibilities, and lateral thinking produces more creative options. Literally, original thought can be created when the human being is in that peak state.

In contrast to this is a negative emotional brain state, where the brain narrows its focus. Tunnel vision focuses the human brain on survival and protection against imminent threat. Such brains are jumpy, reactive, suspicious (bordering on paranoia, seeing threats where there are none), and even subversive.

It would seem the change challenge is a human one. If continuous change is essentially human, so is the challenge with change. If an organization is a type of brain system (as a brain can be seen as a type of organizational system), Systems Theory gives the perspective that constant renewal keeps the system healthy and alive. (This links with transformation as a process, not an event; a point made throughout this book.)

Closed systems atrophy and die. Can some organizations be "closed systems" providing a context in which it is nigh impossible for members of that organization to be in constant state of renewal? This is where the organization lacks the continuous adaptation of a healthy human brain; it lacks the free flow of information across the entire ecosystem with a common, consistent signal both sent and received. Fluid, synchronized effort as one cohesive unit (so that whatever is new can be integrated and embedded) becomes extraordinarily difficult in segregated structures. In an unhealthy organization, people form subcultures, at odds with the common agenda (almost like a cancer cell operating at odds with the health of the human body).

This is about human design and, as a flow-on effect, organization design. As Winston Churchill observed, *"We shape our buildings and afterwards our buildings shape us."* It is far better to work with, not against, human design, as a real business example in shows.

Organization Design: For Transformation or Stagnation?

I am bemused by the term "Change Management," yet it has become a key function of most PMOs (which are still considered integral to transformation in the digital era). Management is sameness, control, consistency, and predictability — what is known. Change is the opposite.

Those sponsoring and leading changes describe typical human reactions including:

- Complaints
- Withdrawal (including hiding information and/or resources)
- Aggression
- Irrationality (paranoia)
- Cynicism
- Territorial protection (people form subcultures/cells).

Leaders say the problem with change is *people*, yet the human system — the essence of being human — continually adapts to both internal and external environments.

Few realize how long humans have grappled with this:

"We shrink from change; yet is there anything that can come into being without it?......... Is it possible for any useful thing to be achieved without change? Do you not see, then, that change in yourself is of the same order?"

Marcus Aurelius, Circa 150 A.D.

And how long organizations have grappled with it:

"We trained hard, but it seemed that every time we were beginning to form up into teams, we would be reorganized. I was to learn later in life

that we tend to meet any new situation by reorganizing; and a wonderful method it can be for creating the illusion of progress while producing confusion, inefficiency, and demoralization."

Gaius Petronius Arbiter, Circa 6 4 A.D.

"Organizations" seem to have *always* been plagued by disorganization and disillusion, the opposite of the brain state needed for its best work. At a time when organizations are more networked than ever, they haven't taken on any of the adaptiveness that is core to human survival. Instead, organizational transformation is more often experienced as a series of clumsy adjustments that frequently run late and over budget, resulting in a lot of angst, trauma, and discontent.

My bank recently changed its online app. It is horrible. As a consumer, I feel like it has gone backwards. One feature I really valued has been upgraded out. It will come as no surprise that when I next get a message *"We are upgrading the banking app...,"* I will dread what follows (and resist adopting the change for as long as I can).

Change is life

Given that continuous, iterative, life-sustaining change is how we (and organizations) stay alive (and relevant), it is not change that is the problem, it is change *for the worse* that is the problem.

Change that is imposed and seen as negative is typically experienced by the "normal" human brain as a threat to the very survival of the individual. The primal brain reacts to this perceived threat in a range of disruptive, and even potentially life-threatening, ways. Daniel Goleman links job aggravation with five times the rate of cancer. (I haven't yet seen research linking consumer frustration with damage to health, but presumably the same principles apply, e.g., for a customer of a bank, where changing supplier can be really onerous.)

Social structures

Relevant for organizational adaptation is the fact that the human brain learns emotional and social intelligence in another type of organization which has a top-down authority structure, the nuclear family. The brain during formative years (when it is literally laying down the hardware of thought) negotiates a daily series of power struggles. Freud called this the conflict between Superego and Id, where the Ego negotiates between the two drives to get along in the world. Eric Berne, in his Transactional Analysis framework, called these internalized constructs "Parent" and "Child," with each state having typical statements (scripts) and emotions that accompany the many and varied "transactions." People repeat these scripts on cue and in situations of uncertainty and threat.

As the person grows up, this "programming" translates into management experienced as the Parent and employees as the Child. Scripts (which are either internal thoughts or expressed statements) are triggered by a controlling authority figure or a resistant, powerless "victim." Resistance to change makes sense in this context, as there is a basic conflict of interests in these states, and the Parent (authority figure) imposing change on helpless (victims) Children would trigger resistance if this is socially programmed at a young age, as it commonly is. The power of this subliminal programming should not be underestimated. It certainly explains many of the bizarre and disruptive behaviors during times of change (perceived as imposed by those in control).

This is not a social system where everyone is united in pursuit of a common goal. It is one where conflict is baked into the very social organization design. It doesn't help that PowerPoint offers such a ready visual of an organizational structure as a vertical control system of dangling boxes (top/down; Parent/Child), or that organizations seem to have inherited their basic structure from the military (with power/without power). Less than three days ago when writing this, an employee referred to following the "chain of command" — still.

This mental construct of "organization" may well explain subcultures within one organization; people retreating into camps that feel familiar and safe (Children ganging up on authority figures?). Inconsistent patterns across an organization collide causing dissonance. The First Law of Thermodynamics states that energy can neither be created nor destroyed, but friction dissipates energy. If you have led change programs that have not had whole-hearted support, you will know that sensation of trying to sprint through molasses. Nothing moves forward, but there is a lot of energy spent in the process.

"'Do I get a say or don't I?' That's the question the brain is asking as it gauges the degree of autonomy you have in any situation. If you feel you do have a choice, then this is more likely to be a place of reward and

therefore engagement. If you feel you don't have a choice so much, then it becomes less safe for you."

Michael Bungay Stanier

Issues with organizational structure

While many organizations have long since moved away from the military model, functional silos remain, as does vertical control. Translating military-style control to commercial teams makes no sense: where information-sharing is a survival necessity, where the enemy is NOT the department next door, and where the mission is more nuanced than the average job description. **A top-down control system causes the hyper-vigilance that drives the emotional brain to operate on what Daniel Goleman called the "Low Road" (Goleman, 1996).** Just when an organization needs "all hands-on deck," the high road in the brain (the deliberate, rational, higher-level thinking) is overridden by the reactive "low road," which Goleman refers to as "dripping with emotion."

So, what is the answer, given that human beings are social, have an internalized Parent and Child default response, and organizations are social systems? Berne points out that while the Parent and Child states are both highly emotive, the Adult state (Freud's Ego) is the neutral, rational mode. By using a neutral tone, devoid of negative emotion, and a universal, positive regard for people (cool head, warm heart), the Adult approach triggers an Adult response in others. This is the problem-solving mode, where people partner up in pursuit of an organization's purpose, hereby liberating collective brainpower and collaborative super-performance for successful transformation.

For any organization to achieve its performance potential, and harness all brain power, a performance partnership has everyone on the one side united against challenges. Imagine the power of collective ingenuity mobilized for transformation success. The Sections "Organization approaches to transformation" and "Neuroscience savviness – the difference it can make" show how the Adult–Adult (partnership) approach to transformation trumps the Parent/Child approach where the powerless Child resists, at all costs (literally).

"Managers who understand the recent breakthroughs in cognitive science can lead and influence mindful change: organizational transformation

that takes into account the physiological nature of the brain, and the ways in which it predisposes people to resist some forms of leadership and accept others."

David Rock and Jeffrey Schwartz

Human Brains and Change

Three aspects of neuroscience are relevant for organizational transformation in any era but more so in the digital era:

- The Social brain
- The Emotional brain
- Latent brain performance — discretionary effort.

The Social brain

A feature of all systems, including social systems, is homeostasis; a system tends towards equilibrium. **This means that once a pattern (critical mass) is reached in a system, it is difficult for members of that system to operate independently of the entrenched "order."** In physical systems, the currency is energy. In social systems, the currency is power. In the same way, as friction dissipates energy in physical systems, so it does in social systems. Those with power are energized; without power, energy dissipates.

For some, the strategy is to play by "the rules" and earn their rewards. For others, it is finding ways to get power either by subterfuge or forming subcultures; anti-establishment power blocks. No one wins as inherent value in the system dissipates. In the former, unique insights the system may need for renewal are suppressed. In the latter, creativity and capability are diverted to alternate (even counter-productive) activity.

Situational triggers for Parent–Child responses, as discussed in the last section, include where:

- Leaders are seen as "out of touch" with the masses; employees are seen as "out of touch" with reality and strategic challenges.
- Leaders are too busy with their "own work" to ensure there is a common mindset, and everyone remains on the same side with the common challenge "out there."

Leaders are seen as acting arbitrarily (even irrationally) because employees are not part of the early stages of the transformation journey.

Resistance to change makes sense in this context, as there is a basic conflict of interests in these states. When employees are in Child mode, the business is NOT getting their full capability contribution.

The effects of the social brain on organizational functioning

The social brain in a state of self-perceived powerlessness compromises how that person works; they operate at a fraction of potential. This underutilization is magnified during times of uncertainty, when many are juggling multiple roles and projects, and most are overworked and exhausted. People work harder and achieve less. Goleman points out that Nature's rule of thumb is that a biological system should use the minimum amount of energy. The brain achieves this by firing the same neurons and repeating firing patterns (Goleman, 2006). A huge amount of effort pours in the one end, and very little dribbles out the other. *Does this explain the poor outcomes from many digital transformation programs?*

Some would say that systems require perturbation for change to occur. When it comes to human systems, however, perturbation can trigger negative patterning, i.e., change resistance, especially where past experience has taught people that they end up worse off; all too common.

The digital era is the first where real-time, whole organization connectedness is possible, and the social impact of this is the digital grapevine: social networks that either align with or deviate from the organization agenda. Bad news travel fastest. Misery seeks company. Before you know it, you have "lost the room." Who really owns the airwaves during transformation? (More about this later in this chapter.)

A key feature of systems, including social systems, is that change in one part of a healthy system permeates the entire system. When this is positive change, the whole system can recalibrate to a new level of harmonious functioning, with minimal loss of energy (inherent value), and with the organization tapping into collective capability. When it is perceived as negative, the whole organization can be quickly hamstrung by collective resistance.

Leaders must realize that not only are they outnumbered by those without a title, but whenever they talk (or are silent) their actions (or inactions) have a ripple effect throughout the social system. Due to ancient programming, they set the tone.

Each leader has a role in creating a social system that reinforces self-drive and an Adult, self-reliant (but team-connected) work culture. This directly challenges and resets individual and collective programming. Such cultures are confident that they can navigate internal and external environmental shifts and ever-changing demands, as they evolve their capability accordingly. (Read more about culture in the chapter **The Culture of Transformation** by Institute Fellow Rey Lugtu.)

The Emotional brain

The human brain is more **emotional** than rational. This is significant when an organization, and therefore each individual, is undergoing disruption.

Negative emotional reactions can be fatal. The stress response involves a number of mid-brain (limbic) structures (between the brain stem and the cortex) including the amygdala (the 911 system), the hypothalamus, and the pituitary gland; these go on alert. There is an information exchange triggering a flood of hormones and nerve impulses to the rest of the body for fight or flight. Then the adrenal glands react; senses are sharper, hearts beat faster, and lungs work harder to increase oxygen supply.

The adrenal glands release extra cortisol and other glucocorticoids to help the body convert sugar to energy in the bloodstream. Nerve cells release norepinephrine which tenses muscles and sharpens senses to prepare for action. Digestion shuts down. When the threat passes, adrenaline and norepinephrine drop, but if repeated, especially over the long term, arteries can be damaged. Chronic low-level stress keeps glucocorticoids in circulation leading to a weakened immune system, loss of bone mass, and memory problems. Brain cells are compromised, stomach lining deteriorates, and the telomeres (part of DNA) shorten, accelerating death (Keltner, 2017). Stress kills.

Emotions at work

On the positive side, Luiz Machado explains why positive emotion, also associated with the limbic system, is so crucial to achievement. The word emotion comes from the Latin "emovere;" to agitate/to excite. It is the basic power source that moves you into the world to accomplish, when not distracted by imminent threat. The goal that triggers this energized response may be the purpose of your role in an organization or the desired results of a transformation program on which your reputation, even the organization's future, depends. Or the goal may be one that you have held internally for a long time that gets an outlet in your current role.

Machado and others since regard the limbic system, specifically positive emotion and the pituitary gland, as the ignition for latent capacity within the human brain; even superpowers. This is a phenomenon also researched by Barbara Fredrickson who said positivity is more important for quality of life and performance than happiness. As mentioned earlier, when in a positive emotional state, the human mind opens up, considering new options and ideas.

> *"Research shows that the brain's limbic (mid brain) system is way more powerful than the cortex, which governs intellect. The traffic instructions that evolution has provided us with are pretty clear; emotions have right of way. Logic just has to wait."*

> Jonas Ridderstrale and Kjell Nordstrom in Funky Business

The limbic (mid) brain is pure emotion, either releasing the thinking brain to soar to new heights (Goleman's high road concept) or gripping the cortex in a chokehold while the midbrain deals with imminent threat. When in a negative state of mind, the human mind narrows. Digital transformation needs the highest-level thinking and best brain performance of the collective organizational brain for strategic goals and planned gains to be realized.

> *"In a state of harmony, security, confidence and delight, the brain hums with efficiency and absorbs massive amounts of information effortlessly."*

> The International Alliance for Learning

Harmony, security, confidence, delight...organizational prerequisites for healthy brain performance.

Latent brain potential: Discretionary effort

There is general agreement that human brains are capable of better-quality thinking and functioning than organizations typically access. We know that latent capacity doesn't become available when the human brain is in a state of threat, confusion, disturbance, or all three; the opposite of: harmony, security, confidence, and delight.

The social/emotional brain favors harmony, achievement, and things that make sense. It repels threat, loss, failure, and confusion (advances) that seem to make no sense and appear to be at odds with the organization's stated goals and purpose. Would you say that during disruption, the typical organization is in a positive, optimistic state? Think about the emotions that most organization "initiatives" trigger.

To access unused brain reserves (a field of education some are calling Reservopedia), the **reason** you apply effort, focus, energy, and talent counts. This determines how much of the brain is engaged in any activity. Take elite athletes and their management of their **mental and emotional states.** You may have heard them say: "*I was in the zone.*" That is mind, body, and spirit united in pursuit of one exciting outcome. That same state of optimized brain–body functioning applies no matter what type of activity, including working for a living.

Machado claimed that Right hemisphere activity in the cortex and midbrain functions is related. In contrast to the speed of logical functions (40 bits per second), the right and mid brains (10^6 of processing speed) are where true genius lies, and the source of unused potential. Consider this example where imagination and gutfeel overruled a logical brain to produce a more elegant outcome:

Tom Henderson, division manager in a large textile company in North Carolina, decided that his people would do better within a different work situation. But what would the new situation look like? He reached for his yellow pad to start drawing the usual array of dangling boxes and stopped. Instead, he summoned an image of each of his top people to mind and considered what he knew and felt about each. Mentally, he moved each into different situations and observed how the man or woman handled it. Then he determined to "bracket" the project, to turn his conscious attention to other things while letting the process he had started continue to work in his mind, after phrasing to himself specific instructions about the outcome he sought and when he needed to have it. Three days later, when he turned again to the yellow pad, the final steps of realigning and reassigning people according to their strengths and potential contribution "came as if I were describing a situation we'd been living with for months."

Magic? Hardly. The technique is based on some of the best and most current research in neurophysiology and has been observed among peak performers for decades.

Intuition, visualization, dreaming, concept-formation, idea creation, aspiration, brilliance, genius…this brain state does not occur with overwhelm, fatigue and stress from delivery deadlines, task completion pressure, complexity, confusion, anxiety, and fear. Digital transformation which is associated with an organization's continuing relevance in a digital world requires the best thinking of the collective capability. This speaks to the organization climate in which successful digital transformation occurs.

In summary, to initiate (agitate) and accelerate performance towards an ideal future state, you must establish **a compelling reason** for continuous transformation that responds appropriately to external and internal signals. Information that enlightens people (united around a common purpose, and in an Adult–Adult performance partnership) about where to put energy, attention, capability, and talent is necessary for a state of digital transformation-readiness. How freely does information flow in your organization in this digital era?

Information must flow freely, so that people can perpetually adapt through continuous reality-checking. **When everyone is sharing the same world view, the transformation journey is shared.** This way, you tap into the full human potential of the payroll for organization success, within current digital capability and even that yet to be developed.

Five ways to get the highest level of brain functioning especially during times of flux and uncertainty:

- Co-create a positive, anticipatory state from which you can expect the best performance; collectively imagine the future state.
- Reveal the compelling reason to evoke strong desire for target outcomes.
- Socialize stories of how everyday efforts are changing human beings' lives for the better.
- Build in humor; light relief. You will get more done in less time, and a good belly laugh relaxes muscles and oxygenates the brain!
- Take time to decompress: renew energy and refill the ingenuity fuel tank. (This is what Waytz *et al.* refer to as the transcendence Default Network.)

Brain-Compatible Communication for Transformation

This chapter started with reference to social systems that have an inherent conflict of interests. That may describe the organizational landscape in which the transformation journey begins, not ideal. A transformation strategy seen to be imposed by authority figures who seem out of touch with the rest of the organization, the masses, won't end well.

> *"Your brain is your own. Your boss doesn't own it; nor can any government own it. You alone are the director of this critical means of production."*
>
> Jonas Ridderstrale and Kjell Nordstrom

Communication could make the difference to transformation success. When I ask people what communication means, they usually describe an input, action, or process: passing information, two-way, etc. The Latin verb "communicare" means "to make common;" an *outcome*. A useful distinction.

Communication is a brain-to-brain phenomenon such that there is some degree of mental contagion if communication has succeeded; a *common* end-state (hence the very real phenomenon of groupthink).

Professor Osmo Wiio researched communication success and found that only 5% of communication arrives at a *common* understanding of a message (statistically, a chance occurrence). This led to his Laws of Communication:

- Communication usually fails, except by accident.
- If communication can fail, it will.
- If communication cannot fail, it still most usually fails.
- If communication seems to succeed in the intended way, there's a misunderstanding.
- If you are content with your message, communication certainly fails, and so on.

As people are unique in their thinking and perception, this makes sense. It remains a profound challenge.

Miscommunication and conflicting priorities are the two most common complaints I hear in organizations.

"Why is there such an epidemic of poor communication? (Because) we've treated information as a "thing". Rather, information is a dynamic element taking center stage. It is information that gives order and prompts growth..........In the past, we were skilled crafters of organizations. Now we are broadcasters, tall radio beacons of information, pulsing out messages everywhere."

Meg Wheatley

The digital era has connected people more than ever, yet communication still may not occur, and this threatens transformation success in at least two ways:

- It is likely that every communication will be (not only can be) misinterpreted.
- The airwaves in organizations are never empty, so the likelihood is that mixed messages will dominate the airwaves.

The human brain has mastered reading between the lines and may imagine what is not there, or miss, for a particular reason, what is there. Key questions are as follows:

- Has the digital era accelerated miscommunication, disorder, and confusion?
- What impact does this have on the success or otherwise of digital transformation?
- How do you align multiple stakeholder views across and beyond organizational boundaries so that all efforts are harnessed in the **right** direction?
- How do you harness diversity to avoid groupthink, and still arrive at a common view of the journey with everyone landing at the same destination, with the organization purpose successfully achieved?

Communicating during digital transformation

During digital transformation, you need a shared view of the organization's strategy, the expected outcomes, respective roles, and specific priorities. And you need continual sense-checking and cross-checking on progress and validity of the current work.

If communication is defined by the target outcome (common understanding of the message between senders and recipients), there are broadly two aims of brain-to-brain communication: to inform and to influence.

Informing

Informing is passive. It requires no action. This type of communication is concise and easy on the ear or eye, e.g., a brief overview, bullet points, bold text to emphasize key points, and lots of white space in written communications. Think of this type of communication as the logical, rational part of the brain, sometimes called "left brain" (though that description is figurative). It comes from the communicator's left brain to the audience's left brain. The approach is minimalistic, reducing content to lists, goals, numbers, schedules, and dates. This type of communication hits the part of the brain that is like Teflon. Information in this format doesn't stick, it isn't remembered for long, and it doesn't engage much of the brain. But it is quick. An example is where a colleague asks you the start time for a meeting and you reply with the time.

Influencing

This type of communication aims to get an active response: to move the audience from Point A to Point B (or keep it at Point B where there are forces pushing it back to Point A). This type of communication is persuasive — selling a message or simply motivating the audience to one, pay attention and two, act; in other words, be changed by it. Think of this communication as hitting the brain where it is like Velcro. Narrative devices used for sticky communication (to motivate action) include stories, idiom, metaphor, simile, innuendo, humor, poetry, proverbs, imagery, and pictures. This information is processed in the part of the brain with long-term memory, and it engages more of the brain. This is where bylines and campaign slogans fit. This communication is figuratively referred to as "right brain" in nature, referring to the right side of the cortex.

Then, there's the **midbrain**. Where information links to purpose, significance, and how this work makes a positive difference to you or others, or where there is threat or danger to be avoided, the midbrain gets activated. Simply put, even more of the brain of the audience is engaged, the content has deeper impact, it has the power to change the way people think, feel, and act, and its influence lasts longer.

This type of messaging (aimed at both the right and midbrains) is not unlike wartime propaganda or the communications around other more recent world-transforming phenomena.

These communication methods are consistent across very different cultures. Having worked with clients in 10 countries, I have found that "whole-brain" communication is remarkably universal in its success.

This simplifies the communication task: if your audience is human, these communication approaches are consistent in effect, broadly speaking. While people differ in terms of personality type or communication style, human beings have more in common than what differentiates them and in general, whole-brain approaches to influence (that target more areas of the recipient's brain) are bound to have more success than those that are clinical, linear, and data dense.

Crafting messages that move people and that "stick," similar to what marketers do to get you to pay attention and buy something, takes whole-brain effort. But people are often exhausted and simply blast a message out, tick that box and move on. The audience, likewise, is overwhelmed by hundreds of similar emails, so the message never reaches its target. Communication simply never occurs, hence the misalignment when organizations are in a state of flux.

The most successful change team I was part of consisted of finance people implementing a new system. We used it as an opportunity to reset the thought patterns of the entire social system.

My advice was to separate out the social and communication aspects as a separate workstream requiring as much attention as the technical side of the work. Their chosen name for this piece of work was *Magnum Opus (MO)*. This identity wasn't known outside of our small group, but it inspired each one of us in the time devoted to both formal and informal communications across an extended period of time, and to the hearts and minds of our "constituents." These leaders were financial people with brains trained in accounting who fully appreciated the neuroscience of transformation.

The *Digital* in Digital Transformation

In considering why digital transformations fail, Rogers states that organizations usually focus on implementing digital practices (such as Agile or

Lean) or integrating digital technologies (such as Public Cloud or Big Data). He points out this is not digital transformation but rather IT transformation aimed at optimizing IT performance for business or organizational needs and outcomes. But these practices *could* be instrumental in digital transformation; perhaps it is more about the scope and vision of the digital transformation.

Many have observed that organizations today have become obsessed with all things digital, yet digitization should be seen as a tool to facilitate the organization's purpose. Without this clarity and discipline, you can spend a lot of time and money on capability that can potentially take the organization away from the intended outcomes (i.e., annoy customers, frustrate employees, and disappoint investors).

Why is this? Could it be the shiny object syndrome? Or the dominance of left-brain thinking produced by an industrial-age education system that hardwires brains to focus on the tangible? That could explain why executives prefer to debate systems and technology over purpose and impact — the intangibles that you can neither (in their view) manage nor measure.

The human brain under pressure from a perpetually networked existence may reasonably focus on a small number of tangibles that represent what they know best (comfort zone), that perpetuate current thinking (due to the biological principle of efficiency), and that can more easily be worked on. It is far less likely that a fatigued and overwhelmed brain will seek out the work that is intangible, nuanced and that represents totally new thinking. Yet isn't that precisely the focus that successful digitization needs? This focus includes factors such as purpose, brand identity, latent potential, market relevance, and the significance of any piece of work to purpose. Without these, digital initiatives may transform the organization in ways that take it backward, at a higher speed than before. Where this happens, this is often noticed and questioned by individuals who are then seen as resisting change.

Using Purpose to anchor digitization

"Purpose" (raison d'etre) is so core to a human brain's level of functioning that *organizational purpose* should dictate the digital in transformation where people are involved, outcomes matter, and you want to optimize performance. Purpose defines what is of **value**: what the organization prioritizes and what people within the organization focus on and achieve.

Without clarity about what is of value within the organization context, you don't have the framework to guide decisions about the "right" digital transformation. Value in whose eyes? Three groups: customers, investors, and employees. All else flows from value creation in these three areas, or else an organization will not optimize investment, attract and retain all potential customers, and attract and retain the right staff.

Few organizations create value in the eyes of all three. Indeed, there are organizations that embark on digital transformation journeys that annoy customers, alienate staff, and alarm shareholders. Some satisfy one or two of the three, but not all three. Recently, an executive mentioned to me that the organization was so busy mapping the customer journey, and they had lost sight of the employee journey. It is certainly not new that keeping staff happy is part of the formula for success if you consider the costs of disengagement, internal disruption, and misalignment.

For more about organizational value, refer to the chapter **Value — The Guiding Star** by Institute Fellow John Thorp.

Organizational Approaches to Transformation

Change vs. transformation

A few years back, Institute Founder Charles Araujo described the scale of change required along organizational, structural, and cultural dimensions to achieve customer-centricity and to enact new business models.

The transformation he described reminds me of this statement:

> *"A butterfly is not more caterpillar or a better or improved caterpillar; a butterfly is a different creature. Incremental change isn't enough for many companies today. They don't need to change what is; they need to create what isn't."*

> Tracy Goss *et al.*

Digital today and tomorrow will be increasingly different. When Jim Collins wrote "Good to Great," organizational change was the theme du jour whereas today all the talk is about transformation. Are they fundamentally different or is the difference simply one of scale and reach?

According to Institute Managing Partner, John Palinkas, *"Change uses external influences to modify actions, but transformation modifies beliefs, so actions become natural and thereby achieve the desired result."*

The digital world is as different to the analog world as a butterfly is to a caterpillar (if not more so). Transformation may therefore be seen as more of a state of being that comes about from the process that Collins describes as build-up and breakthrough; where persistent, continuous effort creates momentum, through the tipping point, to continuous readiness.

Transformation of the third kind

Even in the digital era, decision-making can still be reminiscent of the command-and-control military hierarchy. Three approaches to digital transformation are as follows, with the first two still being all too common:

- A small group of titled people make decisions about how things will work for customer and/or employee and/or investor benefit realization, an executive sponsor is appointed and then the "project" is delegated (abdicated?) to the PMO or IT department. (Command and control.)
- Item 1 above plus a "consultation" phase when people are asked for input during which they suspect none of their thoughts will affect any decisions and after which the project is given to the PMO or IT department. (Command and control with the appearance of collaboration.)
- End-to-end organization involvement ensures the target outcomes are achieved. The organization prioritizes its purpose, and digitization is seen as a vehicle for achieving the core purpose. Everyone, no matter how "high up," takes direction from the organization's purpose. As a result, this is the common thread that aligns everyone, which allows the system to operate fluidly, where change in one part resets the entire organization; communication is harmonious and synchronized.

In this third type of organization, goodwill drives problem-solving for the common good. There is none of the friction that dissipates energy, and the system tends towards value creation, not value destruction. Individual input is continuous and varied to optimize diversity of thought and perspective, to spot where the organization may be going off track and to quickly adjust what is needed for success. This is the pattern of a healthy human brain; where the whole brain is more than the sum of its parts.

The power of having organization-wide commitment to a common outcome and vision is hard to describe and still do justice to its sheer power. Problem-solving is as natural to human brains as breathing is to lungs, and once you have people committed to a common cause, you have all the brain cells on the collective payroll focused on ensuring the vision is realized. Those who have worked "in the zone" alongside others in pursuit of a common goal know this heightened state. This is the kind of human resolve that turns ROI on its head: a fraction of the input yields a massive output.

Here are some characteristics of today's digital organization where transformation is a state of being: *(How does yours compare?)*

- Team overrides individual interests.
- People have high social sensitivity — they notice and respond to others' needs.
- Communication creates more cohesion.
- Team unity accommodates robust debate — ideas are tested with rigor, and the best thinking dictates the way forward.
- Policies and processes further human effort.
- Leaders act as facilitators not directors (certainly not dictators).
- Collaboration is high.

At SEI, a global provider of outsourced investment solutions, desks are on wheels so employees pull together or push apart. Collaboration is engineered into space design as is the case in so many of today's physical organizations. Since the COVID-19 pandemic, online tools have facilitated continued collaboration where this is a priority for organizations.

There seem to be common success factors with digital transformation: the endpoint benefits all three stakeholders (referred to in Section 4), there is a cross-organization mobilization of effort (team-driven), and the approach is what I would call "whole-brain" (campaign-driven).

Apart from the command-and-control approach to changing an organization to a future state (or the consult then command and control), there are four approaches that I have observed, listed here in the order of success (and possibly in reverse order of prevalence):

- Team-driven
- Campaign-driven
- Leader-driven
- Change Process-driven.

Still most common is last: Change Process-driven. **For smaller organizations**, a project manager is appointed to *manage* the transformation. (*Typically, they never leave their computer.*) For larger organizations, a dedicated PMO has this function.

A **Leader-driven approach** is having a Pied Piper (heroic leader) who is charismatic enough to lead people in a direction no matter how much disagreement there may be to the direction. Their loyalty overrides resistance and individual interests.

Research into what "power" does to human brains reveals that brains with power are more cognitively driven while those without are more emotionally driven. Not having power in social hierarchies leaves the brain eternally vigilant, which distracts from productive work.

The "Affect Network" is more important than ever when leading change, yet it would appear that those *at the top* have less access to *gut feel*, if as Keltner claims, they become more task-focused (at a time when tuning in to the whispers is more important than ever).

The **Campaign-driven approach** uses neuromarketing techniques. A whole-brain, compelling campaign sweeps folks along on an emotional wave of euphoria. This sounds cynical but it can work to create positive responses at a time that may otherwise feel threatening. However, if people are alienated and suspicious, the campaign will be seen as putting lipstick on a pig. Nevertheless, I have seen grown men cry — literally — in response to a well-designed campaign. Human brains can be changed forever, and instantly, when this is well done. This can be combined well with the Team-driven approach — the best and most recommended.

The **Team-driven approach** is all-too-rare. It can be applied to a part of a large organization or indeed across an entire organization. The transformation example I referred to in Section 3, where the finance team called the people side of their implementation plan "Magnum Opus," used this approach together with the campaign-approach: we co-created the way forward while using mid and right brain devices. Everyone was brought together to consider the pre-change challenges, anticipate what was possible, and map out the ideal end-state. This was supported with neuromarketing tactics such as an analogy to represent the future state. The collective group chose water: fluid, and adapting to the shape of the container, being a lake of resources for stakeholders. Messages were pulsed out through a regular update called "Splash" (which appeared with a water drop landing on the center of each computer screen, radiating outwards). Every last person threw their efforts behind the pursuit of the agreed end-state (even every last one of those on a list of naysayers we drew up at the start). Every leader was committed to a co-created approach, and people simply responded as human beings do: they said "pick me."

The **Team-driven** approach is simply business-as-usual for a transformative organization:

- that has a compelling and inherently inspiring purpose (raison d'etre)
- that co-creates its future with everyone
- that keeps everyone informed and grounded in market and financial realities
- where expectations of both customers and funders/investors drive how employees organize themselves, flexibly, resourcefully, and responsibly, around agreed and aligned priorities.

The Team-driven approach has never been easier than now. The digital era allows current-state information and future-scenario modeling as never before, to facilitate collective effort. When human brains "put their heads together" to navigate the best way forward given the overriding purpose, strategic anchors, and collective capability, the highest level of thinking and functioning is released in the direction and manner that the information is indicating.

To lead continuous transformation that is human-brain and human performance optimizing:

- Create a transformation-ready culture.
- Communicate (even over-communicate) the team purpose, and how any single change fulfills that purpose.
- Partner **with** people to co-create and lead the change.
- Build strong networks where people collaborate.
- Stay visible, available, and "plugged in" to intervene where messages are getting lost.
- Highlight gains made all the way through — messages pulsing to fill the airwaves.
- Learn as you go, encouraging wide-scale review to feed forward to transformational readiness (and back to item 1).

"Change is inevitable. Change for the better is a full-time job."

Adlai E. Stevenson

Neuroscience Savviness — The Difference It Can Make

This is an example of successful transformation documented by Divina Paredes in CIO Magazine in 2018. John Bell was challenged to transform Fletcher Building's group technology function, so the business could grow and differentiate in the market. He put the human element front and center, with a "transform from within" approach.

"You just can't move faster than what people can absorb...
Ultimately work gets done through people."

John Bell

Two goals were to Delight customers and Make Group Technology a great place to work, and after consulting with staff across New Zealand, Australia, Europe, the United States, and Asia, strategic themes included to Drive digital enablement.

He focused on involving everyone, hearts and minds and *continuous learning.* When John Bell said: *"It's not about individual heroics but working together to get things done,"* he may well have been referring to the **Team-driven** approach to success.

He said *"Never lose sight of the true north, particularly when the going gets tough. We've tested on this a few times; it is so easy to compromise and violate for expediency."* Many leaders will relate to the long nights and dark days when you feel you are reaching for the impossible and you wonder how much more people have to give.

"It is not about you, it's about your team..... The job gets done when
people work together..........the most important people are the ones on the
front line, engaging every day with our customers........I also have a role
to play but stand in awe every day as I witness the dedication and com-
mitment of our staff. I'm committed to helping make their job easy and
better."

John Bell

Did they succeed? The provider of Fletcher Buildings' Engagement survey pointed to the unprecedented 100% response rate by the team at a time when long-term staff said they'd experienced more change in the last two years than the previous 20. There were significant improvements in all key metrics since two years earlier.

The approach John Bell took to ensure success with transformation contains global success principles applying across all types of human endeavor. Whatever the situation, true success is from and for people.

Take-Aways

I am optimistic. Laboratory research has shown that in sensory-rich, positive environments, dendrites (a neuron's receptive branches) grow to a certain length, and the brain then produces behavior associated with "wisdom," and focus turns to the collective good. This evolved way of being is not only the natural order but wholly consistent with a transformation-ready state: in human beings and in organizations.

The brain that has a sense of connectedness with the whole, that is positively inspired by a significant purpose, that supports collective success... *that* brain is also more insulated from the negative impact of tight deadlines, relentless pressure, and the harm associated with digital demands when you're always "on."

A simultaneous emphasis on organizational purpose and the impact work is having on others (giving daily effort an inherent and valuable meaning) is more important (and more possible) than ever in the digital era. Now more than ever, there can be a continuous stream of positive messaging about the impact and inherent significance of daily efforts, as a counter to the stress of incessant data "chatter" associated with the digital era. This is the organization where digitization advances and transforms the organization, fulfilling its purpose, **and** the organization creates and expands digital possibilities, fulfilling its potential.

At a time of AI, VR, and robotics, many may question the future role of humans. But, no matter how sophisticated digital capability becomes, nothing can ultimately replace human ingenuity and the power of organizations fueled by a good purpose.

The human brain is the most complex protoplasm in our known universe, capable of creating original thought; the human brain has significant latent potential, released as discretionary effort when the settings are just right; the human brain does its best work when people "put their heads together" as the digital organization enables.

Human brains are the collective source and creative architects of truly successful digital transformation.

Here's what to do:

- Challenge any organization structure where inherent, meaningful purpose is undermined by artificial segregation, individual agendas, and imposed targets — the classic Parent/Child culture that triggers conflict, protectionism, and resistance.
- Bring who you are as a leader, first (person before role) to a digital transformation journey. Who you are, with your belief in human ingenuity, will create the settings for others to excel, and pave the way for extraordinary success.
- Ask questions and listen to the ideas of your "constituents" (both inside and outside the organization) to co-create solutions.
- Make organizational purpose to dictate who people are, what their roles are, and how they work with others collectively, with people as partners (Adult–Adult) in the aligned pursuit of success.
- Keep everyone informed with real-time progress data, so there is quick, collective adaptation to stay on track for success.
- Remember that continuous transformation is life; replicate that natural order in your organization.

Bibliography

Araujo, C. (2017, November 21). *Three Digital Transformation Truths and One Great Myth*. Institute for Digital Transformation. https://www.institutefordigitaltransformation.org/three-digital-transformation-truths-and-one-great-myth/.

Berne, E. (2011). Games People Play: *The Basic Handbook of Transactional Analysis*. Tantor eBooks.

Bungay Stanier, M. (2015, February 11). *Here's the Decision You're Making 5 Times a Second*. LinkedIn. https://www.linkedin.com/pulse/heres-decision-youre-making-five-times-second-michael-bungay-stanier/.

Collins, J. (2001). Good to Great. HarperBusiness.

Fredrickson, B. (2011). *Positivity: Grounbreaking Research to Release Your Inner Optimist and Thrive*. Oneworld.

Garfield, C. A. (1986). *Peak Performers: The New Heroes of American Business*. William Morrow & Company.

Goleman, D. (1996). *Emotional Intelligence: Why It Can Matter More than IQ*. Bloomsbury Publishing.

Goleman, D. (2006). *Social Intelligence: The New Science of Human Relationships*. Bantam Books.

Goss, T. & Pascale, R. (1993). The reinvention roller coaster: Risking the present for a powerful future. *Harvard Business Review*, 71(6), 97–106.

Keltner, D. (2017). *The Power Paradox: How We Gain and Lose Influence.* London: Penguin Books Ltd.

Palinkas, J. (2013, June 28). *The Difference Between Change and Transformation. CIO Insight.* https://www.cioinsight.com/it-management/expert-voices/the-difference-between-change-and-transformation.

Peterson, E. (2018). Seeing someone cry at work is becoming normal: Employees say whole foods is using 'scorecards' to punish them. *Business Insider.* https://www.businessinsider.com.au/how-whole-foods-uses-scorecards-to-punish-employees-2018-1.

Ridderstråle, J., & Nordström, K. A. (1999). *Funky Business: Talent Makes Capital Dance*, p. 256. FT.com.

Rock, D. & Schwartz, J. (2006). The neuroscience of leadership: Breakthroughs in brain research how to make organizational transformation succeed. Strategy and Business, 43. https://www.strategy-business.com/article/06207.

Rogers, B. (2016, January 7). *Why 84% Of Companies Fail At Digital Transformation.* Forbes. https://www.forbes.com/sites/brucerogers/2016/01/07/why-84-of-companies-fail-at-digital-transformation/?sh=4b94c32e397b.

Thorp, J. (1999). *The Information Paradox: Realizing the Business Benefits of Information Technology.* McGraw-Hill.

Watson, L. (2017, December 23). *Disengaged Employees Are Estimated to Cost between $450 Billion to $550 Billion, According to a Gallup poll.* Medium. https://medium.com/@watsonlaura450/disengaged-employees-are-estimated-to-cost-between-450-billion-to-550-billion-according-to-a-1ff7e290ea39.

Waytz, A. & Mason, M. (2013). Your brain at work. *Harvard Business Review.* https://hbr.org/2013/07/your-brain-at-work.

Wheatley, M. (2011). *Leadership and the New Science: Discovering Order in a Chaotic World.* ReadHowYouWant.com.

Wikipedia. (n.d.). *Wiio's Laws.* https://en.wikipedia.org/wiki/Wiio%27s_laws.

Chapter 6

Agile Transformation

Hans Gillior

Introduction

"The democratization of technology (driven by its plummeting cost), increased access to funds and a rising entrepreneurial culture means that there are now hundreds of start-ups attacking traditional markets."

World Economic Forum — White Paper:
"Digital Transformation of Industries: Digital Enterprise" 2016

Some time ago, I had the opportunity to visit a leading telecom operator in the Nordic region to discuss digital transformation. The company was state owned until year 2000 when it was introduced on the Stockholm Stock Exchange and opened for private shareholders. I traveled to a southern suburb (30 km south of Stockholm) to meet their digital transformation team. The office (at that time) was five concrete buildings of another era breathing decadence and state monopoly. There was no doubt that the telecom company had adjusted themselves successfully to a highly competitive market, but the questions were how to address the challenges of digital transformation.

After the traditional trip to the coffee machine and small talk, I was led into a conference room to meet their digital transformation team. It was an atmosphere of excitement and expectation in the room, and they started out running a PowerPoint presentation of the journey so far. What was interesting about the presentation was that it was very tech oriented and described how stacks of technology (such as billing systems) had been upgraded and replaced during the last year. The presentation ended with a question of how to proceed and accelerate. The eyes of the room turned on me to deliver the "golden" answer to their question.

"So, if a digital competitor (e.g., Google) would launch a new digital telco service tomorrow — how long would it take for you to react? And I mean a service that could potentially disrupt the business," I asked.

The room went quiet for a few moments while the team digested the question. After a while, they started to calculate how long it would take to launch a new digital service including business development, IT development, quality control, marketing, release, and launch. The answer was astonishing an 24 months to launch a new digital service comparable to one of the digital competitors! It was clear that the company was a reactive organization lacking the business capability to compete in the new digital environment.

"It takes you 24 months to develop and launch a new digital service. What do you think a digital competitor (e.g., Google) can do during this time? How many new releases and launches can they do in 24 months?"

The room went quiet again.

"In addition, do you think that digital disruption will increase or decrease in frequency and magnitude during the coming years?"

"I understand where you are going with this, and I see the severity of the digital transformation challenges ahead. The thing is that our senior managers define digital transformation as improvements in our IT infrastructure and not changing the mindset of our employees and leaders. To be honest — nothing happens!"

What we need to understand is that the business landscape in many industries has been revolutionized during the last 20 years due to increased digitalization. It has changed the requirements and expectations of customers demanding faster, smarter, and usable services leveraging the latest digital technology. A good example of this change is the introduction of the smartphone in 2006 and how it allowed the user to have all possible information, media, collaboration, and services available 24 hours a day at arm's length. It has created a new expectation of instant information and services regardless of who the provider is. This is the new normal with a different type of competitiveness that companies and organizations need to relate to.

I had the chance to return to the company a few months ago to further discuss their digital transformation. They had moved to a fashionable area north of Stockholm with a new-built office complex. The word "digital" was replaced by the word "agile" to signify the importance of proactive and rapid response to business volatility. But what was interesting about this visit (almost 5 years after the first visit) was that the same problem still existed, but with other words and concepts. There was still the challenge of collaboration, governance, and leadership to respond quickly to market changes. There was still a misplaced belief in processes, tools, and roles to solve their problems rather than seeing the broader picture and why some companies are more successful than others.

The purpose of this chapter is to explore the area of agile transformation from a broad perspective and why some companies are more successful than others. What is it about their way of working, leadership, and governance that makes a difference? Is it pure luck or is it a planned approach that made them successful?

When We Look at the World

"Digital is the main reason just over half of the companies on the Fortune 500 have disappeared since 2000."

Pierre Nanterme

To master digitalization, we need to understand its implications on the market or industry where companies and organizations operate. What can a company, or organization, expect when moving into a more digital market? Digitalization is continuously changing color and form, and it is difficult to predict exactly how it will impact companies and organizations going forward but here are some observations from companies on the digitalization journey.

- **Unpredictability**: The rapid development in technology, disruptive trends, customer behavior, and regulations are creating an unpredictable business environment. We frankly do not know how the business climate will look like in the next 3–5 years. In more IT-intensive industries, the business predictability is reduced to 3–6 months.
- **Reduced Barriers of Entry**: Protective barriers (due to capital intensity, infrastructure, regulations, intellectual property, or competence) of

markets and industries are being reduced, meaning that it is easier for small firms (regardless of geographical location) to compete on different markets. No one is protected in the digital market.

- **Changed Customer Behavior**: Digital Natives are reshaping the markets with new customer behavior where all impressions and experience are mashed up. Digital consumers pay for personal value and not for irrelevance. The Digital Natives show no loyalty but follow the value and experience.
- **Power of the Social Network**: New business models and services are based on (virtual) social networks. It enables reduced transaction cost of services as information moves quicker in the social network. Our trust is based on the opinion of our peers and not on corporate marketing.
- **Periphery is the New Center**: The traditional structure of society is changing. Central functions (such as business, administration, schools, social facilities, etc.) are more online to the place of the citizens (periphery). New business and services started in the periphery by ordinary people are interacting with other ordinary people.

What is interesting is that these observations are enabled by new digital technology. **Digitalization is not the technology itself but the implication of technology on people, society, and business.** It challenges how companies relate to business, customer, and society; and how their company is governed and led. Companies that cannot rapidly adjust and reinvent themselves to the new digital prerequisites will be phased out.

It is important to understand that different industries are impacted by digitalization in different ways and magnitude. For example, traditional manufacturing companies have a different view on digitalization than a media company. The industries are impacted in different ways considering the five "implications" above. For example, the level of unpredictability is very different between a media company and a mining company and therefore needs to be viewed with different lenses.

Peter Hinssen (The New Normal — Exploring the Limits of the Digital World) expressed the consequences of digitalization in five basic rules of the digital landscape. The rules apply for both the internal and external customers:

- Customers have no patience for non-relevant information.
- The customer requirements will change constantly (unpredictability).

- Customers want to be approached in different ways depending on the situation.
- Customers want the services they need to be successful.
- Customers want their services immediately without trouble! (no waiting time).

These basic observations and Peter Hinssen's rule of digitalization create a feeling for the nature of the digital industry and the change in competitiveness.

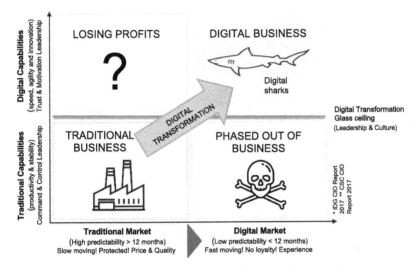

Figure 1:   Digital Transformation Diagram (Gillior, 2017).

The Digital Transformation Diagram (Figure 1) is capturing the essence of the impact of digitalization and digital transformation. The Digital Transformation Diagram should be viewed from the two dimensions: market competitiveness and corporate capabilities.

The basis of the diagram is the market transition from a traditional to digital market with unique characteristics, foremost is the level of unpredictability, and speed of change. We notice that traditional business capabilities are designed for a traditional market but not working in a digital market because it cannot cope with the increased unpredictability and speed. Digital markets require digital capabilities based on speed, agility, empowering leadership, and ability to change. Our view is that most companies move into a digital market without the possibility to change the company capabilities and culture/leadership, jeopardizing their future existence.

Digital Five Forces

The implication of digitalized markets can be summarized in The Digital Five Forces (loosely based on the Porter's Five Forces model). They indicate that new forces in the industry effect the digital rivalry, market attractiveness, and profit levels. The digital forces embrace the new competitive environment and prerequisites and thereby indicate how to be successful in the digital era.

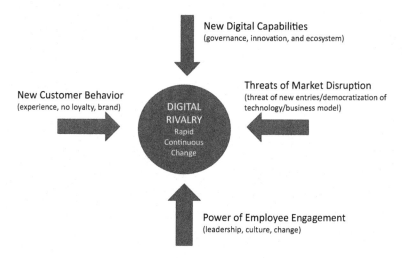

Figure 2:   Digital Five Forces (Institute for Digital Transformation, 2018).

The Digital Five Forces (Figure 2) show that four concrete forces (internal and external) affect the digital rivalry and attractiveness of an industry or market. There are four forces for the senior leadership to be aware of and to actively manage in order to sustain competitiveness.

- **Threats of Market Disruption (External)**: When an industry increases its IT intensity, the industry will attract new digital companies with modern business models, services, and technology. The aim is to disrupt the traditional (conservative) market with shorter product/service life cycles and revenue models based on creating optimal customer experience.

- **New Customer Behavior (External)**: Customer behavior is undergoing change as new social and digital platforms set the standard for future digital services. The digital customer wants the right services at best price to be delivered at once without any hesitation. There is no longer a sense of loyalty to traditional brands but rather to purchase services and products that can boost their experience, well-being, and social status.
- **New Digital Capabilities (Internal)**: The fast technical evolution enables and requires new digital capabilities to provide customer value. The customer requirements change rapidly and therefore the digital capabilities and governance models need to be continuously challenged and updated.
- **Power of Empowered Employees (Internal)**: Digital competitiveness is more than anything a cultural challenge. The company with the most engaged, creative, and change-willing employees has a higher chance of competing in the market. Gallup research shows that traditional companies (globally) have an average of 20% engaged workforce (decreasing) while digital companies have multiples of that level. The research also shows that companies with high level of engaged workforce outperform traditional companies in terms of competitiveness and revenues.
- **Digital Rivalry (Center)**: Digital competitiveness is derived from mastering the digital forces through rapid continuous change. When companies enter a new segment of the digital transformation journey (left to right: see Digital Transformation Diagram), the digital forces will increase in magnitude and hence affecting the conditions and attractiveness of the market. Re-positioning the company in a new segment might seem attractive as it would attract new customers, but at the same time, it will invite new digital competitors and challenge the current governance, leadership, and business model.

The Digital Five Forces are based on profound experience and expertise in digital transformation. The successful companies in the digital transition are those who acknowledge all the digital forces and actively address them through an internal transformation initiative. With a correctly conducted digital transformation, the digital forces become your friend (source for future competitiveness) rather than your enemy (threat of current competitiveness).

As Nitin Seth writes in Winning In The Digital Age: Seven Building Blocks of a Successful Digital Transformation (Penguin, 2021) "despite significant investments in digital transformation initiatives, its impact has been underwhelming." Similarly, McKinsey authors in Fast Times: How Digital Winners Set Direction And Adapt (Amazon, 2020) lament that many companies today are "stalled in 'pilot purgatory,' unable to sustain and scale the benefits... senior executives are frustrated by the slow pace and limited return on investment of their digital transformations, and are unsure what's holding them back." Similarly, Behnam Tabrizi and colleagues write in Harvard Business Review, "Companies are pouring millions into 'digital transformation' initiatives — but a high percentage of those fail to pay off."

Steve Denning: Senior Contributor/Business Strategy — Forbes

Most transformation programs fail to deliver sustainable results and change; thereby jeopardizing the future of the company or organization. **The single most decisive factor affecting change success rate is about managing people, culture, and leadership**.

"A 2016 McKinsey study identified one third of the barriers to transformation were caused by Cultural and Behavioral Challenges."

McKinsey Quarterly, Culture for a Digital Age

New rules of business

It is possible to conclude that most industries are undergoing a paradigm shift revolutionizing how business creates value and success. The new business landscape is built on speed, innovation, and change to continuously adjust itself to customer demands and expectations. The purpose of the digital company is to leverage these capabilities, and innovative business models, to create disruptive monopolies where traditional companies are too slow to react. It is a strategy practiced by digital companies to aggressively seize market shares and revenues.

Definition: *Disruptive Monopolies: A business circumstance where one or few companies disrupt a market with new (digital) services and products out of reach for other market actors. It is achieved by launching new services and products in a speed and innovation superior to competitors and hence setting the future standards of the market.*

There are many examples of disruptive monopolies during the last 20 years. One of the great examples is the launch of the iPhone in early 2007. The innovative touchscreen and open platform for app developers (support the launch of new functionality faster than before) help to disrupt the mobile phone industry and gave Apple a disruptive monopoly. After some time, other companies (such as Samsung) copied the iPhone concept and closed the disruptive monopoly. However, traditional companies such as Nokia and Sony Ericsson were unable to change and were unfortunately phased out.

The disruptive monopoly takes its starting point from the business model; the leverage of the organization's assets and capabilities. Here, we see a difference between traditional and digital companies in how they view their assets. Traditional companies tend to rely on physical assets (buildings, machinery, labor, and distribution) as a foundation for their business model while digital companies rely more on digital assets (information, business intelligence, and digital platforms). Traditional hotels rely on the availability of physical buildings and rooms as basis for their revenue, while Airbnb (and other digital companies) focus on creating the optimal customer experience through digital services and data analysis (consumer habits and needs) leaving the physical building or room to someone else to provide. Traditional taxi companies rely on physical cars while Uber focuses on customer experience of transportation without cars. We see this scenario in industry after industry where new digital companies emerge with new business model focusing on customer experience based on digital assets. This is the new normal (Table 1).

Table 1: Traditional vs. digital business models (Gillior, 2021).

Traditional Business Model	Digital Business Model
• Based on physical assets • (Machinery, buildings, labor, and distribution)	• Based on digital assets • (Business intelligence, data, and information)
• Traditional Governance (slow reaction) • (Slow iterations >12 months)	• Digital Governance (fast reaction) • (Fast iterations <12 months)
• Value by increasing productivity and stability	• Value by increased customer experience and value
• Low growth and profit margins	• High growth and profit margins
• Traditional Product and Service Development — based on centralized R&D and matrix organizations	• Agile Product and Service Development — based on self-governing value streams and agile product teams
• Traditional Command and Control Leadership	• Servant Leadership empowering employees to change and greatness

It is evident that successful companies address the increased digitalization from a broader perspective than others. They realize that a complete agile transformation is required to create the required speed and dynamics to continuously adjust to the ever-changing customer demand and expectations. Whereas digital transformation focuses on utilizing digital technology for business success, **agile transformation is about transforming the complete organization, leadership, and governance to absorb the rapid transformation and disruption of the market** thereby avoiding temporary monopolies. Future-proofing the business from digital disruption and temporary monopolies is to undergo an agile transformation and achieving true business agility.

> *"The more complex the environment (digitalization), and the 'tighter' the targets (performance), the more flexibility the control system (governance) must have: 'only variety can absorb variety.' Failure to provide 'requisite variety' will result in instability (boom and bust) and ultimately system failure."*
>
> Ross Ashby's Law of Requisite Variety
> WR Ashby, "An introduction to cybernetics," London,
> Chapman & Hall, 1956

Agile Transformation frameworks

There are a number of Agile Transformation frameworks on the market addressing the challenges of digital transformation. Frameworks are developed to increase the speed, quality, and value of digital development. Most of these frameworks have their origin in IT development and attempt on revolutionizing the way new digital services are developed and launched in collaboration between IT and business.

SAFe: *"The Scaled agile framework (SAFe) is a set of organization and workflow patterns intended to guide enterprises in scaling lean and agile practices. SAFe promotes alignment, collaboration, and delivery across large numbers of agile teams. It was developed by and for practitioners, by leveraging three primary bodies of knowledge: agile software development, lean product development, and systems thinking"* (Wikipedia, 2021).

DevOps: "*DevOps is a set of practices that combines software development (Dev) and IT operations (Ops). It aims to shorten the systems development life cycle and provide continuous delivery with high software quality. DevOps is complementary with Agile software development; several DevOps aspects came from the Agile methodology*" (Wikipedia, 2021).

ITIL: "*ITIL (formerly Information Technology Infrastructure Library) is a set of detailed practices for IT activities such as IT service management (ITSM) and IT asset management (ITAM) that focus on aligning IT services with the needs of business. ITIL describes processes, procedures, tasks, and checklists which are neither organization-specific nor technology-specific, but can be applied by an organization toward strategy, delivering value, and maintaining a minimum level of competency*" (Wikipedia, 2021).

When studying the principles and manifestos of these frameworks, we notice that these are very similar in the sense that they all include a set of patterns, processes, roles, and task lists to improve the collaboration between IT and business, and hence improve value creation. It is an interesting conclusion because all these frameworks (and there are more out there) have gained worldwide recognition for being the blueprint for agile transformation.

It is important to notice many organizations struggle to implement these "best practice" frameworks and get any business value delivered. In fact, **84% of all Scaled Agile implementations are having severe problems**, and we will continue that discussion further down in the chapter. There is obviously a value to use these frameworks, and there are many success stories of companies that have implemented them well, but we need to be cautious about blindly implementing these without understanding the bigger picture. How do we deal with the increasing unpredictability in the market, and change the business capabilities and culture in the organization to become more competitive?

Problem statement for agile transformation

The key challenge of agile transformation is how to create a new type of company/organization that is ready to meet the new business (digital) challenges of speed, agility, and innovation in a sustainable way no matter how the business landscape will look like in the future?

Dynamics of Business Agility

Many companies I meet have a strategic ambition to become business agile. There is a growing awareness that only agility can absorb the growing unpredictability in the market that is jeopardizing their business performance. The insights are creating a sense of urgency and energy in the top tiers of the organization to transform the business to an upgraded version. Time and money are invested in implementing new agile frameworks (such as SAFe and DevOps) to speed up product and service development with the help of external experts and support, often starting with the IT department. But looking a couple of years into the journey, most of these initiatives fail to deliver.

What we need to understand is that friction and inertia are natural forces on all organizations that hinder change ambitions and achieve their goals and effectiveness. More resources, than necessary, are often needed to manage the friction in the organization and enable it to achieve its goals. The friction has many dimensions and relates to ways we collaborate, communicate, work, govern, and lead the organization. The force grows annually if nothing is done to control and reduce the level of friction in the organization. When starting an ambitious transformation program, the friction in the organization often increases as it brings all the operational challenges up in the light (Figure 3).

Figure 3:   The Flow Effectiveness Formula (2021).

Recently, I had the opportunity to discuss Agile Transformation with Andrew Kallman. He is the founder of the Flow Leadership Framework & Mindset and has over 40 years of successfully running both agile and transformation projects, programs, and portfolios. He has also co-written a couple of Amazon bestsellers on the topic of Flow: the methodology for ensuring success of agile transformations and allowing for optimal business effectiveness.

According to Andrew Kallman, the average level of friction in organizations is around 80%. This means that effectiveness is reduced by 80% and that five times more resources are required to achieve a smooth working organization dealing with its internal operational challenges. We can also conclude that organizations with high friction have a less probability (15–20%) of succeeding with their agile transformation than companies with low friction (50–60%). In fact, most agility transformations are often a chaotic implementation with overwhelming friction and confusion that hinders business agility. **A key to a successful transformation is therefore to continuously work to eliminate friction and inertia in the organization to allow agility to happen**. Why are companies falling into this unfortunate trap?

The Beyond Budgeting Network released research in 2015 that studied the agile business readiness and the result supports our conclusion that most companies struggle with business agility (Table 2):

Table 2: Challenges of traditional governance.

Challenges	Statement	Yes	No
1	Our governance structure can cope with unpredictable change	25%	75%
2	Our governance processes add value to our business and take adequate long time for action	10%	90%
3	Our governance structure addresses key strategic issues	15%	85%
4	Our governance supports a well functioning and ethical behavior	25%	75%
5	Our governance is aligned with tools, such as the Balanced Score card	20%	80%

*) Governance = traditional planning, budgeting, and performance management.
Source: Beyond Budgeting Research (2015).

The root cause of the problem is the "Fixed Performance Contract." This contract is rooted in the "Command and Control" model and culture with a prerequisite of high predictability. The solution is an adaptive approach based on self-governing, holistic view, and change is a natural part of daily life.

Before we start our agile transformation journey, we need to define what business agility is and what the main challenges and obstacles in achieving business agility are. The purpose of the agile transformation is for the company to adapt business agility and hence enabling the company to react faster and more accurately to market trends and competitive challenges.

What is business agility?

"Business agility is a set of organizational capabilities, behaviors, and ways of working that affords your business the freedom, flexibility, and

resilience to achieve its purpose. No matter what the future brings. With this freedom, companies can instinctively seize emerging and unforeseen opportunities for their customers' benefit. They can confidently navigate change, rapidly learn, adjust course, and deliver value at speed. They can thrive — no matter what the future brings. The heart of business agility is no less than the very reason we exist: our customer."

Ahmed Sidky, Business Agility Institute

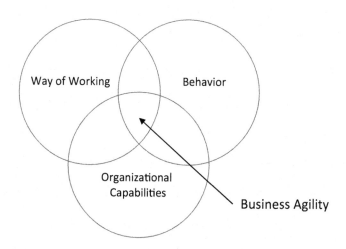

Figure 4:   Definition of business agility.

We notice that business agility is a combination of organizational capabilities (how the business creates value for its customer and gains an advantage over competitors), behavior (including mindset, culture, and leadership), and way of working (how the business delivers value to customers, including processes, routines, and roles). Achieving business agility, therefore, requires a full-scale transformation addressing all three business dimensions and in parallel reduces friction in all these dimensions. This means, in practice, that current capabilities, behavior, and way of working need to be challenged and re-designed to fit the new business circumstances with equal focus. However, what we currently experience (based on Flow Research 2020) is a bias transformation. We observe a heavy focus on the way of working (processes, routines, and roles) with no or little focus on behavior and other organizational capabilities. Also, we notice a high focus on business, a new way of working without simultaneously reducing resisting friction (Figure 4).

My point of view is that most companies and leaders are schooled in designing and managing traditional *business philosophy (sometimes referred to as Corporate DNA)*. These are the fundamental principles that guide the purpose, workings, and ambitions of the company. For many years, the principles are centered on risk-minimizing and rational operations for predictable shareholder value. In this case, the business organization is seen as a huge complex system (machine) of processes, tool, and people that need to be closely monitored and controlled to work efficiently. Any change in the system is painful because the consequences and implications of change are difficult to overview and foresee. **Control is the lubricant that keeps the system going with full speed**.

Business schools have taught traditional business philosophy for decades, and many leaders have made successful careers implementing this philosophy. The business principles then demand a "command and control" management style that promotes monitoring people and processes for the right results. It is based on the people management theory of McGregor Theory X where people are seen as production tools who do not have the ambition or skills to perform and therefore need to be closely managed. Basically, people cannot be trusted in delivering the right results. A rigid organization structure that ensures internal efficiency but not the level of adaptivity required to quickly adjust to new market prerequisites.

In this context, it is interesting to consider the Manifesto for the Agile Company that gives inspirational hints on how the business philosophy needs to change for an agile company. The Manifesto for the Agile Company takes its starting point of an unpredictable business environment with highly competent, self-motivated, and qualified employees.

- **Focus on customers over owners**: The whole company must work together across borders with a common purpose of optimizing customer value. Revenues and stakeholder value are a result of how well the company and organization fulfill their mission (why).
- **Intrinsic motivation rather than extrinsic rewards**: The digital company shows a higher degree of motivation and creativity than traditional companies. Motivation and creativity come from leadership and purpose, not from control and extrinsic rewards.
- **Trust over monitoring**: Trust is a key component of the digital company as it creates the right circumstance for growth, creativity, and motivation.

- **Adaptability over planning**: A digital company operates in an unpredictable market where prerequisites will change in rapid pace. Long-term planning is therefore not possible in a digital environment.

The principles above capture the essence of an Agile Company. What is interesting is that the Manifest for the Agile Company defines how to manage the organizational capabilities to master the new business environment. What these principles have in common is that they jointly are based on three agile components: behavior, way of working, and organizational capabilities.

The development of an agile company is filled with challenges. In fact, approximately 70% of all business transformations fail to achieve the desired business outcome. When studying the key challenges of agile transformation, we start to understand these to focus.

Top 10 challenges of the Agile Transformation

1. Our organization is unable to define a common vision that can be cascaded in the organization, resulting in getting all employees moving in the right direction.
2. We have not focused on eliminating the organizational friction limiting the Agile Transformation.
3. We do not have Executive Dashboards with trend lines that allow executives to make good decisions.
4. Our values are not aligned to business agility values.
5. Our management and support do not provide the right level of support and servant leadership.
6. Our organization cannot scale agile since it is not able to re-invent itself quickly.
7. Challenges in knowledge sharing and collaboration.
8. Our teams don't have the right level of experience in business agility.
9. Traditional development methods are deeply ingrained in our organization.
10. We do not have consistent business agile processes and practices across the organization.

What we can conclude from the research above is that most agile transformation challenges can be derived from a misaligned business philosophy (corporate DNA), especially in the organization's capability and behavioral domain. Generally, companies excel at change, enforcing new way of working, processes, routines, and roles on operational level but not at transformation (transforming people, way of working, and mindset on tactical and strategic levels). These are two completely different practices that require different approaches, leadership engagement, and competence. When we apply change capabilities on agile transformation, the initiative is bound to fail because it does not address the challenges and foundation of the current business philosophy.

Conclusion of defining an agile company

The conclusion is that an agile company is not a complex system or machine but rather a living organism with human behaviors and capabilities, interacting with other organisms (an organism with emotions, ambition, and eagerness to perform). However, ambition and performance are not achieved by "command and control" principles but rather by giving trust. Agile transformation is therefore the journey to change the foundation of the current business and hence challenge and replace the current business philosophy.

Getting the Agile Transformations Right

"Only three things happen naturally in organizations: friction, confusion, and underperformance. Everything else requires leadership."

Peter Drucker

A couple of years ago, I had the opportunity to work with a niche bank in the southern part of Sweden. The market had been challenged by new digital competitors that had upset the market and its dynamics. A transformation of the complete company was necessary for future survival. Our focus was the IT organization that needed to undergo a transformation to support business ambition and challenges in a better way. My team worked with the leadership team (especially the CIO) for a couple of weeks to re-design the operating model and organization.

The final extended management meeting where the CIO was going to present his plans was a memorable experience. The session ended with the CIO, a bit out of script, handing out concrete tasks and responsibilities to the managers for the next 6 months. It was at that time that one of the managers stood up and stated that he did not believe in this approach. The fact was that the IT organization had attempted to transform itself numerous times without success. This was just another attempt; what was it different? The CIO was caught off guard but followed his plan and closed the session.

After the session, I had the opportunity to talk to the manager over a cup of coffee. I asked him about the comment he made and why he thought that earlier attempts had failed. What was the missing link?

"You know, all transformation projects result in more tasks for us managers that we do not have time for. The level of reporting increases and frankly I do not know how to cope. In addition, they have never defined why the meaning and purpose of the change and what is in it for me? Why should I believe in this transformation?"

My take-away from this episode is that transformation is not about tasks and reporting but rather motivating the employees to believe in the journey. That they have what it takes to climb the highest mountain and at the same time enjoying it.

Basics of agile transformation

Business Agility is an organizational state where the business obtains necessary dynamics to address all future business scenarios. It is done by transforming (including reducing friction) the complete organization (business philosophy) in terms of capabilities, behavior, and way of working. There is seldom an easy and speedy path for an agile transformation that can be supported by only academic and theoretical frameworks. In many cases, it requires true craftsmanship with profound experience and expertise in business transformation.

The question we need to ask ourselves is why some organizations are more successful than others in agile transformation. What is it that they do differently to make them more successful in achieving desirable results? There are good examples of agile transformation that combined transformation of capabilities, behavior, and way of working. There are some common trends that should be highlighted for a successful agile transformation based on an interview with Andrew Kallman, founder of Flow.

1. *See agile transformation as a long-term project (minimum 24 months) based on continuous improvements (shorter iterations)*
   When studying successful agile transformations, a common denominator is time. Most successful cases had a lead-time for at least

24 months to change the business philosophy (corporate DNA) in a successful way. It is a lengthy journey that should not be underestimated or rushed. The challenge is to keep the change momentum up to speed during the transformation process. Remember that only 14% of western employees are motivated and engaged at work. To endure a lengthy transformation journey will require smart leadership and higher degree of motivation and engagement. What we need to ask ourselves is if we are ready for an agile transformation with right stamina and focus? Does our shareholder and executives have the right expectations of the agile transformation?

- I often meet business leaders with lack of transformation endurance who are expecting the transformation to show great results after 3 weeks. It is not possible! This is obviously a problem that needs to be overcome. My approach to this dilemma is to re-focus the leadership from operational management to strategic management dealing with the vision of change, prioritization, and communication. This is the level where the leaders should focus to act as an engine of the transformation. Working with an organization where leaders do not understand their role of the transformation (and without endurance) is doomed to fail.

2. *Full focus on delivering value to internal and external customers (service receivers) aligned to the organizational vision*
As stated above, delivering value for organizational customers (internal and external) is the primary objective for all organizations. The concept of value is subjective and linked to customer's frame of reference and sometimes difficult to define. It is therefore important to define and distill the meaning of value and what it means to our organization. Even though most leaders talk about the importance of value, it is hardly ever defined. How can we focus on something that is not defined?

The first step is obviously to define the meaning of value. How do we define value when delivering services internally between different units? And how do we define value when delivering value to external customers?

Value is the situation where the service receiver's (internal or external customer) expectations are met or exceeded by the service provider. To deliver value, we need to understand the service receiver's ambitions, frame of reference, and expectation using the service or product that the service providers deliver.

Value Surplus is the situation when the service provider is exceeding the expectations of the service receiver. It creates a positive boost in brand and a hype around the service. It gives the Service Provider trust and credibility and allows the Service Providers to move closer to the consumer and experiment (innovate).

Value Deficit is the situation when the service provider is below the expectations of the service receiver. It creates a negative push harming the value of the brand. Often a Value Deficit is a product of friction in the organization and is linked to reduction of revenues and market shares.

- My suggestion is also to continuously map and evaluate customer's expectations and ambition — in alignment with the organizational vision and business philosophy. The idea is to quickly understand how expectations (internally and externally) change over time and adjust the offering/services accordingly. Companies that quickly can adjust their offering and still be true to their vision and philosophy are most likely to be more successful than others.

3. *It views the organization from four perspectives with different characteristics and challenges (individuals, teams, program/product, and organization/portfolio/enterprise) that are all interlinked*
   Agile transformation is a challenging task for the complete organization. It is not limited to a certain group of people or units but needs to involve all on different levels. Unfortunately, we see that agile transformation, through the use of different frameworks, is focusing on IT delivery teams with little support and involvement for other parts of the organization.

   A good way to view the organization is through four lenses: individuals, teams, portfolios/products, and enterprise.
   - **Individuals** are single employees or leaders that need to understand the meaning and purpose of the transformation — what is in it for me?
   - **Teams** are a group of employees that work together to deliver excellent quality services to other stakeholders (service receivers) in the organization. They need to understand what is expected of

them, have a coaching leadership, and have the prerequisites to deliver excellent value.

- **Products** are defining the products or services that the organization delivers to its clients. It needs to be aligned to customer expectations and the overall vision of the organization. This is often the product of multiple teams operating on program level in the organization.
- **Enterprise** level is overall leadership and governance of the organization that sets the business strategy and prioritizations and measures its progress.

All these dimensions need to be in focus and included in the agile transformation to achieve its goals. That creates several problems since, e.g., semantics and culture are very different between the different dimensions and create a lot of friction. Each dimension needs to have the right vision, goals, expectations, people, resources, and leadership to enable a successful transformation. However, in most cases I have worked with, this is hardly the case. There is often misalignment and friction in the different dimensions that hinders the performance to accelerate.

For example, in one customer assignment, it was quite clear that the vision and objective of the transformation were not clear to all the teams and what it meant to them. They were therefore not able to focus their energy and ambition in the right direction which in turn created a sense of frustration and friction with all units they collaborated with.

4. *A strong vision and common definitions/concepts that can be cascaded into the organization moving all employees in the right direction (foundation for change)*

A key reason why agile transformations fail is diverging view on the current situation (why) and the plans (how) going forward with the transformation. Successful companies have an accepted, cascaded, and distilled a Vision that guides all leaders and employees in the organization in the right direction. This is one of the first things we check when trying to understand why an agile transformation is not working.

In the end, it is about communication! This is generally an area where most managers and leaders are quite bad at. The messages they communicate are often too complex, lengthy, or incoherent, often confusing the minds of the employees. Most employees are more confused after leaderships' communication than before. We also see leaders using a different language and semantics than the employees understand. We, therefore, urge leaders to understand their audience, speak simpler, shorter, and easier, and repeat their message frequently.

What we also need to understand is the fact that all visions and objectives are associated with challenges. And it is the handling of these challenges by the managers and employees that determine the success of the transformation. They also act as a gateway to the mindset of employees creating a sense of commitment, understanding, and belonging (a feeling of being part of the journey and making a difference). However, most leaders do not address the challenges but rather address the activities that need to be done to achieve the goals (not explaining why these activities are important). The effect on employees is almost the opposite (a sense of distance, isolation, and indifference that will hinder the transformation to take off).

The vision statement can never be undercommunicated. A rule of thumb is to generally overcommunicate the vision by a factor of 10 to ensure that the messages are clear and understood by all members of the organization.

5. *Measure and follow up the agile transformation initiative; justifying the transformation investments. For example, the effectiveness of the value streams*

A minority of organizations measure the progress and value delivery of their agile transformation. Gartner (SOURCE) stated in a research paper that less than 50% of corporate transformations are measured and tracked. Therefore, these organizations have challenges in justifying the initiative to their stakeholders and risk the cancellation of the transformation if no benefits can be displayed. It is therefore important to measure the effectiveness and efficiency of the agile transformation from day way and continuously track the progress.

But what should be measured? The measurements need to relate to the workings of the agile business (i.e., the way way of working, business capability, and behavior). In this case, we need to combine data-driven metrics (e.g., financial figures) with subjective-driven metrics (interviews and surveys) covering the three dimensions. In the end, we also need to show how these measurements contribute to value creation and the overall vision and objective of the transformation. In most cases, this linkage is often lost, and companies measure other perspectives that make no difference in achieving the vision and objective. The agile transformation is then pushed in the wrong direction hindering success. What challenges and solutions (linking to the overall vision and objectives) are these metrics tracking? If leadership and culture are the biggest challenges in achieving the overall vision and objective, then we need to measure how leadership and culture are changing in the right way. Is a positive progress of a metric contributing to the vision and objective? And how?

There are endless numbers of books in the market defining the right metrics to use to track the agile transformation. **My point of view is that all agile transformations are unique and have different starting points, prerequisites, and ambitions. It is therefore fair to say that also the metrics are unique for all organizations and need to be tailored for each journey.** The risk of using pre-defined metrics is that they are not addressing your challenges and ambition 100% but rather at a 75% level. The consequence is that momentum and accuracy of the agile transformation will be significantly reduced and might jeopardize the whole transformation program.

6. *Strong servant leadership that supports the employees to grow, change, and perform*
   During the last decades, the business philosophy is dominated by a "command and control"-leadership style. According to Vilanova University, the "command and control" leadership style is based around authority, discipline, and structure with an aim to meet precise deadlines or work with specific procedures. It assumes that employees are not motivated in work with non-sense of responsibility and therefore need to be micro-managed to reach excellent results. However, the leadership style is not suited for change and transformation and hence creating an atmosphere of innovation, collaboration, and motivation.

   In the light of agile transformation, another kind of leadership style is needed, often referred to as **Servant Leadership**. It is a leadership style that primarily focuses on creating an atmosphere of collaboration, team morale, reputation, and a general positive culture. The leadership is often coaching and supporting expecting employees to self-govern and perform. The downside of servant leadership is its ability to make quick decisions and deal with workplace strife.

- Obviously, leadership styles are not absolute but rather a mixture of different styles to fit the ambitions and business philosophy. A blended leadership style is sometimes called a situation-based leadership style where the style can be adjusted to the current situation. However, it is important to highlight that a higher degree of servant leadership is required to succeed with the agile transformation and deliver sustainable results.

7. *Responsive governance to allow managers to steer the organization fast and accurate with right decisions at the right time based on right information*

   Responsive Governance is a prerequisite for the agile company. The idea of an agile company is to respond quickly to new trends and opportunities and make the right decision at the right time. My opinion is that most organizations react too slowly and therefore will not be able to compete in the digital future.

   When studying successful companies in the responsive governance domain, we notice that there are six areas where these organizations excel and focus:

   1. **Organization and Value Chain**: Ability to design a value-driven and agile organization and value chain including roles and responsibilities, mandate, and focus areas.
   2. **Decision-Making**: Ability of the organization to make right decisions, at right time, and based on right information.
   3. **Information Management**: Ability to leverage the information asset without limiting the organization's cognitive capabilities. Included how employees and managers collaborate in terms of information sharing, meetings, emails, and phone calls.
   4. **Leadership and Culture**: Ability to create a value-driven and motivating culture and leadership enables creativity and promotes continuous change.
   5. **Performance Management**: Ability to track and monitor how the organization creates and delivers value to its service/product receivers (customers/market).
   6. **Market Awareness and Direction**: Ability to fast identify and react to new trends (opportunities and threats) in the market. Setting the right direction and focus area.

Today, the maturity of responsive governance is low in many organizations. There is a tradition of 12-month governance calendar that is not designed to address the governance challenges of the digital era. The level of unpredictability in many sectors is less than 9 months, meaning that it is difficult to foresee trend and opportunities further than 9 months in the distance. After that, it is blurry and chaotic. In comparison, many traditional companies and organizations spend more than 9 months to design the next 12-month business and governance plan. The consequence is that when the 12-governance calendar and plan is launched, then it is already too old, irrelevant, and does not contribute to any value. The challenge of traditional companies is therefore to speed up the business governance to be faster, accurate, and responsive. For example, what is the probability of disruption in the sector within the next 12 months? What is the latest news and information about digitalization in our sector? How do we quickly transform information into accurate knowledge and decisions?

8. *Focus on collaboration, knowledge-sharing, and learning in an open and safe environment*
   All organizations have natural levels of friction that limits the organization's ability to respond quickly to new trends and opportunities and deliver optimal business value. The level of friction increases over time if nothing is done to control and reduce the friction, which limits a higher degree of responsiveness, agility, and performance.
   Looking at the Flow Effectiveness Formula (Figure 3), we see that there are three components that jointly contribute to a high business effectiveness.
   - **Business Goals**: The vision and goals that the organization is set to deliver. Also, the way that the organization cascades the vision and goals into the organization and prioritizes is included in this component. Here, we see challenges in organizations to set the right vision and prioritizations.
   - **Business Resources**: This component includes resources, people, structure, and way of working, in other words, the resources required to achieve the business goals. Agile Frameworks are part of this component.

- **Friction**: This component is a resisting force that hinders the resources to be used fully to achieve the vision and goals. The friction includes challenges in collaboration, communication, leadership, behavior, knowledge-sharing, and inadequate learning.

The Flow Effectiveness Formula suggests that it is necessary for organizations to continuously work to reduce the level of friction to allow for a reasonable business performance. In recent measurements with traditional companies show a level of friction of 70–80% that hinders any change or transformation in the organization.

Leadership friction is a key friction that has a negative effect on the business efficiency. It is often displayed as lack of trust and unclear roles and responsibilities in the organization (between leaders and employees) hindering the collaboration and knowledge-sharing in the organization. A common symptom of this dilemma is internal "blame games" where leaders and employees blame each other for business challenges instead of taking own responsibility and ownership. Successful organizations tend to include trust and behavior as a key leadership competence and encourage dialogue and expectation mapping to overcome internal "blame games."

My point of view here is that if an organization attempts to implement agile businesses, it is of utmost importance to reduce friction continuously throughout the process. It is recommended to run Friction Checks every 3 months to identify, control, and eliminate friction in the agile transformation. Otherwise, there is a large risk that the transformation will take longer time than necessary or fail all together.

A couple of months ago, I worked with a construction company to analyze the level of friction in the design planning phase in a large construction project. We calculated the level of friction to over 60% and mainly consisting of challenges in communicating the vision, collaboration, and a common steering and objectives. The results were a surprise to the management team, but it also confirmed a notion they had of the inefficiency of the design planning process of the building project. The construction company worked to reduce the level of friction (down to 35%) with a result of decreasing the lead time of design planning by over 50%.

Friction is in many organizations, a hidden factor that managers continuously avoid addressing and hence let grow to uncontrollable levels. It costs business millions of dollars each year and hinders the organization to change and be transformed.

Agile transformation is a lengthy and complex journey requiring a minimum of 24–36 months to complete. Many would even suggest that it is an endless journey with continuous adjustment and tweaks. What we see is that many companies seek shortcuts in their transformation work and quickly focus on the structural dimension (processes, tools, and roles) instead of addressing the complete picture, resulting in a high probability of failure.

There are several agile delivery frameworks such as SAFe, ITIL, DevOps, and SCRUM that include several manifestos to describe the workings of their framework. It is interesting to study these well-known frameworks and the fact that they all have a common focus of delivering value to customers.

Five Steps of Agile Transformation

"The biggest challenge for companies won't come from the outside world. It will be to change the dynamics inside their organizations to match the speed of flow on the outside. Unfreezing age-old hierarchical command-and-control mechanisms won't be easy."

Peter Hinssen

As stated earlier, Business Transformation is a very complex initiative (addressing the business philosophy) with 70% rate of failure. In earlier sections of their chapters, we have highlighted some of the reasons why these initiatives fail and why some organizations are more successful than others. The transformation generally ends up in corporate frustration, disillusion, and lost investments. When studying world-known theories of business transformation and reflecting over our own experience, it is possible to see that business transformation goes through five defined phases with different characteristics, challenges, and approaches (Figure 5 and Table 3).

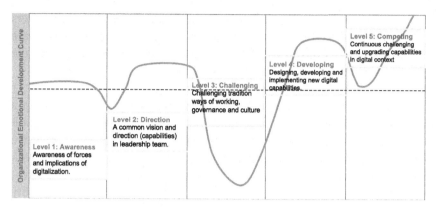

Figure 5:   Phases of Business Transformation (Gillior, 2019).

Table 3:   Phases of Business Transformation (Gillior, 2019) — based on discussion with Christina Rydgren (Business Transformation Expert).

Transformation Levels		Description	Opportunities/Challenges
1	Awareness	Building awareness of the forces and implications of digitalization in the company and industry within the leadership team	No common digital vision or ambition in the company. Important to develop a digital baseline (situation) that is agreed by all leaders
2	Direction	A digital vision and direction have been set in the leadership team — including principles of key capabilities and leadership (business philosophy)	A naïve belief that the digital transformation is complete. Important to build commitment and change management capabilities in the company
3	Challenging	Seeking a new way of working based on the digital vision and principles — challenging traditional governance and culture	The phase where most transformations fail due to lack of leadership commitment, personal prestige, and inadequate culture to drive change This is the phase where friction is brought up to the surface and needs to be addressed

Transformation Levels	Description	Opportunities/Challenges
4 Developing	Designing and developing digital capabilities, culture, and leadership skills to drive digital competitiveness in the industry	Strong leadership skills are needed to overcome the challenges of change (level 3). Important to test and try new capabilities and governance structure to drive digital performance
5 Competing	Continuously challenging (every 6–12 months) current governance, capabilities, and leadership in accordance with digital drivers and forces	A progressive leadership is needed to build momentum for continuous change. Fast iterations (based on fact and data) with a clear vision and ambition

When studying numerous transformation cases, we can confirm known research of why most companies fail to achieve their set goals and objectives of the business transformation.

According to my experience, many companies are successful in achieving phase 2 and developing a new business platform including a common vision, principles, and needed capabilities (the blueprint for the new business philosophy). It is not challenging the traditional way of working in the organization and is not upsetting the current hierarchy, roles, or personal prestige in the leadership team. One could say that phase 2 is necessary but fearless phase for most leadership members. However, when the organization attempts to implement the vision, principles, and new capabilities, it will bring the friction up to the surface and challenge the roles and status of the membership team. There is a high level of doubt, fear, and stress that decreases commitment and willingness to change. It is the collapse of phase 3 that upsets the change agenda. The leadership skills and culture of the organization are tested to execute the new vision and principles usually without success.

The effects of the "collapse of phase 3" are generally a chaotic situation where leaders and consultants are exchanged, the momentum of change disappears, and the organization goes back to the more comfortable phase 2. In some cases, the responsibility for implementing the change vision and principles is delegated to middle management with limited top management support. The business transformation of the organization has failed.

What we need to understand is that the business leader needs to gain full commitment of his/her leadership team in phases 1 and 2 by carefully defining the ground rules of the transformation (What does it mean for them? What happens if we fail? What resources and support are available?), also to assess and address the level of friction in the organization to ensure a smooth and successful transformation. This is best done by practicing several change scenarios with an external facilitator who can prepare them for the coming challenges.

There are organizations that with strong leadership can successfully implement the change agenda/principles and move to phases 4 and 5. In the end, it is all about hard work and building a belief of success. We can do it!

Agile Transformation shares the same approach (phases) as business transformation but with more complex prerequisites. Agile Transformation often takes place in a more chaotic (fast-moving) marketplace where the leaders experience severe business challenges due to a digitalization of the industry (Table 4).

Table 4:   Difference between Business and Agile Transformation.

Business Transformation	Agile Transformation
• Clear conditions	• Chaotic conditions
• Linear change	• Iterative change
• Predictable business environment	• Unpredictable business environment
• Slow reaction to trends	• Fast reaction to trends

Leaders need to acknowledge that agile transformation is different from ordinary business transformations, learn from successful examples, and ensure strong engagements from their managers and employees. The needed efforts are even higher to address great friction in the organization.

Chapter Take-Aways

Agile Transformation is on the mind of many business leaders to manage an increased unpredictability in the market. Only agility can absorb unpredictability. It is a way to stay relevant and competitive in the business landscape and fight off new digital companies trying to take market shares. But the challenges of agile transformation should not be underestimated, and most organizations fail to achieve the required level of dynamics and agility to stay competitive. But what are the key learnings from working in this environment for a couple of years? Why is it that some agile transformation projects are successful while others fail to change? Here are my take-aways:

1. **Everything starts with leadership!** In all the successful projects I have participated in, there is a common trend of an engaged and motivated leadership team that understands the reality of the journey they are embarking on. They go the extra mile to engage the employees, prioritize, and overcommunicate the vision in an excellent way. This kind of leadership does not always come naturally and might require some training, coaching, and mentoring, but the successful leaders are willing to learn and change.

2. **It takes time!** No company or organization will achieve an agile transformation in a few weeks or months. It will take years for a traditional business to transform into an agile business and the journey does not stop there. It is therefore important for leaders to be patient and not expect fast returns, benefits, and change too early. To have a realistic view on what to expect and when the benefits will arrive, it is still important to measure and follow up the transformation but with realistic perspective.

3. **Every journey is unique!** What I have experienced over the years is that every agile transformation is unique and requires a unique approach and plan. There is no prepared blueprint on how to run an agile transformation because it depends on the organization's situation, ambition, prerequisites, resources, and business landscape. However, there are frameworks, tools, and methods to be used but with caution. It is more important to find your own way through the transformation and be true to yourself.

In the end, the agile transformation starts with you as a leader. Are you willing to do what it takes to transform the business with all its challenges, frustration, and obstacles? It is a bumpy but rewarding journey that turns ordinary leaders into superstars. But the journey starts with you as a leader and if you are willing to change yourself to support the transformation. Are you willing to view people and leadership in a different way? Are you willing to re-learn business strategy and governance? Are you willing to devote several years of your life to support the greatest journey of your life? If so, then you are the right man or woman for the job! I wish you good luck and a safe journey!

Bibliography

Beck, K., Beedle, M., Van Bennekum, A., Cockburn, A., Cunningham, W., Fowler, M., … & Thomas, D. (2001). Manifesto for agile software development.

Gillior, H. (n.d.). *GooDIGITAL Framework.* The Goodwind Company. https://thegoodwindcompany.com/research/.

Granito, F. (2020, July 23). *Snapshot Research Results Inside the Data Digital Transformation Levels and Speed.* Institute for Digital Transformation. https://www.institutefordigitaltransformation.org/snapshot-03-digital-transformation-levels-and-speed/.

Harper, J. (2021, July 29). *U.S. Employee Engagement Data Hold Steady in First Half of 2021.* Gallup. https://www.gallup.com/workplace/352949/employee-engagement-holds-steady-first-half-2021.aspx.

Kallman, T. & Kallman, A. (2018). *Flow: Get Everyone Moving in the Right Direction … and Loving It.* Morgan James Publishing.

McGregor, D. (1960). Theory X and theory Y. *Organization Theory*, 358(374), 5.

Sidky, A. (2021, April 14). *The Organizational "Muscles" needed to Build Business Agility.* Business Agility Institute. https://businessagility.institute/learn/the-organizational-muscles-needed-to-build-business-agility/535.

Villanova University. (n.d.). *5 Types of Leadership Styles in Management and How to Implement Them.* https://www.villanovau.com/resources/leadership/5-types-of-leadership-styles-for-managers/.

Chapter 7

Leadership in an Era of Uncertainty

Jeffery S. Ton

Introduction

You've picked up a book on Digital Transformation (or downloaded it to your e-reader or clicked play on the audio version), you know, or at least have an inkling that we are in a new era, a digital era. You are uncertain. You are not alone. This book is packed with information and insights that will help you navigate the uncertain future. In this chapter, we focus on leadership. Why? **Because digital transformation actually has very little to do with technology and has everything to do with...you**. To be successful in this new era, our businesses need and will demand different skills. We must have deeper business acumen, going well beyond the P&L and balance sheet; we must understand our customers and the problems we solve for them. We must be more collaborative and more communicative. We must use design thinking, systems thinking, and critical thinking. And we must be more diverse.

How do you lead in an era of uncertainty? First, you must realize you are not the first leader facing uncertainty; history is filled with leaders who stepped into uncertainty, embraced uncertainty, and flourished in uncertainty. Second, you must be willing to learn from those who have gone before us, learn from what they did right, and what they did wrong. Two such leaders who provide invaluable lessons for the digital transformation leaders are Merriwether Lewis and William Clark. Over 200 years ago, Lewis and Clark led a team of 30 other men, a woman, an infant, and

https://doi.org/10.1142/9789811260469_0007

a dog on an expedition that changed the face of the United States. How they were able to succeed where others before them had failed is a study of leadership through uncertainty.

Lewis and Clark Primer

For those who might need a refresher on their U.S. history. Lewis and Clark, under the orders of President Thomas Jefferson, embarked on an expedition to explore the lands west of the Mississippi River with the hopes of discovering a water route to the Pacific Ocean and establishing trade with the native peoples. They traveled by boat down the Ohio River, up the Mississippi to the mouth of the Missouri River. They navigated the Missouri to its source, crossed the Rocky Mountains on horseback, found the waters of the Columbia River watershed, built dugout canoes, and canoed to the Pacific Ocean...and returned.

They didn't know what to expect. The lands west of the Mississippi River were largely unknown. In fact, on the map they took with them most of the territory west of St. Louis was simply labeled "Conjectural." Heading out into uncertainty, they thought they might see wooly mammoths roaming the plains. They thought they might find red-headed Indians, descendants of Leif Erikson's expedition. They thought the Rocky Mountains would be similar to the Appalachians and Alleghenies in stature and in slope. They were uncertain how they would be received by the native peoples. They faced near death from falling, drowning, and starvation. They survived temperatures colder than 50 below and hotter than 100. How these two men were able to lead this team to the Pacific and return is a *textbook in leading into uncertainty*. These lessons will help us navigate the uncertainty of the digital era and enable us to lead the digital transformations of our organizations.

I first "discovered" (or, better stated, rediscovered) the story of Lewis and Clark through the writings of novelist James Alexander Thom. Wanting to learn more, I devoured the biography of Merriwether Lewis, *Undaunted Courage*, by Stephen Ambrose. This, in turn, led me to the Captains' journals themselves. This reading precipitated an expedition of our own, as my wife and I traveled the entire trail over the course of a six-year period. (Six years...they did it in about half the amount of time and they weren't traveling by RV.) Entranced by the romance and adventure of the story, we were hooked. I, for one, could not stop telling the stories of our adventures...and theirs. My boss at the time challenged me to find the lessons for business in the 21st century. I scoffed, "It's just a story from history. What lessons would be there for a Chief Information Officer on the brink of the Digital Era?" And then...and then I re-read the Captains' journals, all one million words in 13 volumes.

Digital Transformation Leadership Skill #1: Journaling

The first lesson came, not from the words they wrote, but from the fact *that* they wrote. Journaling has become somewhat of a lost art. However, looking throughout history, leaders kept journals. Presidents from John Adams and Theodore Roosevelt to Ronald Reagan and Barack Obama kept journals. Business leaders from Rockefeller to Branson use journals. Marie Curie tracked many of her days in a journal. And, like the view of the Expedition we get from the Captains' journals, the view of the Civil War provided by the journals of Emilie Davis is priceless.

Why do many great leaders of the past and present journal? The benefits are numerous. In fact, do an internet search for the "benefits of journaling," and you will find over 6.7 million entries. That's a lot of benefits! In my experience, there are seven key benefits that will help you lead into the uncertainty of the digital era.

Reflection and decision-making

How much time do you spend thinking? Thinking about your business, your department? Management gurus like Peter Drucker and Jack Webb emphasize the value leaders receive from thinking about their businesses. Digital Transformation requires decisive action, however, proceeding that decisive action with quiet reflection improves the results of that action. Following the decisive actions with the same reflection will greatly improve the next action you take.

Leveraging a journal during your time of reflection can improve your decision-making. It is a tool that allows you to brainstorm different ideas in an environment without judgment. You are free to write and follow your thoughts. As you write various ideas and perspectives on an issue, you will be able to connect the dots between heretofore disconnected events.

Once you have explored different courses of action, further journaling can help you define the action steps needed.

As you begin to formulate your plans, you can leverage your journal to develop the talk tracks for communicating the plans to the stakeholders. Writing these talk tracks in your journal will help you target your message to specific audiences, tailoring your message to their communication styles.

Clarity

As we just saw, pausing to reflect can help your decision-making. However, pausing to *write* your reflections will provide a focus to your reflections and bring clarity to your thoughts. *Studies have shown the act of writing your thoughts helps to quiet your mind so that it can focus on the problem at hand.* You will be able to write from multiple perspectives as you analyze the issue. Let your thoughts flow.

Once on paper, you will not have to worry about recapturing your train of thought. It will be there for your reference, that in itself brings a level of clarity to your reflection.

Even the simple act of documenting your to-do list in your journal will ensure tasks don't get lost in the chaos of the day or week.

Stress and resilience

Perhaps a benefit the Captains realized, even if they may not have recognized it, was a reduction in stress and an increase in resilience. *Studies have shown those who regularly journal report lower levels of stress.* This is manifested physiologically in lower blood pressure and improved function of the immune system, which resulted in fewer visits to the doctor. Those who journal also reported reduced symptoms of depression and anxiety. Mental health professionals now use journaling as one of the tools to improve the mental states of their clients.

Our own personal resilience is built by overcoming obstacles and challenges. Journaling about these obstacles and the ways in which we overcame them can help us face even bigger challenges in the future. The lessons of past challenges and victories are there for us to read, learn, and draw upon.

This brings us to the last benefit I would like to highlight, and to me, the most valuable.

Evergreen lessons

Over the course of the Expedition, the Captains and some of the men would make copies of their journals. They were doing this to clarify comments they had made, augment some of the hurried notes they had jotted, and protect the journals by having second (and third) copies.

By re-reading their journals, they were taking advantage of evergreen lessons. *As you re-read your journal, you will find new insights and new lessons.* Why? Because you have changed, and your environment has changed. Because of these changes, the lessons have changed. I encourage all of my clients to make it a practice to re-read their journals a week later, a month later, and a year later.

Digital Transformation Leadership Skill #2: Co-Captain

In studying Lewis and Clark and leadership, it is interesting to note one of the first actions Meriwether Lewis took upon accepting Thomas Jefferson's offer to lead the expedition. He sat down and wrote a letter to his old Army buddy, William Clark. The letter asked Clark to accompany him on the expedition. But more than accompanying him, Lewis asked Clark to serve as co-captain with him, to share the leadership of the expedition — to be equal in all respects.

> *"If therefore there is anything under those circumstances, in this enterprise, which would induce you to participate with me in it s fatiegues, it s dangers and it s honors, believe me there is no man on earth with whom I should feel equal pleasure in sharing them as with yourself..."*

— Meriwether Lewis, June 19, 1803

Why would he do this? Why would he offer co-command of an expedition he had been dreaming of leading for a decade or more? I believe Lewis had a very high sense of self-awareness. As such, he understood his strengths as well as his weaknesses. He knew the mission would not be successful without the complementary skills Clark would bring to the expedition.

Two hundred years later, we have an explanation, thanks to the work of Gino Wickman, founder of the Entrepreneurial Operating System. In his book, *Traction*, Wickman describes **two roles necessary for an organization to become great, the visionary, and the integrator**. The visionary is creative, they are great at tackling the big problems (not so much, the day-to-day), they are adept at building relationships with clients, partners, and suppliers, and they operate on emotion. The integrator is the peacemaker. They are the ones who integrate the business units; they take the healthy friction and tension in an organization and create energy for the company.

Meriwether Lewis was the visionary, Clark the integrator. As Lewis intuitively knew, it is rare for one person to serve both roles. With Clark as his co-captain, their odds of success would improve dramatically.

To lead a digital transformation, you will need both a visionary and an integrator. Which one are you? Who will be your co-captain on your journey of transformation?

If you are the visionary, you will spend time ideating, coming up with new ideas. You will have a clear view of the future you want to create. When faced with a significant problem, creativity will be your approach to solving it. You will focus on major external relationships, both with key customers and key suppliers. It will be up to you to sell your ideas to all your stakeholders.

This was Lewis. In the winter of 1804/1805, he would spend most of the time away from camp. He would meet with the key leaders of St. Louis and the surrounding area, gathering information, bartering for goods and services, and building relationships.

The integrator, on the other hand, will spend time leading and managing the team. If you are the integrator, you will be responsible for holding the team accountable to their commitments. You will drive the execution of the plan and the delivery of the results. As the label implies, you will bring the major functions together to ensure they are operating in concert with each other, and hand-offs are smooth and predictable. While you may not be as involved in the selling of ideas across the organization, communication across the organization is your responsibility.

Clark was the integrator. That first winter when Lewis was meeting with local dignitaries and business leaders, Clark was taking a rag-tag group of recruits and turning them into the Corps of Discovery.

Leadership does not end with you and your co-captain. In a digital organization, leadership must come from all areas of the organization.

Digital Transformation Leadership Skill #3: Building a Team of Leaders

Captains Lewis and Clark knew the importance of team. Almost from the outset, they began to recruit the members of what would be known to history as the Corps of Discovery. They knew what it would take to attempt this journey, and they set out to find the best of the best. They knew the skills they would need, hunters, trackers, interpreters, boatmen, cooks, and blacksmiths.

However, in addition to these technical skills, they also knew that the men would need to have key personality traits, or what we might call soft skills today. They must fully understand and buy into the vision and mission of the expedition. They must be willing to work hard, well beyond the point of being fatigued. They must work well within a team, to sacrifice self for the success of the team and the enterprise.

Lastly, they knew they would need leaders throughout the organization. The Captains would not always be there to make decisions, to rally the team, to do the work that must be done. Each person would be called upon to lead from time to time, and they would need to do it without being asked or ordered.

The Captains spent months selecting the members of the team. They spent over a year developing the team all the while progressing toward the goals of the mission. Not everyone made the cut. When the permanent party departed Fort Mandan in the spring of 1805, several members were sent back to St. Louis.

As the Corps coalesced into a team, the Captains would form ad-hoc teams to perform certain duties, sending smaller groups out to explore, hunt, and scout. While it would be a stretch to call these self-organizing teams, as the exploration proceeded, there certainly were times the men would organize their own workgroups.

As a leader of transformation, having a team of leaders will be essential to your success. It begins with having a strong vision of where you are going (even if the exact details are not yet known), self-awareness of your strengths and weaknesses, identifying team members that have complementary skills, and then painting a picture of your vision so vivid the team members can see themselves in that vision. Teambuilding in the early days of your journey is a pivotal part of your journey, helping to ensure success as the journey proceeds on.

As you are building your team, pay particular attention to the soft skills just as the Captains did. These skills are essential for leaders throughout your organization. Not only must you master these skills but you also need to develop and build these skills throughout your team. We must have deep business acumen, going well beyond the P&L and balance sheet to an understanding of our customers and the problems we solve for them. We must have industry knowledge to tackle the complex challenges of transformation. We must be more collaborative and communicative. We must leverage design thinking, systems thinking, and critical thinking. And we must be diverse. The problems we are solving require diversity of thought, diversity of experience, and diversity of culture.

Digital Transformation Leadership Skill #4: Building an Ecosystem

As Lewis and Clark and the Corps of Discovery departed the St. Louis area in the spring of 1804, they knew they would encounter tribes of native peoples. In fact, a significant part of their mission was to seek out these tribes, peacefully, and lay the groundwork for future trade as America pushed west. What they probably didn't foresee was the contributions many of those tribes would have toward the success of the expedition.

Without this *ecosystem of partners*, the Corps of Discovery would not have been successful in reaching the Pacific and returning. It is highly likely they would not have even survived, disappearing into history as a footnote. Time and time again, the native tribes, not only offered hospitality but provided food, shelter, horses, guidance, and even lessons in building bull boats and canoes.

Their first winter west of the Mississippi River was near the villages of the Mandan and Hidatsa. The villages were near present-day Bismarck, North Dakota. The winter on the plains was unlike anything the Corps had ever experienced. They recorded temperatures colder than 50 degrees below zero. They learned how to survive in such brutal conditions. During the cold winter days, they spent countless hours talking with their hosts about their journey ahead. They learned to make bull boats. They participated in bison hunts. They learned about the practice of burning the prairies. They formed an alliance that winter, a partnership that would save their lives months after their departure the next spring.

They also met Sacajawea, a young Indian girl of about 16 or 17 years. They learned she was a Shoshone. As a young girl, Sacajawea had been kidnapped near the foothills of the Rocky Mountains. She was now one of the wives of a French fur trader named Toussaint Charbonneau. Through conversations with the Mandan, the Captains learned they would need to locate the Shoshone when they reached the mountains and trade for horses. They negotiated with Charbonneau to have him join the expedition and bring Sacajawea. Not only did Charbonneau and Sacajawea accompany the Corps, but Sacajawea brought her newborn son, Jean Baptiste, on the journey. More on the importance of this decision is in the section on diversity.

In the spring of 1805, the Corps headed west across the plains. Later that summer, they reached the foothills of the Rockies. They could no longer navigate the shallow streams, so they took to foot and continued to ascend the mountains. They were able to locate the Shoshone and barter for horses. The mountain crossing would prove to be one of the most challenging times in the three-year odyssey. Winter had fully set in. The horses struggled to keep their footing in the deep snow. The Corps had relied on 9 pounds of protein per person per day, and now there was no game to be found. Weeks later, they stumbled out of the mountains onto Weippe Prairie, more dead than alive.

As they crossed the prairie, they located the villages of the Niimupu, or Nez Perce as they came to be called. The Niimupu had heard stores of whites but had never seen any. They needed guns to hunt and to ward off their enemies. This group of whites had guns; they were so weak they could have easily been taken. A council was convened. They could kill them and take their guns. An elderly woman named Watkuweis spoke up. She had been kidnapped by an enemy tribe and spent time among the whites. They had treated her well. She advised the Council to "do them no harm."

Among the men of the Niimupu were two braves who had traveled east earlier that year and had traded with the Mandan and Hidatsa (they had traveled to the villages and back, in the time it took the Corps to reach this point). They shared stories of the Corps as told to them by members of those tribes. The alliance the Corps had formed the previous winter paid dividends now as the stories were of peace and mutual respect. The Niimupu nursed the Corps back to health.

When it was time for the Corps to continue on their expedition, the Niimupu taught them how to speed up the carving of dugout canoes, by setting small fires on the logs and then chipping out the char that remained. The Captains even arranged for one of the chiefs to watch over their horses until the following spring when they would return. Another strong alliance had been formed.

These are but a few examples of the partnerships the Captains formed along their journey. Some lasted days, others weeks. Some lasted months and even years. All helped the Corps realize its vision.

As you proceed on your transformation journey, you will need alliances and partnerships in order to realize your vision.

The digital era requires a fresh look at vendors, alliances, and partnerships. Gone are the days when we could keep our vendors at arm's length and maintain a purely transactional relationship. The nature of digital transformation will require quick pivots, innovation, new technologies, and a customer focus. Our teams will not be able to keep pace on their own. We will need partnerships that can pivot with us. We will need new partners to help us to innovate and bring us new technologies. And we will need partners who know and understand our customers. We will need an ecosystem of partners and as an ecosystem these relationships will be fluid, always growing, always changing.

As a CIO, I was bombarded every day with a vendor coming into my office and proclaiming they would like to be my partner. My inner-cynic would say, "yeah, partnership. I write you a check, and you provide some goods or services, some partnership." However, I was just as guilty. I would say, "I want fewer vendors and more partners." I finally had to stop and ask myself. What *do* I mean by "partner"?

To me, it was about the relationship. While there are some partnerships that are formed as a joint venture or other legal entity, I was thinking more in terms of working side by side to achieve a common goal and vision. To me, a vendor partnership comes down to trust, transparency, and respect — mutual trust, transparency, and respect. If I wanted to be trusted by, receive transparency from, and have the respect of my vendors, I needed to show them trust, transparency, and respect. I had to invite them in.

For years, I had the practice of conducting an annual offsite planning meeting with my direct staff. We would celebrate past accomplishments, dissect lessons learned, update our strategic plan, and create action plans for the coming year. Many times, this would serve as input into the annual budget, though there were some years that the budget served as a constraint for the action planning process.

We reviewed each one of our vendors and assigned them to one of four categories: strategic, key, transactional, and other. Vendors assigned to the strategic category had to meet two criteria. First, the product or service we were obtaining from them had to help us achieve our strategic goals in some way. Second, they had to have a track record of showing us they could think strategically.

Key vendors were those companies that either met the first criteria of strategic, but not the second, or they had a significant share of our wallet. Transactional vendors were just that — transactional. There was not a true relationship, they weren't integral to our strategic success and the amount we spent with them was not a significant part of our budget. The other category was reserved for vendors from whom we rarely purchased or who weren't technology-related vendors (think office supplies).

Our strategic and key vendors were invited behind the curtain. Our offsites were two days each year. On the evening of the first day, we would have a fun team-building activity and dinner. Typically, our entire team was invited to attend. We extended the invitation to our strategic and key vendor partners. Each company could send two people. This served several purposes. It enabled us to all interact in a casual environment, getting to know each other outside of "business." It created an air of vulnerability, through team-building activities that got everyone outside their comfort zones. And, as humans, there is something about breaking bread together and sharing a meal that brings us together.

The next day, our strategic partners were invited to join me and my direct reports for our strategic planning and annual planning discussions. In those meetings, we laid out our goals and challenges. We were honest and transparent about some of the problems we were facing. We asked for their insights and help in adjusting our strategic plans, identifying projects for the coming year, and overcoming our challenges and problems.

Those conversations, both formal and informal, created that environment of trust, transparency, and respect. This enabled us to create a strategic partner ecosystem. Over a 5-year period, we were able to completely transform our department and our company.

Digital Transformation Leadership Skill #5: Diversity

Diversity, not a word that immediately comes to mind when we think about the Lewis and Clark Expedition. Just review the number of times I have used the words men, or man, when referring to the Corps of Discovery in this chapter. However, the Captains made three key decisions when forming the Corps. These decisions brought diversity to their ranks. Erring on the side of exclusion instead of inclusion would have doomed the expedition to failure. I do not want to pretend the Captains saw these decisions as anything but the contribution each person could make. They needed the skills the individual would bring, period.

The first decision the Captains made was to take York, William Clark's African-American slave, on the expedition with them. *(Author's note: Slavery is a disturbing and horrific part of American history. I admit to my own struggles of how to view historic figures when it comes to slavery.)* The Captains don't share their reasons for including York; however, what they do share is that York was seen as a full member of the Corps. He carried a gun, he was assigned to advance search parties, and he was sent out on hunts. His contribution to the mission went far beyond the normal duties of a member of the Corps. There are many stories in the journals of barriers the native people and the Corps being broken down as the natives, never having seen a black person before, declared him to be "big medicine" and showered him with attention and respect.

The next decision of diversity was in the recruitment of George Drouillard. Drouillard was the son of a French man and a Shawnee woman. As a mixed-race individual, Drouillard would have been an outcast in many cities in the east. He would have been looked down upon and subject to ridicule and discrimination. What the Captains saw was a man with extraordinary skills of hunting, tracking, and sign language. They knew they would need his help to communicate with the tribes they would encounter. Countless times throughout the journey, Drouillard proved himself to be the superior hunter, bringing back game when all others failed. In the first year of the expedition, Drouillard was sent out to track down one of the men who had deserted. He was able to locate him and bring him back. The Captains' foresight to bring Drouillard paid dividends with every tribe they encountered, as he served a pivotal role in the communication process.

Undeniably, the most well-known member of the Expedition today, outside the Captains themselves, Sacajawea joined the Corps in the spring of 1805. Again, the decision to include a woman in what was essentially an Army unit was done out of anticipated necessity. The Captains learned from the Mandan they would likely encounter the Shoshone near the Rocky Mountains. They would need to barter and trade for horses. Sacajawea was Shoshone, she knew the language. What the Captains could not have known was the vital role she played through teaching the Corps about edible plants, confirming their route at Beaverhead Rock, and helping to guide Clark's party overland to the Yellowstone River in 1806. Perhaps her greatest contribution was from being a female. The presence of a woman was a sign to the tribes of the plains and the mountains that this was not a war party, they must have peaceful intentions. Case in point, from the time they left Fort Mandan in the spring of 1805 until they encountered Shoshone in August, they did not encounter a single human being. Oral tradition from the tribes in the area tells us the tribes knew they were passing through and avoided them because they obviously had peaceful intentions since they were traveling with a woman and an infant.

For leaders today, we are faced with incredibly complex problems. In order to solve them, we must have diversity of thought, diversity of experience, and diversity of culture. We must have teams that are diverse, a culture of equity, and an environment that is inclusive.

Our digital era includes biases, our biases. As humans develop the algorithms embedded in our technology, our own biases creep into the code, the datasets, and, ultimately, the outcomes. For example, the Gender Shades Project conducted by MIT found that facial recognition software was more than 90% accurate when viewed at the aggregate across genders and races. However, when we dive deeper we find that dark-skinned females are misidentified almost 35% of the time. Speech recognition algorithms have similar results. A female is likely to experience a 10% lower recognition rate than her male counterparts.

One of the best ways to combat bias in our technology stack is to have diverse teams that are inclusive. **Everyone has a voice. Everyone reviews the data. Everyone has a perspective that is taken into consideration when building the models, training the models, and auditing the models.**

Digital Transformation Leadership Skill #6: Creating a Disruptive Culture

In his book, *Are You READY for Digital Transformation?: Digital Enterprise Readiness Framework*, Dr. Frank Granito describes the need to have a disruptive culture as foundational to any digital transformation journey. He defines a disruptive culture as, "willing to challenge the status quo, embrace innovation, experimentation, and 'fast failure,' and which is perpetually focused on what's coming next." Creating this culture and instilling it in your team is one of the most important leadership skills you must master.

As it turns out, the entire Lewis and Clark Expedition is a case study in creating a disruptive culture. It started with the master planner of the Expedition, Thomas Jefferson. Jefferson was a prolific inventor. He is credited with inventing among other things the dumb waiter, the folding ladder, automatic doors for his parlor, the lap desk, a wheel cipher, and of all things, a macaroni machine. Jefferson's vision for the expedition itself was an exercise in challenging the status quo. A country that spans a continent? Unheard of in the 18th century.

Jefferson was able to pass this mindset onto Lewis. Lewis spent 2 years as Jefferson's private secretary (chief of staff), he witnessed Jefferson in action, used his creations, undoubtedly discussed the designs with Jefferson, and embraced the disruptive culture himself.

Lewis designed and personally oversaw the manufacture of an iron frame boat. Lewis realized as the expedition moved west and eventually began to ascend the mountains, the Missouri River and its tributaries would become too shallow to navigate by boats and even dugout canoes. The iron-frame boat consisted of collapsible sections, weighing just 176 pounds in total. However, when assembled, it could carry 8,000 pounds. Wood strips would be added to supplement the iron frame, and the hull would be made of animal hides, stretched and attached to the frame. The animal hides would be sewn together and the seams sealed with pine tar. Challenging the status quo? Yes! Embracing of Innovation? Yes! Focused on what is next? Yes!

Unfortunately, for Lewis in this case, it was also a lesson in "fail fast." After traveling up the Missouri River over 2,000 miles from St. Louis, the Corps encountered a series of five waterfalls near present-day Great Falls, Montana. The 18-mile portage required them to innovate. They fashioned carts with wheels made of cottonwoods to haul the gear and the smaller canoes overland. They left the larger canoe behind. They also hauled the iron boat around the falls. When they arrived at the upstream side of the falls, Lewis set about to assemble his "grand experiment."

Lewis had spent months planning the expedition. He agonized over every detail. He planned the supplies they would need. He tried to foresee every challenge. A challenge that would have been so foreign to someone growing up in the heavily forested lands east of the Mississippi is one he did not foresee. There were no pine trees. No pine trees — no pine tar. He needed pine tar to seal the seams. They tried several concoctions, finally settling on a mixture of charcoal, beeswax, and bison tallow.

When complete, they launched the iron boat. It "lay perfectly, like a cork" on the water. Until the wind and waves kicked up. The seams got wet and began to fail. Soon the iron boat was on the bottom of the river. Lewis, though devastated, knew they could waste no time and they would need to "fail fast." He instructed the men to begin the task of carving dugout canoes to carry the gear as far as the water would allow.

It is this kind of culture we need to be successful in digital transformation. **Our teams need to be built to innovate, fail fast, and succeed**. As a leader, how much time do you spend today thinking about where disruption could come from? What will disrupt your industry, what will disrupt your company? What can you and your team do to disrupt the status quo? How can you foster innovation?

The father of disruption, Clayton Christiensen, believed businesses could not disrupt themselves. He believed to be successful at innovation; companies need to relegate innovation to separate business units and even subsidiaries, free from the management and culture of the parent company. History seems to support this theory. Polaroid and Kodak saw the potential of digital, and they invested in the potential of digital images, in the end, they both got left behind and eventually filed for bankruptcy. Blockbuster didn't see the need to change its model when a disruption from the fringe occurred.

However, some companies have been successful in disrupting themselves. Netflix disrupted Blockbuster by eliminating the brick-and-mortar storefront in favor of movie-rental-by-mail. Later, they disrupted themselves by entering into video streaming. Lego went from a "vintage children's toy" to a cultural phenomenon through movie merchandising. And Apple. Apple continues to disrupt itself and other industries. Apple introduced the iPod in 2001, and, just six short years later, disrupted it with the introduction of the iPhone.

How have they been successful, when so many others failed? Leadership guru, Steve Denning, summarized it this way, "*they are being managed from the outside-in, rather than from the inside-out.*" I'll take it a step further and say they are focused on the customer, almost manically so. Not surprising, customer focus is one of the tenets of the agile mindset. While using the agile methodology is not a prerequisite for digital transformation, having an agile mindset undoubtedly is.

Ahmed Sidky, Head of Business Agility at Riot Games, describes agile and the agile mindset in this way, "*Really, agile is a mindset — it's a way of thinking — that's defined by four values, described by 12 principles, and then manifested through an unlimited number of practices or different ways of working. It's simply a deep understanding and culture of learning and experimentation and trying things out. Any creative work will benefit from this notion of an agile way of working.*"

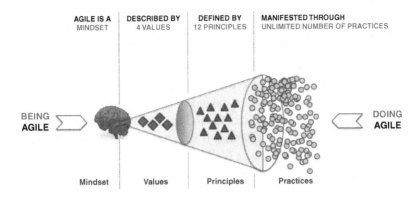

| AGILE IS A MINDSET | DESCRIBED BY 4 VALUES | DEFINED BY 12 PRINCIPLES | MANIFESTED THROUGH UNLIMITED NUMBER OF PRACTICES |

BEING AGILE

DOING AGILE

| Mindset | Values | Principles | Practices |

Having an agile mindset enables you to create a disruptive culture in your team and within your organization. Lewis and Clark were great examples of an agile mindset, their success depended on it — their very survival depended on it.

Key Take-Aways

Our journey of digital transformation is filled with uncertainty. We can take shelter in the status quo (and ultimately fail) or we can use these leadership lessons from the past to lead our teams and our companies into the uncertain future. We can shape and create the future.

Through journaling we can enhance our powers of reflection and improve our decision-making. This leadership skill can help to build our resilience and reduce our stress. Leaders of Digital Transformation will need to leverage the tool of journaling to navigate the uncertain waters ahead.

Traveling with a co-captain who is the integrator to our visionary, or the visionary to our integrator will help to ensure the success of our Digital Transformation expedition. Rare is the leader who is adept at both disciplines.

Building a team of leaders will enable our teams to be agile, attack and solve problems, and continue to proceed in the face of seemingly insurmountable odds. We must take the time to develop our teams to know when to follow and when to lead.

Leveraging the power of an ecosystem will give us the strength to overcome almost any obstacle that lies in our path to transformation.

Creating an ecosystem of partners who will bring their expertise and resources to bear will make us even more resilient when confronted with challenges.

Instilling diversity of thought, experience, and culture in our organizations will provide perspectives we can't see ourselves. Our diverse and inclusive teams will enable us to develop solutions and processes that are more robust, effective, and efficient...and that work for all our customers.

Creating a culture of disruption is necessary to break away from the status quo and incrementalism. A disruptive mindset will empower our teams to think about problems differently and identify opportunities where none seem to exist.

Bibliography

Ambrose, S. (1997). *Undaunted Courage: Meriwether Lewis, Thomas Jefferson, and the Opening of the American West* (1st edn.). Simon & Schuster.

Araujo, C. (2016). *The Ecosystem Advantage: How to Build the Digital Ecosystem That Will Help You Win in the Digital Era* [E-book]. Institute for Digital Transformation.

Araujo, L. (2021, August 23). *Getting to the Purpose of Journaling and Why it's More Than Just a Vessel for Teen Angst.* The MAPS Institute. https://themapsinstitute.com/journaling-and-its-mystical-purposeful-powers/.

Buolamwini, J. & Gebru, T. (2018). *Gender Shades: Intersectional Accuracy Disparities in Commercial Gender Classification. In Conference on fairness, accountability and transparency* (pp. 77–91). PMLR.

Christensen, C. M., Grossman, J. H., & Hwang, J. (2017). *The Innovator's Prescription: A Disruptive Solution for Health Care.* Mcgraw-Hill Education.

Denning, S. (2010). *The Leader's Guide to Radical Management* (1st edn.). John Wiley & Sons.

Denning, S. (2011, March 10). *Yes, A Business CAN Disrupt Itself.* Forbes. https://www.forbes.com/sites/stevedenning/2011/03/10/yes-a-business-can-disrupt-itself/.

Goodman, J. T. (2018). *Reflective Journaling to Decrease Anxiety among Undergraduate Nursing Students in the Clinical Setting.* University of Northern Colorado.

Granito, F. (2020). *Are You READY for Digital Transformation?: Digital Enterprise Readiness Framework* [E-book]. Institute for Digital Transformation.

Hardy, B., PhD. (n.d.). *Keeping A Daily Journal Could Change Your Life.* Inc.

Jackson, D. (1978). *Letters of the Lewis and Clark Expedition, with related documents, 1783–1854.* University of Illinois Press.

Kraner, A. (2021, February 8). *The Agile Mindset*. Medium. https://medium.com/icagile/the-agile-mindset-5e8328452a23.

Lewis, M., Clark, W. & Moulton, G. E. (2002). *The Definitive Journals of Lewis and Clark*, 7-volume set (1st edn.). Bison Books.

Palmiter Bajorek, J. (2019, May 19). Voice recognition still has significant race and gender biases. *Harvard Business Review*. https://hbr.org/2019/05/voice-recognition-still-has-significant-race-and-gender-biases.

Sidky, A. (2015, September 9). *The Secret to Achieving Sustainable Agility at Scale*. *Slideshare*. https://www.slideshare.net/AgileNZ/ahmed-sidky-keynote-agilenz.

Sullivan, A. L. & Simonson, G. R. (2016). A systematic review of school-based social-emotional interventions for refugee and war-traumatized youth. *Review of Educational Research*, 86(2), 503–530.

Walsh, K. (2021, August 8). *Digital Transformation Depends on Diversity*. *TechCrunch*. https://techcrunch.com/2021/08/08/digital-transformation-depends-on-diversity/.

Wickman, G. (2012). *Traction: Get a Grip on Your Business*. BenBella Books.

Wickman, G. & Winters, M. C. (2016). *Rocket Fuel: The One Essential Combination That Will Get You More of What You Want from Your Business* (Reprint edn.). BenBella Books.

Chapter 8

The Client/Partner Engagement

Jessica Carroll

Trust: Building Your Transformative Customer Engagement Plan

After waiting on the Dunkin Donuts line for what felt like an excruciating half-hour a few weeks ago, I finally was first in line to pay and grab my Pumpkin Spice. I was feeling rushed as my first Zoom call of the day was about to start, and I needed my daily caffeine fix, or there was no way I was going to be able to get my head in the right listening zone. So absently-mindedly, I held out my cash and was ready to grab the coffee and go. However, the attendant refused my cash, gave me the coffee, and said, "You're all set. The car in front of you paid." Wow.

Perhaps you've had the gift of "pay-it-forward" too? As non-life-impacting as it may seem when talking about a cup of coffee, the act of kindness was still eye-opening. Suddenly, I was awake, my senses were on, and I was feeling ready to launch the day's meetings. Coffee or not.

Similar to "pay-it-forward," is the concept of "give-to-get" is where a person, without obligation, freely offers something of value in the belief that they will receive something of value in the future.

The first time I heard the phrase "give-to-get" was about 6 years ago by one of my colleagues (and now I would add trusted friend), Tony. At

183

the time I was transitioning from a long-term tenure at an organization to which I had been hugely committed. I needed to re-envision myself and find a path to my next role. This was an uncomfortable and uncertain time for me, but Tony (and many other wonderful colleagues) supported and encouraged me. Tony gave me countless hours of his time freely, although, in his role as a career coach, he should have been asking for payment. In part due to his advice, I landed in a new role and was happily off and running in my new work chapter.

This story is far more than about doing good for someone. This is about a motion that includes a non-obligating, but genuine return to the giver. In this instance, it was a chance, years later, for me to introduce Tony to one of my business colleagues for a potential new business opportunity for which I believed he was the right fit. I was eager to make the introduction, because he was someone I trusted, and I knew my colleague would be in good hands.

Trust — the essential component in building a strong relationship, be it personal or professional. For customer engagement, trust is foundational.

Customer engagement is a critical element of your transformation roadmap because it can create loyalty from your customers, which can translate directly to retention, growth, and brand advocacy. Organizations positioning to thrive in the 4IR are smart to weave an engagement program into their company fiber because increased revenue is a proven outcome, and also because digital transformation is grounded on putting the customer at the core and an engagement program is a tangible method for accomplishing just that.

"Customer Engagement" is "the emotional connection between a customer and a brand. Highly engaged customers buy more, promote more, and demonstrate more loyalty…."

It's the relationship that matters (sometimes more than the product) and gaining the trust of your audience is the cornerstone of that relationship. Customer engagement programs are designed to foster this two-way connection.

Terms such as "customer engagement," "customer experience," and "customer success" are loosely bantered about in the industry, so we need agreement on the purpose and differences of these concepts because they ARE different. For our baseline discussion here, we'll recognize **customer engagement** as the program whole. **Customer experience** is the overarching experience your customers have both with your product and every interaction with your company. And finally, **customer success** is a discipline within an organization. The customer success representative is dedicated to ensuring a valuable relationship is created with your customer, is an evangelist internally to help guide the company's customer-first culture, and works to understand, track, and report on the success of the company meeting the *business outcomes* of their customer (see Figure 1).

Customer engagement is a broad program with multiple threads, it can support stakeholders, and we'll call them all "customers" with a varying purpose. Customer engagement can target:

- The relationship of a company to the consumer (direct-to-consumer).
- The engagement of your company employees (employee experience).
- The relationship with your supporting vendors (vendor management).
- The relationship created between you and other companies for which you provide services (business-to-business engagement or B2B engagement).

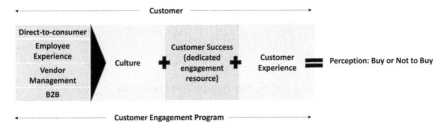

Figure 1: Customer Engagement Program.

Customer engagement is big. For purposes of our conversation here, we'll narrow this discussion to number four, customer engagement in a B2B scenario.

Grab your coffee and let's dig in.

B2B Engagement Works

For businesses that provide (sell) services to other businesses, an engagement program can be a differentiator. While it is common for organizations to invest in the direct-to-consumer experience, it's more unusual to find a business dedicating resources to fostering relationships laterally (meaning B2B) beyond traditional sales and marketing methodologies. So why not leverage this jewel of an angle and win over clients!

To get the program off the ground, to make it actionable, and to keep the momentum, forward rolling a framework helps. The elements of this framework are more than a program outline; they should be a living dynamic target for your full customer engagement lifecycle (see Figure 2).

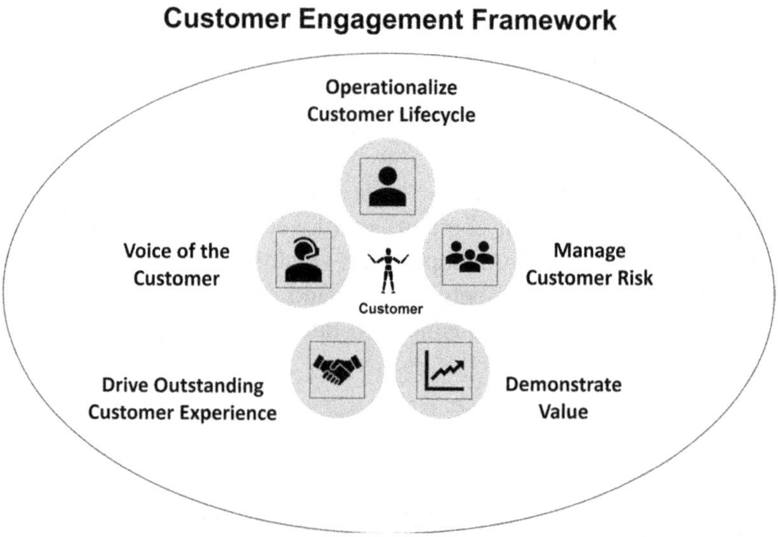

Customer Engagement Framework

Figure 2:   Customer Engagement Framework.

Each segment of the cycle in the diagram is a discrete mini program within the larger whole, so this deserves a bit of a detailed breakdown.

Operationalize Customer Lifecycle: From product development to operations, make your service simple with the customer's experience considered at each touchpoint. Create a customer-first culture throughout your organization to bring this to life. (See "Your Employees Must Be a Part of the Ride," later in this chapter.)

Manage Customer Risk: Keep check on the health of the relationship, particularly around delivery and adoption of services. A continuous improvement program is a great method for executing this element.

Demonstrate Value: This is the place to insert your customer success team (or individuals tapped to pick up this mantle if you cannot create a full business unit). This is a group of employees dedicated to understanding, tracking, and reporting on the success outcomes of your customer. This means they have to understand, from the customer's perspective, what are those success outcomes.

Drive Outstanding Customer Experience: Create a high-touch relationship well beyond marketing outreach and surveys. (See "Authentic Relationships Are a Win for Everyone," later in this chapter.)

Voice of the Customer: Ensure that the pulse of the customer over time is understood. Cycle new feedback into the organization at the operational level to continuously loop through the framework.

With this framework in play, your engagement program is on its way to driving a much richer result for both the customer and for your organization because you have clear target points in the lifecycle. Remember we're really talking about "give-to-get" by delivering products and services that provide the outcomes your customer is after throughout every stage of their relationship with you, they will more likely want to continue to BE your customer.

Strong engagement organically becomes an opportunity for growth within the account because you are delivering success and your customer will want more of that success. If done well, you will be so valued by your customer that they will become a natural advocate, which ultimately can gain you new customers. It's a beautiful thing for both parties.

Your Employees Must Be a Part of the Ride

The framework needs more than a handful of internal evangelists. The culture across your entire workforce will have a direct impact on whether your engagement program is a success or a failed effort. This means that in creating your engagement program you will need to include an initiative to pull in your employees and that initiative must be ongoing, just as your engagement with your customer will need to be a continuous endeavor.

Regardless of whether an employee has direct, indirect, or absolutely no contact with the customer, they feed into the customer's overall experience. It's obvious that your customer service or sales teams (anyone with direct contact) are a factor in how your customer *feels* about your organization. But your back-office teams have an impact as well, even though it may be downstream.

We'll use billing as an example: At some point, you bill your customer. How is that experience for them? Is it seamless, can they easily pay online, is the bill simple to understand? If the customer has a question about it, how does that work? Are the employees answering questions knowledgeable? The experience end-to-end should be considered from the customer's view, even though accounts receivable is not usually considered a customer touchpoint. Especially because receiving a bill isn't the most enjoyable activity in the first place, I would argue it's probably one of the most critical customer-oriented areas of your business.

Everyone in your organization feeds the customer experience. Everyone in your organization needs to be customer focused.

This is not a rah-rah exercise, instilling a customer-first culture throughout every nook and cranny of your organization requires a cultural commitment with real actions. Each employee must participate and their activities, ideas, processes, and most importantly, their individual goals need to tie to the customer-first mission in some way.

A structured process and set of actions to frame your efforts to create and sustain a customer-first culture throughout your organization are necessary to make the objective a reality. These activities should happen as part of your customer engagement program, which fits in your larger digital transformation initiative.

There are two pillars underpinning the methodology to move this process forward. I refer to them as **Behavior** and **Mobilization** (see Figure 3).

Behavior	Mobilization
Interest in seeking knowledge about the customer's business	Executive leadership must be committed
A listen-first outlook; naturally curious and always seek to understand	Present the purpose
Authentic, empathetic, and a fact driven mindset	Meet with each department leader
Transparent, accountable, and respectful communications	Map the customer-first behaviors to activities
The ability to imbibe confidence through problem ownership and a desire to push for resolution with urgency	Each employee must be invested
A positive energy and passion about business outcomes	Measure the program

Figure 3:   Customer-First Cultural Pillars.

The **Behavior** pillar is a guideline for the types of attitudes and emotional skills desired in a customer-first employee profile. An employee should strive to embody:

- Interest in seeking knowledge about the customer's business.
- A listen-first outlook; they should be naturally curious and always seek to understand.
- Authentic, empathetic, and a fact-driven mindset.
- Transparent, accountable, and respectful communications.
- The ability to imbibe confidence through problem ownership and a desire to push for resolution with urgency.
- A positive energy and passion about business outcomes.

Does this sound like the proverbial unicorn? While not all individuals will have all these characteristics working at full throttle all the time, as you coach and grow your employees and especially as you look to onboard new talent, these should serve as standard behaviors for the employee base you cultivate in your transformed future of work.

The **Mobilization** pillar also includes six elements, and these elements are to be used as a guideline for your organization to operationalize the customer-first culture.

- **Executive leadership must be committed**: The CEO and his or her direct leadership team must be supporters. Whether you are the CEO launching this initiative, a leader in the organization, or simply a champion in the ranks, you'll have to figure out how to sell the entire executive team on the value of culture change and gain their commitment. Since a customer-first culture supports customer engagement and customer engagement is a proven revenue generator, this shouldn't be too hard to do.
- **Present the purpose**: Now that executive leadership is behind you, it's time to face everyone else in the organization. Explain the concept of a customer-first culture, show the value that the cultural transformation will bring to the organization, show how employees will benefit, share how it will be measured, and make sure the program plan is communicated. An all-company meeting is a great place to set the stage.
- **Meet with each department leader**: Leadership at all levels must embrace the program. A good way to get that result is to be a great listener. That's right, after the concept has been presented; now it's time

to do some 1:1's with each department head. You'll want to understand what leadership thinks about the transformation, as it will affect them and their staff directly and their feedback will help guide the initiative.

For example, ask what they think a customer-first culture is (and isn't), how they see value in it (or not), how they would envision their staff adjusting behaviors, and what effect, good or bad, these changes may have on their work processes.

If the leader is quickly on board, terrific. If negative concerns are raised, here's the opportunity to discuss how those obstacles can be worked through. Be patient but positively persistent.

- **Map the customer-first behaviors to activities**: Partnered with each department leader, take the behaviors noted above, and talk about how current work activities and processes support them today. Then identify those activities and processes that do not.

Create a roadmap so that it is easy for everyone to see the alignment and the gaps. Not every activity will connect to the behaviors in the final state, and that's okay. Help each leader discover a path to making changes to targeted activities or communications in each of their areas that will achieve a strong customer focus, which also makes sense for your organization.

Use the behaviors noted above as your guide to gauge where each employee falls on the customer-first vs. non-customer-first scale. This will give the leader a template they can use to coach an employee that might have gaps in their behavior profile.

This takes work, but if the leader is onboard with the transformation (see above), he or she will eagerly put in the effort.

- **Each employee must be invested**: Although the cultural transformation purpose and plan may have been presented company-wide, you'll have to repeat the message many times over. Next to leadership support, gaining commitment from each employee is critical. The transformation will potentially require each person to adjust their behaviors, work processes, and certainly communication style. This is not easy. But, if an employee understands how their actions contribute to the growth of the company, and they see how critical he or she is to this end goal, you'll get them onboard.

Collaborate with the department leaders, and the individual employees, to define at least one goal for each staff member that ties directly to the customer-first mission. The ideal way to do this is for the employee themselves to attempt to determine what that goal(s) needs to be, so they have personal ownership.

- **Measure the program**: Giving each employee at least one goal will help provide practical insight into the success of the program over time. Additionally, though, add KPIs for each department unit to track what works and what doesn't (and so the department leader can effectively adjust where needed). Ultimately, the success of the customer-first cultural transformation will be measured by revenue growth of existing customers, the loyalty of customers to remain customers, and the advocacy and positive brand reputation the effort produces. (See "It all Comes Back to Math," later in this chapter.)

While here we look at these *behaviors* and *mobilization activities* in the context of customer-first culture for the sake of your customer engagement program, they are equally critical for your digital transformation. A workforce that can drive transformation by embracing change to delight the customer (and to stay competitive over time) requires these very same behaviors to support a cross-organizational customer-first environment.

Your people are the primary ingredient in the recipe for the success of your digital transformation. Start with a program that surrounds your employees and motivates them, recognizing their importance in creating a culture that drives premier customer engagement.

Authentic Relationships Win for Everyone

So now that you have a framework in hand and your internal culture is thriving with the customer-first energy, how do you create *real and meaningful* relationships with your customer? This is NOT a popularity contest. This isn't about being likeable as much as it is about understanding what matters to your customer and delivering value on that.

A few years ago, I accepted a role as a customer success executive. I was tasked with building the discipline (creating the department) as well as managing my own client portfolio where I was to create relationships with the CIOs of those accounts. I remember the first customer I met and our introduction of what I was there to do. To say skepticism showed on the CIO's face is an understatement. When you say, "I'm here to be your advocate," and "bring you value," that sure sounds salesy and fluffy. I knew going in that on first blush this might seem so irrelevant to the reality of the service delivery he cared about, but I walked into that meeting okay that he was going to be skeptical because I was confident that I WOULD be his advocate and I WOULD bring him value.

The reason it worked (yes, ultimately, he and his team saw great value) was because I took time to understand their position, objectively understand how we were delivering, and help both my team and his team course correct where needed. The truth was we were not delivering all things well and our customer also wasn't always following process either — this was a two-way course correction. It worked because over time, we built **trust** across both teams that our intention to do right for our customer was the mutual goal, even if that meant hard conversations along the way.

I think one could say most humans understand how to build trust, but equally it's probably fair to say we don't always take the path to doing that. We get caught up in our own objectives; we are in a hurry to have things our way. To create meaningful customer engagement, building trust is foundational, and, therefore, building it must be intentional.

Think about the **Behavior Pillar** we discussed earlier. For my skeptical customer, those behaviors had to be embraced by my team in order for us to bring value back to the customer. He wasn't happy with our service, so we had to understand that and see *objectively* why. Changing our behaviors and adapting our focus (think framework) all had to happen first. Once we were able to do that internally as a team, we were able to succeed in the eyes of my customer, and it was a motivating thing to watch.

A collaborative mindset, rather than us vs. them (seller vs. buyer), from a team of professionals who are focused on solutions that drive the business strategy of the customer is a much more direct way to get the customer engaged with your company, because your interest is their success. What customer wouldn't love that!

Like give-to-get, fostering a genuine environment of strong partnership that is focused on "doing the right thing" to attain the desired business outcomes creates a win for everyone.

But there is one other element to this. Consideration of the employee experience specifically for the new and future generation of workers must be an added layer to your engagement program, because if you are positing the need for authentic relationships with customers but you do not create the same commitment to your own employees, the customer engagement efforts will be viewed as a hollow management ploy. The same can be said for any program (e.g., diversity, equity, inclusion (DEI); social responsibility; etc.), so while we look at this now in the context of client engagement, this component is vital across the scope of your organization and your work practices.

The new workforce (think 20-somethings and those entering the workplace in the next 10 years) is expecting to participate in a work environment that provides the purpose and values that are relevant to *them*. These values will be a consideration in their acceptance of a job in your company, how committed they will be to your programs, and certainly in how long they will stay.

Recently, I separately interviewed three 20-something professionals, each in very different roles. One is a copywriter for an advertising agency in New York City, one is a social worker, and one is a college admissions counselor at a prestigious university in the U.S. I wanted to understand their view of the workplace, management, and the expectations and framework of what a desirable employee experience would entail.

Although their professions and therefore work environment are wildly different, their vision of an enticing workplace where they would feel committed was the same. It came down to these four elements:

- **Empathy**: Where there is genuine concern for the person as a human in a full sense, beyond work activities. As the social worker put it to me, "I want to be cared about as a person, not as the worker."
- **Mentorship**: Where there is a commitment by those with experience within the organization to help guide, coach, and support the growth and success plan of the individual, especially those new in the workforce.
- **Transparency**: Where management becomes an authentic listener to their ideas and concerns and makes those concepts actionable where appropriate, as well as providing honest communication as to the why and how behind decisions and directions of the company.
- **Life-balance**: Where management understands and respects their life outside of work. This fits so neatly with the growing need for businesses to accommodate and support a work-from-anywhere, work-anytime dynamic vs. the traditional 9 to 5 in the office only structure.

Consideration and adaptation of your company's approach to the employee experience for this group of professionals must be woven into your employee experience program, because this group of professionals is critical to the future success of your business. It follows then that these elements must be a factor of your client engagement program too, because you can't push an "authentic" customer-first culture without also pushing for an internal environment that authentically cares and values the employees responsible for delivering on the objectives and results of the program.

You need this vibrant new set of professionals engaged in all facets of your work ecosystem in order to support the purpose of your company. Adjusting the organization's internal programs to speak to the employee in a personal way with understanding of the values of the individual is part of adapting to the future of work. It's a circle of authenticity where there is genuine care for the employee, so then (along with the engagement program) genuine care for the success of your customer can be realized.

Standard Operating Procedures for Engagement

For a B2B customer engagement program to truly work, you will need to build in activities that support the framework. Beyond the mindset and behaviors of your employees, there are standard operating procedures that will round out your program and deliver value back to your customer throughout the lifecycle.

Whoever is responsible for managing the front-line relationship in your scenario (customer success manager, account manager, business relationship manager, etc.) for B2B relationships, there are some simple but effective activities that can enrich the interaction you have with your customer.

Business reviews with a C-suite sponsor and leadership must be consistently held and worth everyone's precious time. You may be doing this already, but I would add that your business review should be far more robust than simply reporting on performance metrics. It should be targeted to support the success outcomes of your customer and provide a transparent review of how your company is delivering against those outcomes. So obviously, you need to know what those business success outcomes are and what your company provides to support them. See operating procedure number two.

Conduct a strategy workshop. At least once annually, conduct a session where you give your customer the floor to really explain their priorities across all angles of their business. This should be far more than focusing on the priorities you think your company can support; you'll want to understand holistically what the challenges are and the competitive or innovative priorities they are looking to drive, so you clearly can see how all the pieces fit together and where your services critically link. Then, get clear on what you will own (not sell) and how you're going to measure the delivery of those services. You and your customer will need to jointly agree these are your target delivery metrics. To get your customer to share all this, guess what, you need their **trust**.

Make sure to **leverage a continuous improvement program**. Tracking both delivery challenges and wins is one of the strongest methods for transparent and accurate understanding of account health. It is also one of the smartest methods both to solve problems and highlight the good stuff, giving you and your customer objective clarity. As I shared in my earlier example with the skeptical CIO, it is also a tried-and-true way to build **trust**.

Another important step is to **commit to 1:1 meetings with customer leadership**. Engagement works when there is consistent meaningful interaction. Get on your customer's calendar for regular check-ins. This is not meant to be a sales call, this is about the customer. Listening is everything in these meetings.

Bring value without obligation and **share thought leadership assets**. Presumably, your company is an expert in some area. Use your company's thought leadership (e.g., whitepapers, webinars, relevant video, other timely collateral, etc.) to simply give something useful to your customer, freely.

Create social interaction opportunities. If you can get to this step, you are doing fabulously with your program. Invite your customer to interact outside of the office. Do a dinner, support a charity of their choice, do a charitable activity as combined teams, invite them to a conference you will be attending that would interest them, or have them come speak at an event on a relevant topic that highlights the good work *they* have accomplished, do a fun social event, etc. Again, this is not a sales activity; it is simply relationship-building at its core.

Finally, **consistently launch customer surveys and then report the results**. Obviously, the most standard engagement method is gaining feedback from your customer, and usually, this is done by conducting surveys. The twist I will add is to objectively share the feedback results with your customer. You may even go bold and share the results aggregated across your entire customer base (white-labeled of course). Adding this step, including recommendations to address any negative reviews, is where you deliver on transparency.

Now you've got a framework to guide you, behaviors for your workforce that are tuned to support a strong customer experience, and standard operating procedures to help build a relationship and trust with your customer.

How do you know if it's working? You've got to measure it all.

It All Comes Back to Math

This is an ironic topic for me, as anyone that knows me knows, I don't do math (English major). The thing is accurate data can prove the truth and that's a whole lot easier than promoting a marketing thesis to your customer on why your service is beyond awesome.

Let numbers lead the story.

After one of the strategy workshops I ran with another CIO customer and his team, I went back to my office, put all of their Post It®-covered insights all over my walls, and spent a few days re-ingesting all of their ideas, challenges, vision, and priorities. There were layers of disconnected concepts, but I did uncover a theme: To grow the business, there was a need for flawless operations, so that the company could pivot technological efforts to consumer-facing initiatives. For all of their focus on bettering the consumer experience, and this session clearly bubbled the consumer to the top of everything they valued, without finding a way to efficiently manage the organization's underlying operational support, the tech team would never get to the innovative, visionary, and transformative initiatives being asked for by leadership.

What was *valuable* was consumer innovation, what was *measurable* was if the tech team could shrink commodity-support activities and increase their efforts and time supporting these new business initiatives.

Sound familiar? This is not a surprising revelation — you may have had similar conversations in your organization. How do you shred non-value technical activities to focus on the business, but still operate a reliable responsive technology organization? This is part of the conundrum of digital transformation.

For this organization, there was determination and pressure that this effort had to be accomplished. But, how to measure if they were truly advancing the directive to shrink the commodity activities and grow the transformative?

To support the CIO's scenario, I asked the CIO and his team to do a guesstimate percentage of time spent today on commodity (run) activities and time spent on transformative business activities, and then, looking out 12–18 months, the percentage for run and transformative work that they would desire. There was a bit more thinking that went into this than what I'm sharing here, but at the end of the day, it's somewhat of a "put your finger in the wind" exercise. However, I made the case that precise exactness means less than not measuring.

When we circled back to this at our Business Reviews, we re-examined the percentages, we looked at where we were months ago, and how close we came to our targets. In one review session about 8 months after our strategy workshop, this KPI status review opened a lively but significant discussion among my team and the customer as to why the numbers hadn't really changed after all that time and why the transformation was not further along.

It was a meaningful discussion because while the numbers were all initially guesses, what was important was that the numbers showcased, in some *relative measurable* way, where urgent action needed to be taken. In this instance, part of that action was for my customer's team to step quicker into changing their work methodologies (so the CIO was satisfied because the metric-driven discussion gave his team the push they needed), but it also opened a new opportunity for him to hire my company to do more work.

This wasn't a nefarious sales tactic; this was a method to get at the outcome the customer was after and partner with them to make sure that happened. Both teams were united, inspired, and focused on working together to get this effort moving faster. That was the real goal: Two-way useful engagement from which actionable decisions and movement forward could be made.

There are a few measurement types that I would suggest are needed in the B2B engagement program. Combined, they create a multi-layered method for understanding the state of the service, in a non-anecdotal yet measurable way. Here are my recommendations for setting a well-rounded measurement program that can create *context* around the delivery value of your services and simultaneously gain you usable insights from your customer's point of view.

Strategic Business Outcome KPIs: The example above with my CIO customer is one such KPI. What's important about this one is that it was derived specifically out of the strategic business outcomes of the customer. Look for KPIs that align with those goals, even if they are hard to define, a guesstimate is better than not measuring.

Performance KPIs: These are your standard operational KPIs. While they may not be specifically business oriented, it is important to watch performance for patterns, improvement opportunities, and of course, a way to show your customer where successful delivery has occurred.

Customer Feedback: Whether you look at Net Promoter Score, Customer Satisfaction, or other customer insight methodologies, this is the best place for understanding the perception of truth about your company from the customer's view. Customer feedback is a table stake engagement measurement. How often you survey, the type of survey, and the questions you ask will be a key part of how well you are gauging the "truth" of your customer's perception of your company.

As B2B relationships have the potential of being a bit more intimate than typical direct-to-consumer interactions, you'll want to craft your feedback program to fit your specific audience, of which you should have a strong understanding if your engagement program is humming along.

As noted already, elevate this action to include a personalized readout of those results to your customer with recommendations for improvement where applicable. This motion is where you transparently deliver your commitment to engage with the customer, with their interests as your target.

Measure Your Account Team: You may be fortunate enough to have a customer-success team leading the engagement effort, or it may be the account manager, business relationship manager, or some other role. Whatever group owns this direct relationship, they should have KPIs to measure the iterative value they are bringing to the customer and your organization.

Use the standard operating procedures as a starting point for determining those KPIs. For example: How many business reviews *with the decision-maker* have been conducted over x period of time; has a strategic workshop been conducted; did the workshop produce viable Business Outcome KPIs; how many 1:1 meetings have occurred over x time; were the 1:1 meetings with decision-makers; have thought leadership assets been freely and consistently delivered; do the customer feedback KPIs indicate an improving or declining view of your company, etc.

Measure Your Culture: As we have already discussed, a customer-first culture requires the entire workforce to be invested in some way and you need a customer-first culture to make the engagement program work, and the engagement program needs to work in order to support your larger digital transformation.

Set goals with the employees that tie to the overall program. Goals could be as simple as spending time with the account team to learn more about the customer, or participating in customer support training, or adjusting response time objectives, etc. The employee should be a participant in determining what goal or goals they can target to achieve in support of bettering the customer experience through their individual contributions.

Each department as a unit should also track what works and what doesn't, so the department leader can effectively adjust. For example, if response-time objectives are adjusted, but over time it shows no gain in the customer relationship and yet puts burden on the employee's effectiveness, it's okay to adjust those KPIs. Whatever the measurements are, keep them in the context of improving the customer experience, yet simultaneously balance the cost of the change to the company in efficiency, time, or dollars.

All combined your measurement programs will ladder up to **revenue growth and customer satisfaction** as the top-line metrics of the engagement program. Revenue growth from existing accounts, new business, or referrals must be the ultimate barometer in parallel with your customer satisfaction ratings. However, all the other measurements and activities we have been discussing are important as sub-elements of your engagement program; they feed the two winning outcomes of more revenue and delighted customers.

When you aggregate these layers of measurement, you have an understanding of performance against the business' most desirable outcomes, you have performance transparency, you have the unscripted perspective of the customer through their feedback, you can define how well your own customer frontline workers are driving the account health, and you have a way to broadly look at your entire workforce and track their commitment through tangible actions, in support of the transformative customer-first experience.

Donuts Aren't the Sweetener for Engagement

You may just be one of the best sources for understanding what meaningful or valuable engagement looks and feels like.

Put yourself on the receiving end for a moment. I would contend that you're on the receiving end of customer engagement every time you buy anything from anyone.

We said earlier that customer engagement is a program, and the experience created is a part of that program. So, for example, you have an experience when you buy coffee from your favorite coffee shop. You have an experience when you work for a company, when you hire a vendor, when you're working alongside that vendor you have an experience that you manage, and when a company hires your company (whether intentionally or not) creates an experience for your customer. Some of these experiences can be fantastic and some of these can be awful — an engagement program's purpose is to keep the experience fantastic.

I'll share one of my favorite experiences (not coffee this time), and that is with Zappos, the online shoe company. Zappos has been long held as the customer experience standard. As an ardent shoe lover and therefore a recipient of their services many times, I have to honestly say that they create experiences for the consumer that make every interaction easy with some added flavor of fun. This is far more than having an intuitive website. More uniquely, their messaging *feels* like it is directed to you. From the moment you purchase (including the sometimes necessary merchandise return), they reinforce how smart you are for your tasteful choices and how excited *they are* to deliver the product (or help you send it back). While it may not be a sophisticated concept, it feels human, personal, and affirmative — every time you interact. Zappos has figured out how to make the retail shopping experience make me feel good about spending my money — and they keep me coming back.

Perhaps more applicable to our discussion on B2B engagement, I'll share that several years ago, I was in the client seat myself. It just so happened that I was in a position with some significant purchasing power. I (along with my leadership team) was theoretically the perfect target for a vendor who knew how to create a relationship through value.

While my team was often subjected to the usual sales tactics of holiday baskets, donuts, and a plethora of throw-away trinkets from eager prospective vendors, those offerings were not a formula for engagement.

However, I did have one vendor who truly understood the meaning, and therefore, value behind creating a deeper professional connection. Right from our first introduction, she took the time to meet the team and listen carefully to our vision, strategy, and needs. She wasn't in sell mode. She made a point to set regular check-ins, she sent relevant material and insights aligned to my team's initiatives without being asked, she made sure to bring us to key industry events, and most importantly, she was an internal advocate, especially if there was an escalating "crisis." I knew she could be counted upon to move mountains whenever needed. She knew our business objectives, and therefore, tuned her offerings to fit those specific objectives. She felt like an extension of my leadership team.

She was part of a highly functional engagement program at her organization, and the culture around this type of engagement permeated the culture at her company.

So, who did I turn to when I had a project and needed new services? The trinket and donut-giving vendors or someone who, instead of donuts, spent time with me and my team and understood my objectives? Easy answer, her company always was first on the list because she, and subsequently her company, gained our **trust**.

Key Take-Aways

We've looked at how digital transformation requires a customer-first culture, because the end goal is delivering an incredible customer experience that drives more business. We've explored how your employees must be bought in with a clear plan for how to make this work. And we've outlined how a structured program with identifiable standard operating procedures and a way to measure those actions are all components of how to tune your organization to be a customer engagement showcase. The key take-aways for a winning client engagement program are as follows:

- You need a program framework that serves as a constant North Star.
- You need the buy-in from your employees across the organization. Consideration of the employee experience, particularly for the new generation of professionals, must be an established underlying layer, because their commitment to your company's purpose is necessary for your organization's success.

- Building trust is foundational. Authenticity and two-way value between your organization and the customer must be intentional. Think give-to-get.
- Clear procedures and activities must be defined and operationalized.
- The program must be measured.

The intricate engine of your engagement program should be driven by your organizational purpose but never without line of sight to delivering products and services of value for your customers. When done with intent and commitment, engagement can generate loyalty, because the experience the customer has is delightful, and there is **trust** that your company will continue to deliver.

The Fourth Industrial Revolution has shifted consumer expectations. A personalized and more targeted understanding of our needs is what we have all now come to expect. Whether we are talking about direct-to-consumer, our experience as an employee, how we interact with our vendors, or our business-to-business relationships, the presumption is that, as the receiver, we will be delighted with the interactions, touchpoints, and outcomes the seller delivers.

When you are the company selling to continue your growth trajectory, committing to an engagement program is a fundamental and necessary element of your digital transformation journey. Simply put, digital transformation puts the customer at the center. A well-framed engagement program encircles that aspiration and puts your company in position to make meaningful transformation a reality.

So, another cup of coffee (maybe skip the donut) plus the engagement components we've explored, and you have what you need to put your customer engagement program on your transformation roadmap with all the utensils you need to deliver on the customer-first promise.

Bibliography

Fertik, M. (2018, December 16). *Why Customer Engagement Should Be Every Business's Top Priority in 2020.* Forbes. https://www.forbes.com/sites/michaelfertik/2019/12/16/why-customer-engagement-should-be-every-businesss-top-priority-in-2020/.

Kashanchi, S. (2018, August 31). *Are Your Customers Coming Back for More?* Gallup. https://www.gallup.com/workplace/241766/customers-coming-back.aspx.

Wikipedia. (n.d.). *Fourth Industrial Revolution.* https://en.wikipedia.org/wiki/Fourth_Industrial_Revolution.

Chapter 9

The Customer Experience

Roy Atkinson

This chapter explores the relationship of Customer Experience (CX) and Digital Transformation (DX), each of which has influence on the other. The Institute for Digital Transformation recognizes the fundamental connection between CX and DX itself:

> *"The integration of digital technologies into a business resulting in the reshaping of an organization that reorients it around the customer experience, business value and constant change."*

Raymond Sheen, Institute Fellow

Although the words "customer experience" are everywhere, not everyone understands the true depth and breadth of what CX means, why it is increasingly important, and what DX means for it. Reshaping an organization sounds, and is, daunting. Keeping focus on the customer provides an anchor point for the endeavor. We do need to remember, though, that there isn't an endpoint: Neither CX nor DX is a project. The change required by both is, as the above definition states, **constant**. This is not new thinking; Heraclitus is famous for reminding us that change is the only constant.

Each customer's journey is individual, whether we are discussing business-to-customer (B2C), business-to-business (B2B), client, patient, or any business relationship. To an extent, the overall view is similar to quantum mechanics: We cannot predict the exact behavior of any individual customer, but only the probability that they will behave in a certain way. To make our predictions as accurate as possible, we require data in real time, or as close to real time as we can obtain it. Digital tools and emerging technologies are making this aspect of CX more realistic and attainable, but no tool has the magic that makes everything perfect.

This chapter will explore:

- A working definition of CE.
- An explanation of the stages of the customer journey.
- How the customer is driving change.
- Why business agility is a requirement.
- The differences among digitization, digitalization, and DX.
- Ways of measuring CX.
- Changes in customer behavior and interaction.
- People, Process, and Culture.

What Is CX?

What do we mean by "CX"? One of the clearest definitions is from the solutions provider Zendesk:

> *"Customer experience (CX) is everything related to a business that affects a customer's perception and feelings about it."*

Erin Hueffner

Although we would broaden the language from *business* to *organization*, this definition stands out because it includes the words "**perception and feelings**." Without the inclusion of the customers' perceptions, we would be talking about CX **design**, not CX. Furthermore — especially regarding all things digital — it is important that CX be measured and analyzed as near to real time as possible. This is increasingly feasible because of the availability of digital tools discussed later in this chapter.

CX is often expressed with reference to the Customer Journey, i.e., the various phases of the relationship customers have with any organization or brand. Here are eight stages through which the journey passes (Figure 1):

Figure 1: Eight stages of the Customer Journey.

These stages are an expansion upon other models including Truelson's *5A's*: Aware, Appeal, Ask, Act, Advocate. Note that not all customers will go through all eight stages. Some never become advocates, e.g., and not all customers need or seek support.

- **Discovery**: At this stage, a prospective customer becomes aware of a certain organization or brand, whether through marketing or word of mouth, including social media.
- **Affinity**: The person finds something to like about the organization or brand and/or its offerings.
- **Research**: The prospective customer looks into similar products or services, and compares availability and price as well as other attributes including the brand reputation and cachet.
- **Purchase**: The prospective customer becomes a paying customer.
- **Receipt**: The customer takes delivery of the product or receives the service. This stage includes experiences with delivery, whether physical or digital.
- **Use**: The customer puts the product to use or consumes the service. At this stage, the initial perceptions of the customer are put to the test. Does the product or service live up to expectations and perform as expected?
- **Support**: The customer seeks assistance from the organization, brand, or other customers. Support includes documentation, customer service functions, and community.
- **Advocacy**: Based on their own experiences, the customer shares positive information about the product, the brand, or the service they received.

The Advocacy stage feeds directly back into Discovery by other prospective customers as brand advocates attract their interest. This produces a cycle of CX for the brand in which increasing numbers of customers are brought onboard (Figure 2).

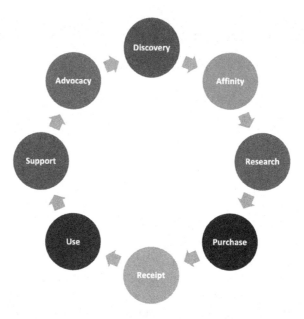

Figure 2:   The brand view of the CX journey.

Increasingly, customers are interacting with each other, as well as with organizations and brands, digitally. The popularity of advocacy media such as Amazon customer reviews and sites such as Yelp and Rotten Tomatoes are examples.

Change Is Being Driven by the Customer

Customer demand, not in the sense of increasing consumption but rather their demand to do business digitally, is one of the key drivers of DX, along with the necessity of the business to remain competitive or to gain competitive advantage. This demand will certainly increase as customer demographics change to include an ever-increasing percentage of digital natives (i.e., those who were born in the age of the internet), bringing with them expectations of ease, mobility, and speed. Global mobile e-commerce, sometimes referred to as *M-commerce*, has increased to nearly three-quarters of all e-commerce, and e-commerce is itself increasing as a percentage of total commerce. Global e-commerce sales reached $876 billion in the first quarter of 2021, up 38% year-over-year.

Customers are leading the way; businesses must follow, find new ways to lead, or fall by the wayside.

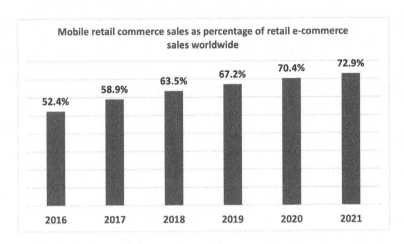

Mobile retail commerce sales as percentage of retail e-commerce sales worldwide

52.4%	58.9%	63.5%	67.2%	70.4%	72.9%
2016	2017	2018	2019	2020	2021

Figure 3:   Mobile retail e-commerce (Coppola, 2021).

These reports highlight retail business-to-consumer (B2C) sales (Figure 3), but business-to-business (B2B) services are also moving forward with digital strategies and have demonstrated their strengths during the pandemic.

Business Must Become More Responsive, Agile, and Available

"To stay competitive in the next normal, companies have expanded and accelerated their use of digital solutions. Indeed, in just the first few months of the pandemic, 96 percent of B2B organizations shifted their operating model to emphasize digitally enabled self-serve, remote, and contactless operations."

Digital B2B services in the next normal | McKinsey

What should be immediately obvious from this model is that all the various areas of a business or organization need to be involved in CX:

- **Marketing**: including social media — is involved with Discovery, Affinity, and Research.

- **Sales**: including e-commerce — is involved in the Purchase.
- **Shipping, Fulfillment, and Logistics** are involved in the Receipt stage for physical goods; those responsible for the technical architecture of the organization, whether IT or someone else, are involved in this stage if the customer is buying digital products or services.
- **Customer Success and Customer Service** facilitate the Use and Support stages.
- **Marketing and/or Community Lines of Business** are involved with the Advocacy stage.

Underlying all the transitions, collaboration, and handoffs among the business units are the needs for excellent technology, elimination of silos, shared data and knowledge, and **business agility**, defined as the ability of an organization to:

- Adapt quickly to market changes (internally and externally).
- [Provide] Working solutions over comprehensive documentation.
- Respond rapidly and flexibly to customer needs.
- Adapt and lead change in a productive and cost-effective way without compromising quality.
- Continuously be at a competitive advantage.

As we can see, business agility is precisely what is meant in our definition of DX by being reoriented around "the CX and constant change." In other words, CX is, at least in part, driving DX.

Digitization Is Not Transformation

Before proceeding, it is very important to understand the differences among DX, digitalization, and digitization (Figure 4).

- **Digitization** refers to creating a digital representation of physical objects or attributes...
- **Digitalization** refers to enabling or improving processes by leveraging digital technologies and digitized data...
- **Digital Transformation** is really business transformation enabled by digitalization...

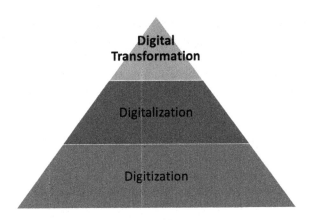

Figure 4:   DX pyramid.

There is an order involved: Digitize then digitalize in order to enable transformation.

> *"In the final analysis, therefore, we digitize information, we digitalize processes and roles that make up the operations of a business, and we digitally transform the business and its strategy. Each one is necessary but not sufficient for the next, and most importantly, digitization and digitalization are essentially about technology, but digital transformation is not. Digital transformation is about the customer."*

Jason Bloomberg

Understanding and measuring the customer journey is, then, extremely important. Most organizations attempt to measure by asking customers to complete surveys, including Customer Satisfaction (CSAT), Customer Effort Score (CES), or NPS®

Survey Type	Primary Question	Application
CSAT	How satisfied are/were you?	Assessing reaction to a transaction
CES	How easy was it for you?	Assessing ease and convenience
NPS®	Would you recommend us?	Predicting loyalty and advocacy

Unfortunately, many companies measure *transactions* rather than *relationships*, and CX is by definition not transactional but is rather the sum of all the responses a customer has to every interaction with the organization or brand. None of these common survey types was originally designed to measure CX. They are most relevant when used in conjunction with other measures such as:

- **Customer churn rate** (Customer Churn: Definition, Rate, Analysis and Prediction | QuestionPro).
- **Repeat purchase rate** (Yaguara).
- **Customer lifetime value** (What Is Customer Lifetime Value)? (Qualtrics).

In addition, surveys are problematic:

> *"...biases may occur, either in the lack of response from intended participants or in the nature and accuracy of the responses that are received. Other sources of error include intentional misreporting of behaviors by respondents to confound the survey results or to hide inappropriate behavior. Finally, respondents may have difficulty assessing their own behavior or have poor recall of the circumstances surrounding their behavior."*

Priscilla A. Glasow

Additionally, survey data always lags behind customer behavior. A customer does something, is presented with a survey, and responds (or doesn't). Digital tools can provide more accurate information by tracking actual behavior as opposed to self-reported behavior and do it in, or much closer to, real time. Heat maps, which show exactly which areas of a given web page attract the most attention and the most clicks, are one example. These maps have been heavily used by marketing departments and advertising agencies to assess the performance of websites and ad campaigns.

Recently, an analogous approach has been utilized for the analysis of audio extracted from telephone conversations. Conversations with customers are regularly recorded by contact centers. Using Part of Speech tagging and Maximum Entropy modeling can illuminate sentiments in audio recordings. Because of the sheer volume of calls and contacts, it is not feasible for the resulting text and audio to be reviewed by humans. A very small subset of calls has typically been reviewed by managers for quality assurance purposes. The remaining recordings have gone into storage and have been part of the vast troves of *dark data* (data which is never analyzed or used) that organizations accumulate.

Applying analytics across multiple contact channels, especially when powered by machine learning and **Natural Language Processing** (NLP), not only illuminates the types of language that elicits more positive responses from customers but can also be used to provide in-ear or on-screen coaching for representatives in real time, help make sense of the unstructured data resulting from customer comments and feedback (Voice of the Customer, or VoC), and help make organizations more responsive and responsible.

Such analysis is not restricted to the contact center, however, even in light of the contact center's expanding role in many organizations. IT service desks can make use of recordings to improve their own services. Sales and marketing are finding value in using NLP tools for similar reasons. Analyzing speech even at a rudimentary level can give valuable insights; consider the advantages of knowing how many times a given competitor's name is mentioned by customers, and in what context, and whether with negative or positive sentiment.

These unused recordings are only one of the pools of dark data organizations are storing, securing, and backing up for no apparent purpose. Streams of data are coming from social media, customer relationship management (CRM) tools, customer website searches, questions, comments, suggestions, and so on.

According to a study by Splunk, 60% of organizations reported that in 2019 more than half of all their data was dark, with one-third of organizations saying that 75% of their data was dark (Figure 5).

Percentages of Dark Data in Organizations

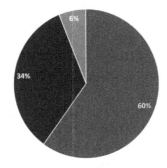

■ >50% of data is dark   ■ 75% of data is dark   ■ <50% of data is dark

Figure 5:   Percent of dark data — percentage of organizations.

Saying that an organization is "data driven" would be, in most cases, an overstatement; organizations are operating on less than half the available data.

As machine learning, NLP, and overall artificial intelligence (AI) rapidly evolve, tools and techniques for measurement have also improved and continue to do so. Data analytics, including predictive analytics, are powerful tools for businesses and other organizations to better understand their customers' journeys, monitor the performance of various improvements, and adjust far more rapidly than survey-based feedback would allow.

> *"Organizations that build optimal nimbleness and forward-looking analytical infrastructure will be successful in maneuvering through the pandemic and post pandemic world."*
>
> Puneet Shivam and Raghuram Iyengar

The CX programs of the future will be holistic, predictive, precise, and clearly tied to business outcomes. Evidence suggests that the advantages will be substantial for companies that start building the capabilities, talent, and organizational structure needed for this transition. Those that stick with the traditional systems will be forced to play catch-up in the years to come.

Changing Customer Behaviors and Preferences

According to the United Nations Conference on Trade and Development, global e-commerce rose to almost $27 trillion in 2020–2021, accelerated by the COVID pandemic. In light of uncertain health conditions and changes in buying habits, this trend is likely to continue in both B2C and B2B markets. The rise in online commercial activity will also require accompanying shifts in how marketing, sales, and support are accomplished.

Customers are also shifting the ways they interact with each other. Although social media continues to be strong, online communities are becoming increasingly popular, especially with younger customers. These communities include, e.g., Facebook Groups and Reddit's "subreddits." Brands can be welcomed into these communities, especially if they interact informally and are trustworthy.

One of the preferences of contemporary consumers is *personalization*, helping to steer customers to products and services of interest, and guiding their experience with the product or service after the purchase.

Personalization, once limited mainly to targeted offers, now extends to the entire CX. This means that customers want personalization throughout their interactions with a retailer — with multiple, personalized touchpoints that enable them to allocate their time and money according to their preferences.

Successful personalization requires ready access to accurate customer data across the organization including buying history and habits, preferred contact channels, correct name and pronouns, and any other relevant data. Maintaining and use of the data requires proper data governance, compliance, cybersecurity, and access control.

Top marketers are developing systems that can pool and analyze structured and unstructured data, algorithms that can identify behavioral patterns and customer propensity, and analysis capabilities to feed that information into easy-to-use dashboards.

Setting up a centralized customer-data platform (CDP) to unify paid and owned data from across channels is essential to these efforts. Unlike traditional CRM solutions, CDPs provide built-in machine-learning automation that can cleanse internal and external data, connect a single customer across devices, cookies, and ad networks, and enable real-time campaign execution across touchpoints and channels.

Getting personalization right at scale paves the way for *hyper-personalization*, which will largely be enabled by AI and other emerging technologies.

While personalized service often means calling the customer by name and keeping track of preferences, hyper-personalization takes it to a much higher level. It's now about utilizing customer data to personalize and customize experiences, offers, and content in real time...

Again, this kind of hyper-personalization depends on the technology that affects its delivery, from the data through to the devices the customer is using. The experiences must be deliverable anywhere the customer is — whether static or mobile — and relevant to the customer's current environment and context. To accomplish this kind of interoperability and ubiquitous access, it makes sense that the data and the digital systems that deliver it are accessed from the cloud.

This approach extends into the realm of healthcare, providing personalized care to patients and health consumers (customers seeking to invest in their own health) in real time.

For health systems looking to integrate hyper-personalized infrastructure into their consumer experiences, it can be helpful to break it down into four tiers, starting with basic data and moving to advanced, AI-powered insights:

- **Tier 1 — Basic preferences and needs**: Optimizing communications based on channel, language, and location preferences.
- **Tier 2 — Proactive communication**: Providing customized appointment reminders, personalized marketing outreach, medication management, and scheduling outstanding labs and screenings.
- **Tier 3 — Personalized navigation**: Creating tailored appointments and personalized payment plans based on the needs and preferences of the individual.
- **Tier 4 — Tailored care delivery**: Using patient data and AI to create personalized care plans and staging predictive care interventions.

If the goal of CX is to increase the success of a business or organization, then hyper-personalization can provide the basis to achieve it. Customers are getting what they want, how they want it, and organizations can see the effects of improvements in real or near real time.

Process and People

While process should *not* be a primary focus (results are more important), the technologies that are emerging now within organizations depend upon repeatable steps and having outcomes that reflect the intents of leadership as well as feeding the needs and desires of customers. Processes are not paramount but are important. In the best of all possible worlds, processes would be designed prior to the acquisition of new technologies, but that is not always possible or practicable. Customizing technology solutions comes with a high cost, not only in terms of the work it takes to customize, but the later process that must be paid if the technology is replaced or upgraded. Ideally, new systems should reflect the organization's culture and its customers' needs, as well as being the right tool for the job.

We began by saying that DX is **reshaping the organization**. An organization is, after all, composed of people, and people are the keys to both CX and DX. The culture of any organization is, to put it simply, **the way things are done**. If that culture is centered on achieving an excellent CX, chances of success are far greater than if the culture is one of "plugging in the latest widget" and seeing what happens. That much should be obvious, but judging by the number of failed transformations, it is not.

Creating and maintaining a culture is very difficult; changing an existing culture is even more of a challenge. Denise Lee Yohn laid out the actions leaders can take.

To build a customer-centric culture, business leaders should take six actions:

- *Operationalize customer empathy*: Empathy is one of those buzzwords that sound really good, but very few companies actually understand what it means, much less practice it. Essentially, customer empathy is the ability to identify a customer's emotional need, understand the reasons behind that need, and respond to it effectively and appropriately. And it's pretty rare. *According to PwC*, only 38% of U.S. consumers say the employees they interact with understand their needs...
- *Hire for customer orientation*: From the very first interaction with prospective employees, organizations should make thinking about customers and their needs a clear priority...
- *Democratize customer insights*: For every employee to adopt a customer-centric mindset, every employee must understand the organization's customers...
- *Facilitate direct interaction with customers*: Companies need to develop ways for employees to interact with customers directly, even in "back office" functions. After all, every employee impacts the CX in some way, even if indirectly, so every employee can benefit from interacting with customers to better understand them and learn about their successes and challenges...
- *Link employee culture to customer outcomes*: The adage "You can't manage what you don't measure" applies to customer-centricity, too. Managers will be motivated and equipped to cultivate a

customer-centric culture if they know if and how it impacts results, so organizations should ensure they establish and track the link between culture and customer impact...

- *Tie compensation to the customer*: Organizations should reinforce a customer-centric culture through their compensation program...

Because of the need to have multiple lines of business (in fact, *all* lines of business) involved to some extent in one or more of the eight stages of the customer journey we discussed, it is also imperative that silos be broken down and both knowledge and expertise shared across the entire organization. This is another difficult task for leaders to accomplish but is part of the business transformation that is encompassed in DX.

Summary

We began with the Institute's definition of DX stating how it reorients the organization around the CX, followed by a definition of CX itself with the reminder that the customer's perceptions and feelings should be included.

Although each customer's journey is unique, there are generally eight stages through which they pass in their relationship with an organization or brand: Discovery, Affinity, Research, Purchase, Receipt, Use, Support, and Advocacy. Brands, using CX programs, try to guide customers through these stages and give them opportunities to deliver positive messages that will influence prospective customers.

As customers go through these stages, their experience will be (directly or indirectly) influenced by various areas of the organization, making silos counterproductive. The entire organization should be customer-centric, that is, focused around CX. In order to maintain this focus, businesses need to be more responsive, agile, and available to customers. This type of agility requires a commitment to constant change; neither CX nor DX is a project with an end date.

To remain agile, organizations cannot depend upon surveys as an adequate way to measure customer sentiment. Fortunately, new tools and methods of measuring responses and reactions in real time are currently on the market and are continuing to evolve. Artificial intelligence, machine learning, and applications of these technologies such as NLP are making it possible to analyze the huge stores of data organizations currently hold, though much of it remains "dark." As digitally powered analytics bring this structured and unstructured data to light, CX will become even more important and influential to the way business is conducted.

Customers have led the way during the 20-odd years we've been in the "experience economy," but organizations now have the digital means to communicate, collaborate, guide, track, and measure customer behavior and value. This makes personalization and hyper-personalization feasible.

Technologies, while exceedingly useful, are not sufficient to true transformation. The people who make up organizations and the processes they follow (their ways of working) need to be aligned and focused as well.

Digital Transformation aims to provide the means for an organization to deliver better CX. The use of digital tools and emerging technologies can help move organizations from providing simple customer satisfaction to providing hyper-personalized experiences that differentiate them from competitors, acquire and retain customers, and achieve financial success. These achievements will not be attained without committing to constant change, investment in the appropriate tools and technologies, and the desire to create a culture that is supportive and foundational to the outcomes.

We have seen that huge amounts of data reside, unexplored, within organizations; one of the keys to success will be the willingness of the organizations and their leaders to go where the data takes them and truly engage with those with whom they do, or intend to do, business. This will be accomplished through the use of emerging AI, machine learning, NLP tools, proper data governance, knowledge sharing, and a culture focused on the customer.

Bibliography

Bain & Company. (n.d.). *About the Net Promoter System*. https://www.netpromotersystem.com/about/.

Beer, C. & Beer, C. (2021, March 9). *The Rise of Online Communities*. GWI. https://blog.gwi.com/chart-of-the-week/online-communities/.

Benjamin, G., Forsgren, M., & Guzman, N. (2020, October 20). *From Defense to Offense: Digital B2B Services in the Next Normal*. McKinsey & Company. https://www.mckinsey.com/business-functions/operations/our-insights/from-defense-to-offense-digital-b2b-services-in-the-next-normal.

Bhat, A. (2022, May 27). Customer Churn: Definition, Rate, Analysis and Prediction. QuestionPro. https://www.questionpro.com/blog/customer-churn/.

Bloomberg, J. (2018, April 14). *Digitization, Digitalization, And Digital Transformation: Confuse Them At Your Peril*. Forbes. https://www.forbes.com/sites/jasonbloomberg/2018/04/29/digitization-digitalization-and-digital-transformation-confuse-them-at-your-peril/#78e677fd2f2c.

Boudet, J., Gregg, B., Rathje, K., Stein, E., & Vollhardt, K. (2019, November 19). *The Future of Personalization — And How to Get Ready for It*. McKinsey & Company. https://www.mckinsey.com/business-functions/marketing-and-sales/our-insights/the-future-of-personalization-and-how-to-get-ready-for-it.

Gartner. (n.d.). *Definition of Dark Data - IT Glossary*. https://www.gartner.com/en/information-technology/glossary/dark-data.

Glasow, P. A. (2005). Fundamentals of survey research methodology. Retrieved January, 18, 2013.

Global e-commerce jumps to $26.7 trillion, COVID-19 boosts online sales (2021, May 3). Home | UNCTAD; UN Conference on Trade and Development. https://unctad.org/news/global-e-commerce-jumps-267-trillion-covid-19-boosts-online-sales.

Gupta, M. S. (2020). What is Digitization, Digitalization, and Digital transformation. https://www.arcweb.com/blog/what-digitization-digitalization-digital-transformation.

Hueffner, E. (2020, April 17). *What Is Customer Experience: Strategies, Importance & Examples*. Zendesk. https://www.zendesk.com/blog/why-companies-should-invest-in-the-customer-experience/.

Iero, T. (2022, April 29). *What is Hyper-Personalization: A Customer Experience Key Component*. Mindful. https://getmindful.com/blog/hyper-personalization-key-customer-experience-component/.

Kaushik, L., Sangwan, A., & Hansen, J. H. L (2013, May). Sentiment extraction from natural audio streams. In *2013 IEEE International Conference on Acoustics, Speech and Signal Processing* (pp. 8485–8489). IEEE.

Lindecrantz, E., Gi, M. T. P., & Zerbi, S. (2020). Personalizing the customer experience: Driving differentiation in retail. *McKinsey Insights (March). Erişim Adresi*. https://www.mckinsey.com/industries/retail/our-insights/personalizing-the-customer-experience-driving-differentiation-in-retail.

McKinsey & Company. (2021, July 12). *Prediction: The future of CX*. https://www.mckinsey.com/business-functions/marketing-and-sales/our-insights/prediction-the-future-of-cx.

Sheen, R. (2019, May 1). *Digital Transformation in Product Development*. Institute for Digital Transformation. https://www.institutefordigitaltransformation.org/digital-transformation-in-product-development/.

Singh, S. (2021, August 23). *Get Personal: Building a Hyper-personalized Care Strategy*. AVIA. https://aviahealth.com/insights/get-personal-building-a-hyper-personalized-care-strategy/.

Statista. (2022, May 4). Global Mobile Retail Commerce Sales Share 2016–2021. https://www.statista.com/statistics/806336/mobile-retail-commerce-share-worldwide/.

Statista. (2022, May 23). Reasons for Digital Transformation in Organizations 2020. https://www.statista.com/statistics/1017623/worldwide-digital-transformation-drivers/.

Truelsonm, M. (2019). *Mapping The Consumer Path Throughout The 5A's*. http://marktruelson.com/mapping-the-consumer-path-throughout-the-5as/.

UNCTAD. (n.d.). *Global E-commerce Jumps to $26.7 Trillion, COVID-19 Boosts Online Sales*. https://unctad.org/news/global-e-commerce-jumps-267-trillion-covid-19-boosts-online-sales.

Yohn, D. L. (2018, October 2). 6 ways to build a customer-centric culture. *Harvard Business Review*. https://hbr.org/2018/10/6-ways-to-build-a-customer-centric-culture.

Zaki, M., McColl-Kennedy, J., & Neely, A. (2021, May 4). Using AI to track how customers feel — in real time. *Harvard Business Review*. https://hbr.org/2021/05/using-ai-to-track-how-customers-feel-in-real-time.

Chapter 10

Digital Transformation Readiness

Dr. Frank Granito

Introduction

"Rely not on the likelihood of the enemy's not coming, but on our own readiness to receive him."

Sun Tzu

"One secret of success in life is for a man to be ready for his opportunity when it comes."

Benjamin Disraeli

"By failing to prepare, you are preparing to fail."

Benjamin Franklin

"The readiness is all."

William Shakespeare

"Semper Paratus (Always Ready)"

United States Coast Guard

These are just a few of the perspectives of the concept of "**Readiness**." So, what is Readiness and why is it so important? Readiness, by

223

definition, is the quality or state of being ready. But here we are talking about *Organizational* Readiness, specifically Readiness for change. Organizational readiness indicates the relationship between people, processes, systems, and performance measurement. It requires synchronization and coordination without which no implementation will be successful. That is true for any major change, including Digital Transformation. The proliferation of digital technologies purports to increase the innovation potential of most organizations. However, *approximately 90% of new ideas never convert to new product or service deliveries because of the lack of organizational readiness.* So, why would an organization commit to Digital Transformation if they knew that failure was virtually guaranteed if they were not ready?

Organizations, such as "first responders," know that being ready is central to their mission success. *Semper Paratus* is a Latin phrase, meaning "Always ready." It is used as the official motto of the United States Coast Guard, the Royal Hamilton Light Infantry (Wentworth Regiment) of the Canadian Army, the U.S. Army 16th Infantry Regiment, and the Long Beach (California) Fire Department.

What do these organizations have in common? They all face ever-changing threats. And more importantly, they are continually implementing new procedures and technology to stay **ready** to meet those threats. Threats and challenges are not static, and these organizations need to always be ready by continually adapting as situations and technology change. Indeed, one of the major units of the Coast Guard is the Force Readiness Command and their Doctrine is, *The Service has built its reputation on being 'Always Ready' to meet any maritime challenge by successfully and repeatedly adapting to the situation at hand.* Their customers are very visible, and their needs are clear — if the Coast Guard fails, lives could be lost. They work from the needs of the customer backwards to develop the services that keep us safe.

This is the true essence of digital transformation — not the implementation of mere technology to automate core services, but the shift in power to the customer and the need to continually adapt technologies, processes, and culture. That requires continuous "Readiness" to adapt to dynamic customer needs and ever-changing technology to meet those needs. Perhaps organizations considering a Digital Transformation should think about their Readiness like the United States Coast Guard and other first response entities.

Importance of Readiness

Have you ever been to a restaurant and waited too long for your food? One of the reasons is the establishment may be ill-prepared to serve its guests. The chef and their staff just don't show up when the restaurant opens and start cooking for customers. Hours, sometimes days, before the doors open and guests arrive, prep staff are there ensuring readiness for service. They are making sauces, baking bread, cutting vegetables — all the things that are necessary to make the restaurant ready to open for service. Then during service, kitchen stations are organized and ready to take and deliver orders; wait staff have tables prepped and condiments filled. If they are not ready to serve their guests, they won't be in business long. This process is called *mise en place*, French for "everything in its place."

Mise en place might be one of the most widely translated French phrases in the culinary lexicon, despite which, it remains one of the least understood. But translation is about more than just substituting words. It's about conveying the idea *behind* the words. And the idea of *mise en place* is all about being prepared, being ready. But prepared for what? The term "mise en place" (pronounced "MEEZ-on-plahs") arose from the environment of restaurant kitchens. And cooking in a restaurant is a very different situation than cooking at home. So, **it stands to reason that the type of preparation needed for each situation will likewise be different**. For restaurant staff, mise en place is about setting up their stations, ensuring all the ingredients and tools they need are within easy reach, to minimize wasted movement and extra steps. Containers of chopped herbs, diced onions, minced garlic, squeeze bottles of oil, not to mention tongs, spatulas, whisks, and spoons, are all laid out within easy reach. And just like a restaurant, any organization and its staff need to be ready — ready to serve, ready to produce, and ready for change.

Organizational readiness is a measurement of the preparedness of your company to undergo a major change or take on a significant new project, in this case, a Digital Transformation. You do not want to undertake a big change without knowing if your organization has the capability and resources to accomplish it effectively. More than just a reasonable expectation that you will be successful, being ready for a transformation can also save your company's reputation by allowing you to avoid a potentially high-profile failure for engaging in a project you were not ready to complete. Understanding readiness also gives your company the ability to address any potential issues before they become big problems as you move forward on the transformation, save time and money, and probably improve the profitability of the change.

In addition, understanding your readiness allows you to address the details of the change with your employees and customers to determine if they are ready for such change and have the ability and resources to do their part. This is part of what we at the Institute for Digital Transformation call the "**Why this, why now**" of change that is part of our *Deep Roots* methodology. Being kept in the loop and engaged with what the company is doing will make your employees and customers feel more valued, which will increase their personal investment in the proposed transformation and motivate them to want to do their part in it well.

Certainly, you will be able to identify the weaknesses of your organization that understanding readiness will provide, but it will also give you the additional benefit of identifying the strengths of your organization, most particularly the things that will be the strongest assets for you in your transformation. Exploiting strengths can provide greater assurance of success and may even hasten it. Finally, readiness will allow you to know whether your organization meets the requirements to even **consider** the transformation. If you do not have the capabilities and resources now, either acquire them or do not even start until you do.

So, why is Readiness important? The data should tell you why. In our ongoing study of Digital Readiness, the results are represented in Figure 1.

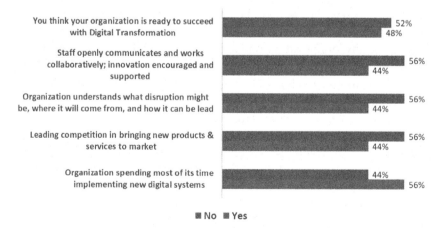

Figure 1:   Digital Readiness Quiz Results.

From this, we can make some significant observations:

- The data shows most respondents believe they are not ready for Digital Transformation.
- An overwhelming majority believe their culture is **not collaborative**, and the organization **does not understand** where disruption comes from.
- An overwhelming majority believe they are **not able to lead competition** in bringing products and services to market.
- And, yet many organizations are spending most of their time implementing Digital Systems.

The Readiness Framework

To successfully transform into a Digital Enterprise, an organization must exhibit its Readiness. Organizations will only be ready to transform themselves into true Digital Enterprises when they possess:

- **Operational Sustainability**: Your organization has a stable operational base.
- **Organizational Agility**: Your organization can quickly adapt to change.
- **Strategic Agility**: Your organization can anticipate change.
- **A "Disruptive" Culture**: Your organization is receptive to implementing change.

An organization shows Readiness for Transformation when they show competency in each of these four "Dimensions" of Digital Readiness. This is their *mise en place*!

Operational Sustainability

The first, foundational dimension of readiness is a stable and sustainable business process and technology operations model. **If an organization's business processes and technology operations are not running in an efficient and sustainable manner, there is a limited likelihood that they will successfully endure a transformational effort.** You must first make your organization fit before you can undertake a fundamentally stressing and taxing effort to transform into a Digital Enterprise.

It is also important, however, to note that being *"operationally sustainable"* does not necessarily equate to the highest levels of operational maturity (using whatever scale of measurement) or completely robust process definitions and operations. The objective is to have a business and technology operation that is efficient and scalable while not being overly rigid or constraining to the organization.

Operational Sustainability is necessary to provide foundational organizational discipline. Business and technology operating models are intended to provide the "instrumental value" of achieving specific organizational goals and purposes through conformance to rules. Too much adherence to business and operating models could result in displacement of goals by making them an end in themselves. When this happens, the organization sees discipline not as a measure serving a specific purpose, but as an immediate "terminal value." We designed the Attributes of the Operational Sustainability Dimension to measure whether operating models provide *"just enough"* discipline to continue to deliver the instrumental value intended.

The Operational Sustainability dimension does not assess typical measures of maturity found in legacy assessment models. Rather, the seven attributes of this dimension, described below, focus on *organizational capabilities*. Measuring the capabilities represented by the seven attributes has a profound impact on an organization's ability to perform with a sound base of foundational processes. These capabilities provide the foundation that enables the organization to then achieve organizational and strategic agility.

For Operational Sustainability, the organization must first have *Strategic and Functional Clarity*. This means that both the individuals and the team understand the overall mission of the organization, understand how the organization creates value, and can effectively communicate that information across the organization. It further examines whether the team understands and can communicate its role in fulfilling that mission and delivering that value. This Attribute also goes beyond the mere understanding of the mission and value proposition. To fully understand and deliver the mission and value, individuals and the team need to develop, maintain, and monitor relationships across the organization.

Without Strategic and Functional Clarity, the organization lacks the ability to deliver basic functions that directly support the mission. Activity takes place with no value; processes are measured with Key Performance Indicators (KPIs) that add no value to mission, and that means productivity is meaningless.

Next, Operational Sustainability requires the organization must have *Inter-Functional Integration.* Inter-Functional Integration basically means **integration points between the teams are understood**. It examines whether the team understands which other teams or roles are dependent on their team's operating processes and models to properly provide services. In addition, it examines the team's understanding of how its processes and models are interconnected and how they act individually or collectively with other processes to deliver organizational mission and value.

The speed of communication in the Digital Era will outpace the normal bureaucratic mechanisms of the traditional organization and therefore threaten the value chain. Inter-Functional Integration maintains a synergy with Strategic and Functional Clarity such that rapid changes in operating and processing models can be transmitted, received, and understood — as well as performed.

Harvard Business Review (Caimi 2014) estimates 15% of an organization's collective time is spent in meetings — a percentage that has increased every year since 2008 — and the Project Management Institute (Rajkumar, 2010) estimates about 90% of the time in a project is spent on communication by the project manager. Lack of Inter-Functional Integration could undermine the agile communication needed to survive and thrive in the Digital Era.

Operational Sustainability also requires *Operational Discipline.* Operational Discipline addresses the basic tenets of Information Technology Service Management (ITSM), but from the perspective of Service Capabilities. Traditional ITSM "maturity" frameworks deal with the life-cycle of Strategy, Design, Transition, and Operations, but do not examine the more important development of delivery capabilities. **Measuring capabilities is consistent with the Digital Enterprise Framework goal of measuring instrumental value rather than terminal value**.

Fully developing the attribute of Operational Discipline delivers consistency, cost savings, self-improvement, and improved operational performance of existing organizational standards, processes, and procedures. Further, these capabilities help ensure that the organization captures, shares, and adopts its best practices so that staff can be rapidly reassigned throughout the organization without retraining or knowledge loss. Without Operational Discipline, there is no model or baseline from which to measure and ultimately improve.

Governance is also a requirement of Operational Sustainability. This **addresses whether the organization knows how to make decisions,** clearly identifies who is responsible for making those decisions, and whether decisions are made in a timely manner. Also, important in the decision-making process is understanding the events that may trigger a decision and how to initiate the decision-making process.

Governance provides the mechanisms of organizational transparency and principles of disclosure that directly address staff, stakeholder, and customer need to know. This will ensure greater success as this process will align the goals of decision-makers with the goals of the organization. Governance also reduces waist, risk, and mismanagement thereby ensuring value and reputation with customers and staff. Without Governance, effective decision-making is compromised if not severely jeopardized.

Another requirement of Operational Sustainability is *Metrics-Driven Management*. This measures whether there are KPIs, whether those KPIs are understood, and whether the organization collects sufficient data by which to measure them. A KPI is a measurable value that demonstrates the effectiveness of an organization in achieving key business objectives or critical success factors.

Metrics provide objective measures of performance, and this data enables organizations to "manage by fact." What gets measured gets done. Employees are faced with many competing demands on their time. When they know the small handful of Metrics that grade their performance, it keeps them focused on doing the right things.

Still another requirement of Operational Sustainability is *Operational Flexibility*. Continual improvement is a theme that permeates the attributes of *Operational Discipline* and *Metrics-Driven Management*. *Operational Flexibility*, on the other hand, measures how the organization initiates and acts upon improvement initiatives. The basis for Operational Flexibility is **the ability for staff to feel comfortable questioning existing operational and business processes** and the organization's receptiveness to proposed changes to those processes or their supporting technologies.

A rigid, mechanistic organization cannot adapt, so it falters when challenges arise. A flexible organization is willing to try new approaches, even when the old ways are working fine. Continuously refining its operational and business processes helps an organization identify new and better ways of getting things done and fostering innovation. Operational Flexibility allows the organization to become more efficient over time, which translates to higher profits and lower costs.

Finally, good *Team Dynamics* is necessary for Operational Flexibility. The **Team knows and understands their various roles in operational**

and business processes as well as how their roles support the mission and value proposition of the organization. The Team should also understand how their roles support the organization's vision for the future.

Good Team Dynamics leads to a positive team atmosphere in which employees feel empowered. In such an environment, team members are more comfortable taking calculated risks and seek out innovative solutions to complex problems. Establishing an environment in which employees can thrive without conflict involves improving the group dynamic so that team members listen to each other, value individual experience, and consider other perspectives before making impactful decisions. When team members feel safe, they are willing to help others succeed, which fosters a collaborative environment where employees trust each other to get work done.

Organizational Agility

The second dimension of readiness is developing the capability of Organizational Agility. Organizational agility is not just about the ability to change direction. It is the ability to rapidly adjust the structure, operating processes, and functions of your organization to adapt to changing market conditions. It demands that organizations and their leadership can reduce structure and process, as necessary, to enable the organization to respond more rapidly and effectively. As with Operational Sustainability, it comes down to balance. The organization has created just enough structure and process to ensure stability, while removing anything that may inhibit the organization's ability to pivot and move as fast as is necessary to seize market opportunities or respond to market risk.

The organization must be tactically flexible to exploit opportunities within their strategic boundaries and without compromising the instrumental value of the operational and business processes. Using operational governance processes in a constructive manner coupled with proper organizational taxonomy gives organizations the flexibility and autonomy to make rapid decisions. Autonomy leads to organic leadership and teaming. In this environment, self-forming leadership and teams are extremely constructive because they operate in the open rather than in the shadows typical in a mechanistic organization focused on the terminal value of maturity models. Organizational agility encourages risk-taking and leaders are not afraid to be vulnerable to their peers and subordinates.

Organizational agility builds on the Operational Sustainability dimension and is influenced by the balanced use of operational and business processes. Organizational Agility is also influenced by taking advantage of digital communication channels and technologies that facilitate the collaboration needed to support the team autonomy and organic leadership so necessary for this Digital dimension. The seven attributes of this dimension, described below, focus on tactical agile capabilities. These capabilities depend on Operational Sustainability described in the previous section and enable the organization to then achieve strategic agility required in the Digital Era.

For Operational Sustainability, the organization must first have a good *Organizational Taxonomy*. This means the organization maintains, and effectively utilizes, a clear mapping that connects delivered business value to the supporting business processes and the underlying functional teams that execute those processes. An **Organizational Taxonomy provides a basis for accurate and consistent business processes and their execution**.

When an organization properly organizes and classifies its assets, processes, and information through a Taxonomy, those classifications can be used as a strong foundation for adapting and even creating new groupings to meet changing business needs.

Next, an organization must have good *Communication and Coordination* that examines whether organizational teams have clear and open lines of communication through which opportunities to pivot and the potential risks and ramification of changes are shared and coordinated. Communication and Coordination among staff helps people manage, create, and sustain organizational operations. Organizational communication happens in many forms, including conversations, emails, memos, and websites. Ideally, organizational Communication and Coordination facilitates sharing of information, planning, project coordination, business process execution, and social interaction. Poor communication or nonfunctional communication systems lead to confusion, lowered morale, and loss of productivity. Communication also plays a crucial role in altering individual's attitudes. **A well-informed individual will have better attitude than a less-informed individual and thus will be able to adjust to changing business needs and processes**.

An organization must have *Team and Organizational Autonomy* to make rapid, preliminary decisions regarding potential changes to operating models, structures, and processes prior to submission to a larger governance process. **Team and Organizational Autonomy provides faster actions and decisions** since traditional organization theory may lead to bottlenecks; individual and team development since team members understand which skills and knowledge they need to acquire and go about on their own to acquire them; better redistribution of work because planning and tracking tasks are taken up by the team rather than traditional leadership models; and finally the overall use of full human potential because there are more opportunities to explore and uncover hidden or unused talents of staff.

Team and Organizational Autonomy facilitates the ability of staff to search for and use information, learn new skills, and feel comfortable in ambiguous work situations enabling the Organizational Agility required to adjust to changing customer and business landscapes.

Operational Experimentation is another attribute of Organizational Agility. This allows organizational teams to embrace and effectively execute concepts such as Lean Startup, Minimum Viable Product, and Fail Fast to employ rapid testing and experimentation around potential changes to operating models, structures, and processes. Operational Experimentation is based on a sound technological prerequisite to utilize standardized, comparable, and integrated technologies and information systems. An organization that exhibits Operational Experimentation has management and senior leadership that recognize the relationship between innovation and learning.

Operational Experimentation **allows organizations to try new things quickly, enable change more rapidly, and save money by avoiding big failures**. It also allows organizations to entertain creative ideas that would be too risky for a normal life-cycle models as well as implementing prototypes and pilots first that allow the discovery and refinement of approaches. Finally, Operational Experimentation allows the organization to be resilient through a large pipeline of ideas that makes you ready to adapt to change.

Another requirement of Organizational Agility is *Collaboration*. A Collaborative Organization is one where **teams exhibit an openness and willingness to work together constructively with others** during their experimentation or testing and change efforts, especially when those efforts impact or will impact their functional domain. In a Collaborative Organization, there is a participative approach to decision-making between management and non-management, and collaboration is facilitated by the Organization's commitment to training in and the use of interpersonal skills. A collaborative organizational environment also means having other training and education resources available for employees as well as evangelists within the organization.

Collaboration looks at how an organization listens to the ideas of staff, their needs, and their suggestions and integrates their feedback into technology and strategy. A Collaborative Organization thus can quickly adapt organizational structures and processes to implement changes and stay competitive.

Still another requirement of Organizational Agility is *Mission-Driven Governance*. An organization with Mission-Driven Governance is characterized by teams embracing **an approach to decision-making in which the overall needs and benefits to the organization are the primary evaluation criteria of any decision** to change operating models, structures, or processes, even when change decisions span multiple groups or business units within the organization. As a result, organizational adaptation and change is essentially accomplished by self-leading staff.

A key intangible benefit of Mission-Driven Governance is the ability to function in a productive and efficient environment in which all organizational elements work together toward a common strategy. But there are also tangible benefits of Mission-Driven Governance such as revenue, reputational protection, and customer attraction. Ultimately, Mission-Driven Governance assists the organization to confidently take on reasonable risk because decisions are based on better information.

Finally, *Adaptive Leadership* is also an important attribute of Organizational Agility. This means an organization's leadership team encourages change, celebrates experimentation, protects appropriate risk-takers, and ultimately takes responsibility and accountability both for failed experiments and for the failure to appropriately pivot.

Adaptive Leadership is like the organizational concept of "fail fast" to avoid major commitments to efforts that may not be successful. The difference is that Adaptive Leadership **focuses on the leader and the leadership team as a facilitator for the "fail fast" organizational practice**. Adaptive Leaders make decisions based on achieving reasonable positive results and avoiding the "pseudocertainty" effect (the tendency for people to perceive an outcome as certain even though it is uncertain) observed in multi-stage decisions, in which evaluation of outcomes in a previous decision stage are discarded in subsequent stages. Additionally, Adaptive Leaders consider both the consequences of inaction with the consequences of action.

Adaptive Leaders can operate in chaos and make decisions in the face of uncertainty with an aim towards reducing risk over time. They are not constrained by traditional organizational hierarchies. Adaptive Leadership elicits high performance from staff which drives many of the other Organizational Agility attributes.

Strategic Agility

Whereas Organizational Agility is about the organization's ability to pivot when directed, Strategic Agility is the ability to anticipate when to pivot. Organizations must reduce their reliance on long-term strategic planning documents and instead create the capability within the organization to continuously monitor shifts in the market and emerging technologies. Then dynamically re-craft the organization's strategic direction and vision to create competitive advantage and mitigate potential competitive disruption. The organization must develop a strategic set of capabilities that enables it to rapidly detect opportunities and threats, seize strategic opportunities, and ensure continued competitiveness by adapting, improving, protecting, and reconfiguring the organization's business model and assets.

In Organizational Agility, an organization must be tactically able to adjust its structure and operating processes within the bounds of a chosen strategy. An organization must also be able to scan the environment through objective and formal assessment capabilities and rapidly test selected strategies to ensure they are sound. Facilitating strategic change emphasizing a joint effort by multiple stakeholders in a common connected digital space enables the organization to make agile evidence-based decisions using both internal and external assessment information.

Strategic Agility is the highest level of the Digital Enterprise Framework and represents a synergy of the other Dimensions of Operational Sustainability and Organizational Agility. Strategic Agility is heavily influenced by internal and external listening mechanisms and the ability to communicate Strategic Changes effectively and rapidly to both staff and customers. The seven attributes of this dimension, described below, focus on strategic agile capabilities. These capabilities depend on Operational Sustainability and leverage Organizational Agility described in the previous two sections.

First, the organization should possess what is known as a *Strategic Planning Framework* where the organization outlines a strategic vision, directional principles, and intentional outcomes to enable rapid shifts in strategic plans when necessary. A Strategic Planning Framework means **the organization has a clear mission statement that outlines its reason for existence, provides a vision for what it is to deliver, and distinguishes it from competitors.** There is a clear linkage from the organization's strategy to its implementation of strategy.

A Strategic Planning Framework measures external opportunities and threats as well as internal strengths and weaknesses to generate and implement strategy. This establishes a uniform vision and purpose that is shared among all members of the organization and helps them pull in the same direction which results in improved quality of services for customers and a means of measuring the service.

An organization must also possess a *Formalized Listening Capability* where there is a **formal organizational process that continually monitors the market, competitors, and customers to rapidly identify market shifts** outside of any formal strategic planning process. Formalized Listening Capability complements the Strategic Planning Framework by not only continually scanning the environment, but also considering unfamiliar and even negative information to formulate Strategy.

Formalized Listening also means gathering information from customers and competitors as well as examining regional and national trends to forecast their industry's likely future. Formalized Listening allows the organization to not only predict, but also affect, competitive positions. A Formalized Listening Capability not only can help assess the intensity of competition, but it also helps with strategic thinking on how to better match a business' strategy to the specific competitive character of the marketplace.

Deep Listening Empowerment is another trait an organization must possess to have Strategic Agility. This is where the organization can identify potential market shifts, competitive disruptions, and changes in customer demands and needs at every level and has established operational protocols to continually seek, collect, and adjudicate these findings throughout the organization.

An organization practicing Deep Listening Empowerment **uses strategic information systems to design and manage the flow of information to improve productivity and decision-making.** Competitive advantage in the digital economy is even more important than in the old economy and Deep Listening Empowerment helps an organization gain a competitive advantage through its contribution to the strategic goals of an organization and the ability to significantly increase performance and productivity.

Next, an organization must possess a *Strategic Assessment Capability* where it **maintains a formal internal capability by which to assess potential changes to the organization's strategic direction based on identified market opportunities or competitive threats** on an ongoing basis.

With a Strategic Assessment Capability, the organization can assess itself continuously, rather than when it's too late, which will help an organization not only react to change to support Organizational Agility, but to be Strategically Agile to anticipate and drive change. A Strategic Assessment Capability yields an awareness of business issues, knowledge of how to improve efficiency, and a clear vision of what direction an organization should be going.

A Digital Organization should also possess *Strategy Testing and Assurance*. With Strategy Testing and Assurance, the organization has **established mechanisms to rapidly test and measure potential changes to strategic direction and established clear mechanisms to rapidly assess results and shift strategy**, as required. Strategy Testing and Assurance requires the organization have established performance measures to evaluate decisions made through its Strategic Assessment Capabilities and maintains benchmark data not only on itself, but its competitors. More importantly, the organization's innovation and improvement activities are tracked and measured, and top management, senior leadership, and key decision-makers' job performances are evaluated by a Board of Directors or some independent oversight.

A mature Digital Enterprise might have an Enterprise Resource Planning system that unites the organization's major business activities within a single family of software modules.

Strategic Governance is also something a Digital Enterprise should possess for Strategic Agility. Strategic Governance looks at whether the organization utilizes a governance process that is **empowered to make organizational changes to strategic direction, outside of the normal strategic planning process**, based on strategic assessment and testing, including the determination of executional requirements. While Mission-Driven Governance in the Organizational Agility Dimension focuses on the organization's ability to properly govern decisions in reaction to change, Strategic Governance addresses the organization's ability to proactivity anticipate change through its Strategic Assessment Capabilities.

Strategic Governance is characterized by a strategic board and reasonable oversight that help to find overlooked opportunities as a pipeline to Strategic Assessment. Furthermore, there is a strategic evaluation and influencing activity that examines management's actions and provides additional input. Strategic decision-makers recognize their larger responsibility including broader economic, legal, ethical, or voluntary obligations to society. Finally, there is a code of ethical behavior that drives the culture of the organization and guides organizational decisions.

Finally, an organization should be able to conduct *Strategic Shift Communication and Execution*. Here, the organization has established **clear mechanisms to communicate changes in strategic direction, their organizational and operational impacts**, and maintains the ability to effectively cause those changes to be executed and realized.

Executives are effectively matched to implement strategy based on skills and are able to motivate Staff to properly use their skills and abilities to implement strategy. This ensures the growth of a "strategy-culture" where strategy is compatible with the culture, the culture can be modified to fit the strategy, and management is willing to invest in changing the culture. Strategic Shift Communication and Execution allows the organization and its culture to focus on the right strategic and operating issues.

Strategic Agility is easily seen with the success of one famous traditional print newspaper. The Washington Post is following the strategy of its owner, Jeff Bezos, the founder and CEO of Amazon. The Post has hired both journalists and engineers, invested in new technology, and expanded into new markets. In the same way he built Amazon, Bezos has committed to a strategy of absorbing financial losses in the short term with an eye toward gaining market share over the long-term. Their ability to be Strategically Agile resulted in the Post's digital subscriptions growing 145% in one year. While the Post's conversion into a primarily digital publication is the strategy, maintaining the core principle of commitment to first-class journalism is still the core business.

Disruptive Culture

"Shortcomings in organizational culture are one of the main barriers to company success in the digital age. That is a central finding from McKinsey's recent survey of global executives, which highlighted three digital culture deficiencies: functional and departmental silos, a fear of

taking risks, and difficulty forming and acting on a single view of the customer (Goran *et al.*, 2017, p. 56)." Figure 2 details the findings.

Culture is the most significant self-reported barrier to digital effectiveness.

Which are the most significant challenges to meeting digital priorities?
% of respondents

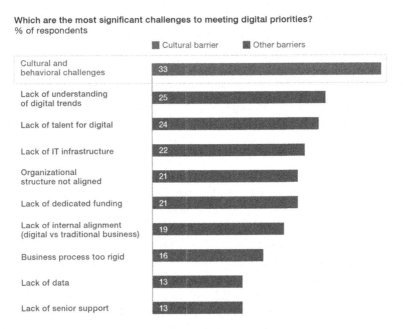

Figure 2:   McKinsey Digital Survey.

Source: 2016 McKinsey Digital survey of 2,135 respondents.

An Operationally Sustainable culture needs to be free to work within the bounds of good operational and business processes to allow innovation to flourish without the shackles of onerous, and sometimes unnecessary, processes. Organizational Agility is marked by a culture of continual service improvement and management support for the "business application of creativity." The creativity can be put into place through the demonstration by top management of "visible and consistent support for change," enabling the organization to adjust quickly. Strategic Agility is characterized by a culture that has a set of beliefs that put the customer's interests first and is part of an overall, but much more fundamental, corporate culture. This broader culture is one following agile values like proactivity, responsiveness, trust, support of proposals and decisions of employees, and the handling of change as both opportunity and chance.

The first three layers of the Digital Enterprise Readiness Framework create the structural support within the enterprise to enable the transformation into a digital enterprise. But a final cultural transformation is critical to becoming a digital enterprise. The digital enterprise requires a "**Disruptive Culture**" that is willing to challenge the status quo, embrace innovation, experimentation, and "fast failure," and which is perpetually focused on what's coming next. The culture must permit continual disruption in every facet of the organization, including technology, business models, industry dynamics, offshoring and outsourcing strategies, regulatory management, etc. They must also, however, possess the discernment to only execute disruptive change that results in competitive advantage. A Disruptive Culture spans the entire Framework and quite literally surrounds all Dimensions, as a foundational enabler of each Dimension and as an outcome of the other three Dimensions. Therefore, specific culture markers are built into the Framework at each Dimension. Let's look at the specific culture markers of each of these Dimensions.

Evidence-Based Decision-Making is **making decisions based on data rather than what one can remember** and examining other alternatives or procedures rather than relying on one's own experiences or only knowledge that is readily available. It is a cultural norm to actively seek and consider all information for decision-making even though it may be hard to find or is unstructured. A culture of Evidence-Based Decision-Making seeks to avoid common mistakes such as "Groupthink" and The Abilene Paradox and uses Delphi Techniques to prevent bias. Simply put, the benefit of Evidence-Based Decision-Making is that it improves the quality and outcomes of decisions.

Continual Operational Reassessment Bias means the **organization is biased toward continuous change, celebrating change efforts, and questioning any operating model, structure, or process** that has remained unchanged for an extended period. Continual Operational Reassessment Bias is the natural cultural skepticism of the status quo. Therefore, there is continual alignment and re-alignment of services to the changing business needs with resulting identification of additional changes and improvements. In a culture of Continual Operational Reassessment Bias, the organization allows free time or autonomy for staff to consider and propose innovation, and there is a system in place to reward employee suggestions or change proposals. This allows the organization to innovate through the natural skepticism of its staff.

Critical Thinking and Analysis is where one learns from others' successes and failures. One does not accept the status quo and constructively challenges everything. **You can suspend your beliefs long enough to consider other points of view**. While Continual Operational Reassessment Bias is an organization-wide objective cultural perspective, Critical Thinking and Analysis is more an individual subjective perspective. As a result, Critical Thinking and Analysis is examined through the lens of personal habits and traits. Critical Thinking and Analysis is, in short, self-directed, self-disciplined, and self-monitored, allowing the organization the agility to self-correct.

Management Innovation is where **management actively supports the "business application of creativity."** To foster Organizational Agility, there must be a Management culture that has discovered, practices, and encourages entirely new ways to organize, lead, coordinate, or motivate staff. Critical Thinking and Analysis is an organization-wide individual cultural perspective, *but* Management Innovation is a cultural practice that pervades the culture of the Management layer. Therein lies the opportunity. You can wait for a competitor to stumble upon the next great breakthrough, or you can become a management innovator and find it now.

Organizational Innovation is when **the organization displays a culture of continual service improvement**. Continual Operational Reassessment Bias is the natural cultural skepticism of the status quo; however, Organizational Innovation is the affirmative and proactive encouragement and rewarding of innovation that challenges the status quo. To improve, the organization needs to know its baseline. Consequently, periodic training and communication of policies and procedures are foundational to Organizational Innovation.

With that foundation, Organizational Innovation then practices proactive encouragement, rewarding of innovation, and there is evidence of rewards programs to encourage feedback or innovative ideas. An organizational mindset of Continual Service Improvement is an engine for innovation and thus Organizational Agility by focusing on staff ideas for customer service.

Organizational Leadership is a **"visible and consistent support for change" from top management**. Organizational Leadership is a higher form of Management Innovation in that it is more proactive and organizationally pervasive by encompassing both the formal and informal Leadership. Here, the Leadership builds on overall innovation and continual service improvement to support and lead the organizational changes necessary to support agility.

Building relationships that cross organizational boundaries are encouraged by management and executive leadership, and there is an expectation that leaders will not only seek the input and perspective of subordinates or team members, but lobby on behalf of those ideas and suggestions. This leads to a sense of ownership and accountability for overall performance which makes leadership of change and Organizational Agility an organic effort.

Agile Values is where the organization has a culture of practicing proactivity, responsiveness, trust, support of proposals and decisions of employees, and the handling of change as opportunity and chance. Agile values are the degree to which the people of an organization share the intrinsic or well-learned mental prerequisites of an agile culture and to what extent the organization establishes the required technological prerequisites to support agility. For example, the organization views and accepts change as a tool to gain competitive advantages.

Staff are, in general, always willing to continuously learn from one another and to pass their knowledge to others, as well as being able to sense, perceive, or anticipate the best opportunities which come up in the environment. Finally, the organization can exploit change to gain a competitive advantage because it prefers market-related changes (e.g., new competitors and preferences) to generate new opportunities. An organization with Agile Values facilitates a well-directed approach for improvements and continuous assessment of actions taken.

Collaborative Digital Storytelling is where the organization facilitates organizational change by emphasizing a joint effort by multiple stakeholders in a common connected space. Foundational to Collaborative Digital Storytelling is either a **private or public digital online space for small groups to collaborate where staff can share organizational experiences via text, audio, or video**. Staff can use digital online space at a flexible time that is convenient to them as well as use it asynchronously (e.g., an elapsed time between two or more people) or synchronously when everyone is at the same digital space (not necessarily physical space) at the same time (the latter important for global companies operating in multiple time zones).

Collaborative Digital Storytelling allows reflection around an organization's shared assumptions; particularly those that are unhelpful, impede smooth functioning, and interrupt the sustained competitive advantage of an innovation.

Customer Orientation is when the organization exhibits a **set of beliefs that put the customer's interests first and is part of an overall, but much more fundamental, corporate culture**. This is the Cultural "glue" that holds the organization together: a commitment to innovation and technological development and a strong emphasis on being cutting-edge, trying new things, and prospecting for opportunities. The organization emphasizes high consensus, openness, collaboration, and participation and is a very dynamic place, and staff are always willing to stick their necks out and try new things if they believe it will better serve the customer experience.

Often, this leads to providing more capability than the customer expected. An organizational culture that exhibits this Customer Orientation can cause "overshooting" or "overprovision" scenarios resulting in competitive advantage based on deeper understanding of customer needs. These tendencies are drivers to competitive positioning, which leads to differentiation and market share.

Final Thoughts

Gartner estimates that over 70% of transformation initiatives fail and Forbes reports that 84% of Digital Transformation efforts fail. Digital Transformation efforts usually focus on implementing Digital practices, such as Agile, Lean, or DevOps; or implementing Digital Technologies such as Public Cloud, Big Data, or Predictive Analysis. Additionally, many organizations erroneously think of a Digital Transformation as integrating Digital Technologies. This is merely an IT transformation and is directed at optimizing IT performance for business or organizational needs and outcomes.

True Digital Transformation is more than just implementing Digital Practices and Digital Technologies. Digital Transformation rightly targets optimizing business or organizational effectiveness via digital investments and IT services. Transformation occurs when business strategies or major sections of an organization are altered. This can be quite disruptive and stressful for an organization. The plans may be great, but the lack of Readiness for Transformation presents additional and unnecessary risk. There are a range of issues that provide the basis for a successful Transformation, including modicum of operational maturity, the culture of the organization, and human reaction to change, all of which are interdependent with the organization's ability to be agile and adapt. In short, Transformation efforts fail because organizations are not "**Ready**" to Transform by exhibiting Operational Sustainability, Organizational Agility, Strategic Agility, and finally a Disruptive Culture.

Bibliography

Araujo, C. (2012). *The Quantum Age of IT: Why Everything You Know about IT is about to Change.* IT Governance Ltd.

Armenakis, A. A., Harris, S. G., & Mossholder, K. W. (1993). Creating readiness for organizational change. *Human Relations*, 46(6), 681–703.

Bazerman, M. & Don, A. M. (2013). *Judgment in Managerial Decision Making.* John Wiley & Sons.

Brendel, W. T. & Chou, C. C. (2016). Transforming organizational change through collaborative digital storytelling. *Journal of Educational Technology Development & Exchange*, 9(1), 2.

Bowen, P. L., Cheung, M. Y. D., & Rohde, F. H. (2007). Enhancing IT governance practices: A model and case study of an organization's efforts. *International Journal of Accounting Information Systems*, 8(3), 191–221.

Caimi, G. (2014). Your scarcest resource. *Harvard Business Review*, 74–80.

Catlin, T., Scanlan, J., & Willmott, P. (2015). Raising your digital quotient. *McKinsey Quarterly*, 1, 1–14.

Crocitto, M. & Youssef, M. (2003). The human side of organizational agility. *Industrial Management & Data Systems*, 103(6), 388–397.

CSG Inform. (n.d.). *Digital Transformation is about the Journey, not Just the Destination.* Retrieved from https://inform.tmforum.org/videos/transformation-is-about-the-journey-not-the-destination/.

Demirkan, H., Spohrer, J. C., & Welser, J. J. (2016). Digital innovation and strategic transformation. *IT Professional*, 18(6), 14–18.

Drogseth, D. (2015) *Digital and IT Transformation: A global View of Trends and Requirements.* Enterprise Management Associates. https://www.enterprisemanagement.com/research/asset-free.php/3099/toc/Digital-and-IT-Transformation:-A-Global-View-of-Trends-and-Requirements-toc.

Doz, Y. L. & Kosonen, M. (2010). Embedding strategic agility: A leadership agenda for accelerating business model renewal. *Long Range Planning*, 43(2–3), 370–382.

Goran, J., LaBerge, L., & Srinivasan, R. (2017). Culture for a digital age. *McKinsey Quarterly*, 3(1), 56–67.

Granito, F. A. (2011). University of Maryland University College, ProQuest Dissertations Publishing, 3509189.

Granito, F. A. (2020). *Are You READY for Digital Transformation?: Digital Enterprise Readiness Framework*. Institute for Digital Transformation.

Granito, F. (2020, April 1). *Snapshot Research Results Inside the Data Digital Readiness Quiz*. Institute for Digital Transformation. https://www.institutefordig italtransformation.org/snapshot-01-digital-readiness-quiz/.

Holt, D. T., Helfrich, C. D., Hall, C. G., & Weiner, B. J. (2010). Are you ready? How health professionals can comprehensively conceptualize readiness for change. *Journal of General Internal Medicine*, 25(1), 50–55.

Hunger, J. D. & Wheelen, T. L. (2003). *Essentials of Strategic Management*. New Jersey: Prentice Hall.

Kantabutra, S. & Suriyankietkaew, S. (2012). Examining relationships between organic leadership and corporate sustainability: A proposed model. *Journal of Applied Business Research*, 28(1), 67.

Koehler, J., Tirenni, G., & Kumaran, S. (2002). From business process model to consistent implementation: A case for formal verification methods. In *Proceedings. Sixth International Enterprise Distributed Object Computing* (pp. 96–106). IEEE.

Lehman, W. E., Greener, J. M., & Simpson, D. D. (2002). Assessing organizational readiness for change. *Journal of Substance Abuse Treatment*, 22(4), 197–209.

Linich, D. & Bergstrom, J. (2014). *Building a Culture of Continuous Improvement in an Age of Disruption*. Deloitte Consulting.

Lokuge, S., Sedera, D., Grover, V., & Dongming, X. (2019). Organizational readiness for digital innovation: Development and empirical calibration of a construct. *Information & Management*, 56(3), 445–461.

Long, C. (2000). Measuring your strategic agility. *Consulting to Management*, 11(3), 25.

Loucopoulos, P. & Heidari, F. (2012). Evaluating quality of business processes. *Modelling and Quality in Requirements Engineering, Essays Dedicated to Martin Glinz on the Occasion of His 60th Birthday*, pp. 61–73.

Lukas, B. A., Whitwell, G. J., & Heide, J. B. (2013). Why do customers get more than they need? How organizational culture shapes product capability decisions. *Journal of Marketing*, 77(1), 1–12.

McKinsey & Company (2018). Unlocking success in digital transformations. Retrieved from https://www.mckinsey.com/business-functions/organization/ our-insights/unlocking-success-in-digital-transformations.

Schein, E. H. (2006). *Organizational Culture and Leadership* (Vol. 356). John Wiley & Sons.

Weiner, B. J. (2009). A theory of organizational readiness for change. *Implementation Science*, 4(1), 1–9.

Wendler, R. (2014, September). Development of the organizational agility maturity model. In *Computer Science and Information Systems (FedCSIS)*, 2014 Federated Conference on (pp. 1197–1206). IEEE.

Wrapping It All Up

Dr. Frank Granito

Somethings to Think About

After reading this book, I hope that you have come to realize that the key word in the phrase "**Digital Transformation**" is not digital. The technology is just a tool or an enabler that makes the transformation possible. Let me give you three examples, two of which you are already familiar with.

Get a Ride: Or put another way, a method of getting from point A to point B by using someone else's vehicle. Traditionally, you would just hail a taxicab from in front of a hotel or call for a pick-up. Uber took that premise and used technology to change two key elements; how you "hail" a cab and the vehicle used. Instead of looking for a taxi stand or call, you now use an app to get a ride. The app also lets you see who is on the way and where they are, providing significant improvement from just having to wait. The other key change is that Uber, Lift, etc. are not using commercial vehicles, instead they are using personal vehicles for commercial service, a major shift in the industry.

A Place to Sleep: Everyone has stayed at a motel, hotel, etc. It is the normal when traveling, either for business or pleasure. Most people are used to booking a room online, but what Airbnb did was to use technology to bring together all of the individual rentals of personal property and put

247

https://doi.org/10.1142/9789811260469_bmatter

them in common booking system. They also added many of the things you are used to in a commercial rental (i.e., guaranteed availability, arrival time, lodging standard, etc.). The key fact is that technology has enabled using personal property for commercial purposes.

Shipping a Package: For those of you too young, let me tell you how it was done in the *"old days."* You took your package to a shipping center and were asked to fill out multi-part carbon paper form. They reminded you to press hard because of the multiple copies. They gave you a copy, attached one to the package, and the rest were used to track the shipment of your package.

In the mid-80s, our friend Roman Hlutkowsky led an engineering team at FedEx. They were the team that created the first Federal Express SuperTracker and the computer systems to support it (Figure 1).

Figure 1: Federal Express SuperTracker

Here is the part you probably do not know, the reason they were asked to build this device was that **5-part carbon paper was too expensive**. That's right, one of the very first Digital Transformation efforts was a cost savings program. And that is all it would have been for nothing if not for the fact someone said, *"what if we let the customer lookup their own shipping information?"* And because of that simple idea, the entire package-shipping industry was changed.

This got me to wondering if Uber and Airbnb were also just cost-saving programs. Think about it, they were able to start a Transportation and Accommodation company without the capital investment normally required.

Hopefully, these three examples have shown you that the key word is **Transformation** and not the technology part. Technology is just an enabler that makes these changes possible.

Digital Transformation

Transformation is just another word for change. And when we talk about changing anything, we need to realize that change is an individual and personal matter. A 1976 McKinsey study showed that **"cultural and behavioral challenges"** were the number one barrier (33%) to digital effectiveness. For any change effort to be successful, you must change the individual's beliefs and behaviors.

We will let you in on a technique we use when advising on transformation efforts. Most efforts start with the senior executive say, *"go do this."* We advise that you launch the program by having the senior executive, write a document titled *"Why This? Why Now?"* We have them explain what is happening in the industry, explain the pressures on their company, explain potential solution, and most importantly why this change is necessary and how it will benefit the company in the long run. We have found that when this approach is used, you can expect approximately 85% understanding from the organization. And remember, understanding is the first step in acceptance of any change.

The common message

If you have come this far, you might be asking, **"Now what?"** What should I take away from this book? Well, let's demystify it all for you. As I wrote in the Introduction, every contributing author in this book has approached their theme through one common thread — *Culture*. Transformation is not about technology, it is about organizational transformation at every level with technology as an enabler. The key to this organizational transformation is *culture*. Every chapter in this book looks at approaches to Digital Transformation through that lens.

In "The Culture of Transformation," **Reynaldo Lugtu Jr**. tells us that "legacy cultures of organizations would likely present the biggest barriers to transformation." But what *culture* is needed to overcome this barrier? Mr. Lugtu states that among other types, a culture of flexibility is most needed to support digital transformation. Flexibility, quite simply, is adaptability and openness towards change. Change is difficult, but not impossible. Mr. Lugtu points to two classical approaches: Lewin's unfreeze–change–refreeze and Kotter's 8-Step Change Model. These are seminal approaches, and they work.

Whynde Kuehn offers a different perspective on culture. In "Business Architecture as an Enabler of Transformation," Ms. Kuehn points out that Digital Transformation is about fundamental business shifts which also require a rewiring of the way an organization operates. Although business architecture can be leveraged as a catalyst and enabler to help shift peoples' mindsets and behaviors, these shifts require changes to the underlying structures and *culture* of an organization, but. To sustain transformation, organizations need to adopt new mindsets and ways of working that are value-based, agile, and innovative. For example, organizations need to develop transformational strategies and a *culture* of continual strategy and innovation, not tactical improvements.

The "Digital Transformation Manifesto" is rife with references to culture and rightly so. **Raymond Sheen** points out that successful digital transformation is much more than a project to incorporate the latest version of a technology. It occurs when the organization's *culture* and mindset have embraced the capabilities and potential for a radical shift of operations and strategy that are enabled because of the digital technologies. The culture an organization should be looking for is one that "empowers individual leadership." Organizations need to focus on their workforce development. This includes the hiring, training, and promotion of employees and associates; and is organized to enable leaders to develop at all levels. The entire organization is motivated and incentivized to implement productive change on a continual basis.

In his chapter, "Value — The Guiding Star," **John Thorp** reminisces about his prior work in *The Information Paradox* and admits, "As I look back now, I realize that, to keep it simple I left out a few key parts of the original model — notably *culture*." Most businesses have no clear idea of the value that they expect to realize from the use of the technology. They still see digital transformation as being largely about implementing the technology and have little understanding of the significant changes, they will need to make to realize value from their use of technology. Changes to the nature of their business, how they are organized, their processes, the skills of their people, their reward system, and, most importantly, their *culture and mindset*. To Mr. Thorp, the solution is simple. He states, *we still have what is predominately a "culture of delivery" — "build it and they will come," rather than a "culture of value" — one that focuses on creating and sustaining value from an organization's investments and assets.*

In "The Neuroscience of Transformation," **Cherri Holland** tells us to lead continuous transformation that is human brain and human performance optimization, organizations need to create a transformation-ready *culture*. More specifically, Ms. Holland teaches us that in an unhealthy organization, people form subcultures, at odds with the common agenda. She likens this to a cancer cell operating at odds with the health of the human body. If we agree that an organization is an "organic" entity, a territorial subculture literally provides a protective cell for people to retreat into camps that feel familiar and safe. These subcultures can be incubators for those who insist on inhibiting the health of the organization. The solution is as easy as it is difficult: Each leader as well as the team of leaders has a role in creating a social system that reinforces self-drive and an adult, self-reliant, but team-connected, work culture. Such cultures are confident that they can navigate internal and external environmental shifts and ever-changing demands, as they evolve their capability accordingly.

Hans Gillior, in his chapter "Agile Transformation," gives us some advice on how to create this adult, self-reliant, and team-connected work *culture*. In the light of agile transformation, another kind of leadership style is needed, often referred to as *Servant Leadership*. It is a leadership style that primarily focuses on creating an atmosphere of collaboration, team morale, reputation, and a general positive culture. The leadership is often coaching and supporting expecting employees to self-govern and perform. The downside of servant leadership is its ability to make quick decisions and dealing with workplace strife. Certainly, there is a way to mitigate this, and Mr. Gillior is quick to point out that leadership styles are not absolute but rather a mixture of different styles to fit the ambitions and business philosophy. A blended leadership style is sometimes called a situation-based leadership style where the style can be adjusted to the current situation. However, it is important to highlight that a higher degree of servant leadership is required to succeed with the agile transformation and deliver sustainable results.

At the Institute, we often refer to Leadership as a *behavior* and not a role. As such it can be argued that it is more of an art than science. Thus, leadership can come in many forms, styles, and even at different times depending on the situation. This is never more evident for **Jeffery S. Ton** in his chapter "Leadership in an Era of Uncertainty." If leadership is an art, can we learn from others? Two such leaders who provide invaluable lessons for digital transformation leaders are Merriwether Lewis and

William Clark. Over 200 years ago, Lewis and Clark led a team of 30 men, a woman, an infant, and a dog on an expedition that changed the face of the United States. How they were able to succeed where others before them had failed is a study of leadership through uncertainty. Captains Lewis and Clark knew the importance of having a diverse team. The problems we are solving today require the same diversity of thought, diversity of experience, and diversity of *culture* that Lewis and Clark understood over 200 years ago.

We often talk about being customer-focused in the Digital Era. **Jessica Carroll**, in her chapter "The Client–Partner Engagement," takes this to another level. We are told that it is no longer sufficient to be just customer focused. We must be concerned with customer success. Ms. Carroll tells us that customer success is being dedicated to ensuring a valuable relationship is created with your customer, being an evangelist internally to help guide the company's customer-first *culture*, and working to understand, track, and report on the success of the company meeting the business outcomes of their customer. The organization can ensure this by instilling a *customer-first culture* throughout every nook and cranny of the organization. This requires a *cultural* commitment with real actions. Each employee must participate and their activities, ideas, processes, and most importantly, their individual goals need to tie to the customer-first mission in some way.

Speaking of customer-focus in Digital Transformation, **Roy Atkinson** brings it home for us in his chapter, "Customer Experience and Digital Transformation." Mr. Atkinson tells us creating and maintaining a *culture* is very difficult and changing an existing *culture* is even more of a challenge. But fear not, there are things that can be done. Such as: operationalize customer empathy; hire for customer orientation; democratize customer insights; facilitate direct interaction with customers; link employee culture to customer outcomes; and finally, tie compensation to the customer. Digital Transformation aims to provide the means for an organization to deliver a better Customer Experience. This will not be attained without committing to constant change, investment in the appropriate tools and technologies, and most importantly, the desire to create a *culture* that is supportive and foundational to the outcomes.

Finally, in my chapter "Digital Transformation Readiness," I emphasize *culture* in all four Dimensions of Readiness. Culture is the true essence of digital transformation — not the implementation of mere technology to automate core services, but the shift in power to the customer and the need to continually adapt technologies, processes, and *culture*. The digital enterprise requires a "**Disruptive Culture**" that is willing to challenge the status quo, embrace innovation, experimentation and "fast failure," and which is perpetually focused on what's coming next. The culture must permit continual disruption in every facet of the organization, including technology, business models, industry dynamics, offshoring and outsourcing strategies, regulatory management, etc. They must also, however, possess the discernment to only execute disruptive change that results in competitive advantage.

Approaching your transformation efforts

You have read about all the different approaches used by our Institute Fellows, and I am sure that you want to know which one is the best or most effective. Well, the answer is all of them and none of them, but *culture* should be at the core of each approach. Let me explain — I am sure that you have heard the expression *"When the only tool you have is a hammer, everything looks like a nail."* It is the same with Transformation or change efforts. Organizations have some similarities, but they are all different and unique in certain ways. Using the same approach every time guarantees that you will have failures.

The purpose of presenting different approaches to transformation was to give you a toolkit and not just a single tool. (Where's my hammer?) You need to understand the *culture* of your organization and use an approach that is appropriate for your specific situation.

Five Mantras of Digital Transformation

Years ago, we published the Five Mantras for Digital Transformation. We feel they are still valid today. So, in closing, we leave you with these five things to live by:

- Transformation Never Ends.
- Transformation Is About Culture, Not Technology.
- Let Business Outcomes Guide Your Journey.
- Business as Usual No Longer Exists.
- Create a Culture of Continuous Change.

Index

Business, Technology, Organization, Process, and People (BTOPP) model, 75–76, 89, 95
business-to-business (B2B) services, 209
business-to-consumer (B2C), 209
business transformation, 12, 158–159
Buvat, J., 2

C
Cameron, L., 3
campaign-driven approach, 125
capabilities, 22
Carroll, Jessica, 252
categorization, 92–93
change governance, 61–62, 122–123
Change Governance Domain, 68
change management, 107
Charan, Ram, 83
chief executive officers (CEOs), 8
Christiensen, Clayton, 178
Churchill, Winston, 107
clarity, 166
Clarke, Arthur C., 55
Clark, William, 163–164, 167, 174, 179
client/partner engagement, 183–202
climate, 10
closed systems atrophy, 106
collaborative cross-organizational ventures, 38
collaborative digital storytelling, 242
collaborative organization, 233
Collins, Jim, 122–123
command and control leadership style, 153
communication, 100, 118–119, 232
community lines of business, 210
competing values framework (CVF), 3
competitive advantage, 100
composable organization, 31–32

conduct trainings, 16
coordination, 232
COVID-19 pandemic, 57, 124
critical thinking and analysis, 241
cross-entity coordination, 38
cross-team communication, 32–33
C-suite sponsor, 194
cultural change, 98–99
cultural domain metrics, 68
cultural perspective, 64–65
culture, xxv, 2–3, 11, 154
culture of flexibility, 6
culture of transformation, 1–17
customer and market domain, 52–53, 63–64, 68–69, 208–209
customer behavior, 134, 214–216
customer centricity, 7, 15, 29–30
customer churn rate, 212
customer-data platform (CDP), 215
customer empathy, 217
customer engagement, 184
customer experience (CX), 11, 184, 205–219
customer feedback, 17, 198
customer-first behaviors, 190
customer-first cultural pillars, 188
customer lifetime value, 212
customer orientation, 217, 243
customer satisfaction, 199
customer service, 210
customer success, 184–185, 210

D
data, 53–55
data analytics, 214
data collection methods, 53–54
decision-making, 12, 154, 166
deep listening empowerment, 236
Delphi method, 4–6
DevOps, 141
digital business model, 139
digital customer engagement, 29

Henderson, Tom, 115
Hess, T., 4–6
Hinssen, Peter, 134
Hippold, S., 2
Holland, Cherri, 251
home appliances, 50
Hueffner, Erin, 206
human brain, 104–107, 111–116, 128
hyper-personalization, 215

I
IBM, 51
Ilišević, D., 4, 7
imperatives, 47
individuals, 150
influencing, 119
information, 23
information management, 154
information systems (IS), 3
Information Technology
    Infrastructure Library (ITIL), 141
Information Technology Service
    Management (ITSM), 229
informing, 119
initiatives, 23
innovation quotient, 15–16
innovative culture, 8–12
iPhones, 48

J
Jefferson, Thomas, 176–177
journeys, 23

K
Kallman, Andrew, 142
Kaplan, R., 59, 85
key performance indicators (KPIs),
    228
knowing-doing gap, 98
Kotter, J. P., 13
Kuehn, Whynde, 250

L
labeling, 75–77
latent brain potential, 114–116
leader-driven approach, 125
leadership, 11, 99–100, 154,
    163–180, 194
lego blocks, 28
Lewin, Kurt, 13
Lewis, Merriwether, 163–164,
    167–168, 177, 179
life-balance, 193
limbic (mid) brain, 114
logistics, 210
Lugtu, Reynaldo Jr., xxv, 249

M
Machado, Luiz, 113–115
machine learning, 214
Magnum Opus (MO), 120, 125
market awareness, 154
market disruption, 136
marketing, 209–210
maximum entropy modeling, 212
McConnell, J., 8
McGregor Theory X, 145
McKinsey Digital survey, 238
M-commerce, 208
mentorship, 193
metrics-driven management, 230
midbrain, 119
mission-driven governance, 234
mobilization pillar, 188–189, 191
Morton, Michael S. Scott, 75
Moynihan, Daniel Patrick, 53

N
Nadella, Satya, 96
Nadkarni, S., 1
narrative devices, 119
Natural Language Processing (NLP),
    213

Printed in the United States
by Baker & Taylor Publisher Services